Astrology, Numerology, and Tarot All-in-One

Learn the Astrological Signs and the Meaning of Numbers, Tarots and Magic Cards, Uncover the Secrets of Your Future and Destiny

By Jade K. Star

against the publisher for any reparation, damages, or monetary loss due to the information herein, either directly or indirectly.

Respective authors own all copyrights not held by the publisher.

The information herein is offered for informational purposes solely, and is universal as so. The presentation of the information is without contract or any type of guarantee assurance.

The trademarks that are used are without any consent, and the publication of the trademark is without permission or backing by the trademark owner. All trademarks and brands within this book are for clarifying purposes only and are the owned by the owners themselves, not affiliated with this document

Table of Contents

ASTROLOGY

The Ultimate Guide For Beginners on Zodiac and Astrological Signs, Methods and Techniques to Read the Stars and Discover More about Astrology for Love or Medical Purposes

by Jade K. Star

INTRODUCTION

Life is extremely uncertain. When intelligence is unable to respond to the insecurities of a person's life, then astrology is a pseudo-science, quackery, or a quick-gaining tactic. But before we learn astrology, we should not come to any conclusion. Before we know anything about astrology, we first need to know when astrology comes from and what the various astrological schools are. Here I gave some fascinating information on and the origin of astrology.

Astronomy is concerned with studying the movements of celestial bodies and reduces these observations to numerical order. Astrology is a study of the effects on human affairs of the movements of these celestial bodies. The ancient astronomers were able to forecast the recurrence of cosmic phenomena by repeated observation, and astrologers began predicting the events on this planet.

Astrology is the synthesis of values, structures, and rituals that can inform future men, worldly events, and human relationships. Astrologist is the person who practices this astrology. Many astrologers agree that life and natural things affect the body and actions of human beings.

CHAPTER ONE

What Is Astrology?

The mere mention of astrology is adequate in our current age of science and logic to elicit a broad spectrum of reactions in society. The word astrologer recalls visions of hippies, new-ages sorcerers, psychics, or a number of other charlatans and frauds for many people. On the other hand, kings and emperors have used their secret knowledge of astrology to their great advantage throughout history.

Judges and Politicians, world-famous celebrities, wealthy entrepreneurs and financiers from New York and London to Moscow and Hong Kong are still using astrology to guide them in important decisions to this day. So what is astrology, and how would this ancient discipline be used to assist you? Please read the answers to these and other questions.

Let's first discuss some common myths and misunderstandings about astrology.

Magic is not astrology.

This is reiterated: astrology is not magic. The theory behind the practice of astrology is based on thousands of years of empirical research, and our understanding of astrology, like all of good science, continues to evolve and develop as we do.Even as alchemy set the stage for the rise of modern science as well as the systematic approach highly respected,, astrology will also lead to a better understanding of the energies inherent in the universe and how their flux and fluid can impact terrestrial life.

Astrology is not a fad of the new age.

We all saw signs of this shady tarot and palm-reading shops, and if you have visited Europe (especially Eastern Europe), you have probably met a variety of gypsies and other ne'er-dows hocking their astrology and fortune-telling services, often at exorbitant prices. Alas, the vast majority of these people are charlatan and fraud; some are well-intended but arrogant about their own skills, and you sometimes find a real astrologer out there, but the vast majority of them are snake oil dealers (or women, as often happens) and are conscious of that.

Real astrology is an old science that valued individuals have practiced throughout history, right up to the present day. You will not find actual astrologers with exaggerated claims, false promises, or gimmicky advertisements in their products because they actually don't need to. Even if some reputable astrologers sell crystals, essential oils, and other natural products, most of us will not be in a mile of a New Age shop. Many teachers, lawyers, doctors, or other professionals, and astrology is yet another aspect of our lives.

Astrology is not based on mumbo-jumbo superstitious.

Many of the misunderstandings about whether astrology is a valid science derive from the fact that astrologers used metaphor and allegory to express their interpretation of how the location of the stars influences terrestrial life historically.

Modern astrologers still use much the same terminology and symbolism because modern science still needs astrology.

They are only now starting to research and to understand the impact of such issues as mass coronary excesses from the sun and how this affects life here on Earth. No wonder they have not even begun to understand here how electromagnetic waves and nuclear energy of other stars can affect life.

Not simple astrology.

It's a bit of a two-pronged argument. On the one hand, the principles underlying astrology are simple and easy to grasp; but on the other, look at the nighttime sky when you are away from the city next time! In order to obtain the most accurate readings from all astrological charts, two or three tens of different aspects and connections are usually to be examined and taken into account. This makes astrology difficult and complex, especially if you want the most precise and detailed results.

Do you not remember the kings and emperors I mentioned, the politicians, celebrities, and financial players around the world? Well, part of why you can use astrology for your own benefit is that you can afford to pay for qualified astrologers ' services. If a successful businessman in India wants to find a good date for its merger, it takes an astrologer from several days to weeks to choose the best time. Good astrology took time and effort because there are a great many planets, stars, and celestial bodies, as well as their positions and relationships, which must be taken into account.

Astrology won't solve your problems.

Most people tend to turn to astrology when they want help with their own problems or when they want an easy way out of their difficulties. Sadly, astrology doesn't work that way. What astrology could do is enable you know more about a case, particularly in relation to any hidden or invisible forces at work. This is why I consider Astrology a device that can be used or misused like any tool so that the best use of Astrology is to help you decide better.

And last but not least, a very important factor you never should forget-not all astrology is the same.

While there are certain core principles and practices that all astrologers tend to follow (we are all finally working with the same stars), many different branches of astrology exist. Horary astrology and natural astrology are two of the most popular and well-known practices, but electoral astrology, astrology by sun signs, and geomancy are also common.

If you wish to learn more about your own personality and psychology, as well as about the different natural energies and forces at work in your life, then you want to find out more about your birth, your astrology. On the other hand, you need horary astrology if you're searching for more details (if it is' does he love me?' or' where did I leave my keys?' or something very important, such as' when should I get married?').

Astrology : A Science or Superstition?

People were always curious to understand their future. Whenever anyone is in trouble and cannot quickly get out of it, they want to know if the days of their suffering will end. And if so, when? It is natural to ask if this investment will bear fruit when you put a great deal of time, energy, or money into some plan. There were always people around who anticipated future events effectively. Many people may just look into the future, some use tarot cards, or draw up an astrological map that we call horoscopes, or read lines in people's palms. Their approaches have been different. One cannot argue that many times, and many people have accurately predicted the future. Every good prediction shows the future can indeed be correctly predicted.

In ancient times, the people held astrologers highly esteemed. This did not distinguish astronomers from astrologers. Clearly, astronomy and astrology were not treated as two different topics. Many would be surprised to learn that astrologers were also the most famous past scientists. In ancient India, astrology was called' Jyotish Shastra,' including both predictive astrology and astronomy. Of note, the astrologers of that period were also brilliant mathematicians. A successful astrologer was referred to as "Trikal-darshee," who can see the past, the present, and the future. It might not be an exaggeration to say that astrology is known as the leading branch of science.

This subject gradually disagreed over a period of time.

Why did Astrology lose its high standing?

This is a normal part of life in which people emulate well-respected, popular people. Once astrologers saw the social status, charlatans started to pose as astrologers. They learned some tricks and started to repeat gullible people. It was and remained a very profitable industry. An astrologer earns money by making forecasts without confirming that his predictions are accurate. No money-back-guarantee is available:-). Once an astrologer has set up a shop, people begin to come to him in the hope that he can correctly predict the future. The astrologer's job is awesome. For instance, he can predict about ten people, with only one prediction correct. The nine men he has incorrectly predicted will never return to him. But the 10th person, about whom the astrologer might correctly predict, will not only return to him but will also refer to him many others by referring to personal experience. In this way, an astrologer's business always flourishes, no matter how he carries out his trade. But the downside was that astrologers, as a profession, started to be regarded as many dubious people, such as modern-day politicians. When this idea began to gain ground, astrology was no longer attractive to intelligent people. People with talent began to follow other areas of expertise. The inevitable happened over a period of time. No talent worth salt chooses to pursue astrology as a vocation or a hobby, and the result is that everybody can see it nowadays.

Another very important reason was that Astrology was one of the lesser fields of knowledge. It was India's downfall, the cradle of human civilization, and its loss of status as the depository of all the wisdom of the ancient world. The Islamic hordes, who attacked and plundered India many times and ruled it for hundreds of years, had nothing to do with invaluable artworks, magnificent architecture, and the other exalted spaces of human activity. They are destroying most of the old temples, burying libraries like Nalanda and Takshshila, and constantly taking from the future generations of humanity numerous books of infinite wisdom. A great deal of known knowledge was lost, including astrological texts. This loss was irreparable, as the then Indian society ensured its survival and a steady fight against the aggressors. The few people with invaluable text and scripture are hard-pressed to retain the other works of ancient wise men. This is why when you study Astrology, and you feel like there are some vital links missing. It was natural for Astrology also to lose its prominent place when Hindu philosophy lost its ground. When modern science progressed, and the scientific model gained ground, astrology began to disappear into oblivion with the dearth of actual astrologers.

The critique and security astrology were ridiculed for two main reasons by individuals. First of all, of all, astrologers ' predictions often go wrong. Furthermore, they make different predictions if you take your horoscope to various astrologers. We also produce different horoscopes with the same set of data about a person's birth. Such findings lead people to conclude that astrology is not a science, and it is only a way of fooling individuals for the benefit of astrologers.

One can not deny the validity of the above reasons. Nevertheless, there is an element of bias in Astrology, which also leads to the denigration of this science. Take an example to illustrate this.

A man gets sick because of a certain disease. He's going to the doctor in his neighborhood. The doctor recommends that he take some examinations. After seeing the results of these tests and taking into consideration the symptoms of the patient, the doctor determines that the person has contracted some disorders, say Sickosis:-). He prescribes certain medications, and the patient returns home in order to get rid of the disease as quickly as possible. After two days of taking medicines, the patient finds that medicines do not work as they should be. He returns to the doctor, and the doctor changes the medicines, and the person immediately answers to the second drug. The guy is back to his old healthy self in a few days ' time.

What if the person had not answered this second set of medicines? He'd most probably have gone to another doctor.

So it ends up with the right diagnosis issue. Once the infection is correctly identified, it can be treated successfully. The challenge of the physician is to correctly identify the infection, considering the signs and the results of the tests. In fact, he deviates the disease based on the symptoms shown by the patient, and, in order to confirm his assumptions, the patient is asked to undergo other tests. If the doctor's first guess is incorrect, he suggests a further set of tests to validate his second-best guess of the disease.

There is another factor that can improve the chances of the patient: the test results. If the laboratory carrying out these experiments is incorrect, the result is expected to deceive the doctor. It was also found several times that different physicians would diagnose the problem differently, even with the same symptoms and the same set of test results.

In the sense of astrology, the same issue is offered as evidence that this is not a science. When a doctor makes a mistake, the

Medical Science is not responsible for his skills. But if an astrologer fails, astrology is a pseudo-science. When doctors may come to different conclusions from the same results, why should astrologers not differ? If you take the blood samples of the same patient in several laboratories, you are almost sure that their results vary. No one denigrates modern science itself when the computers designed with all our scientific knowledge make mistakes. Yet people are only too ready to dismiss Astrology. Perhaps by doing this, people want to show their scientific disposition.

Why are astrologers going wrong?

Need to know: this is perhaps the main reason. Many astrologers find it difficult to avoid the temptation to begin making predictions after studying a little. A certain percentage of their predictions prove true because they practiced some astrology after all. We can not refrain from revealing their half-baked information. Another justification for the temptation to start reaping the fruits of their efforts to learn the subject as soon as possible. As consumers flock to them, they lack the desire to continue learning. They also have little time left to make additional efforts to learn more. They are too busy to duplicate people.

Lack of talent: people of genius are not studying astrology in the modern age because the pursuit of this topic is not considered very respectable. We choose to become scientists, engineers, physicians, literary poets, musicians, etc. This does not aid the development of astrology or contribute to additional knowledge or finding the missing links in this topic. There are currently no serious research projects in this area. This knowledge base is, therefore, not tested.

Incorrect data: since statistical data such as time of birth etc. are the very basis of astrology. If this information is incorrect, the horoscope is considered to be faulty and, therefore, it is meaning. The location of cusps, house divisions, and the planetary positions must be correct at any given moment. The many ephemerides differ so much that they seem unbelievable. In this age of science, one must follow the most precise data (for example, from NASA) for measurement. Astrologers tend to follow the easy route of certain ready-minded things, which leads to inaccuracies in their calculations.

Subject destiny: it may occur that the destiny of the individual who wishes to read his future does not benefit the person to know his future. This idea may appear far-flung, but it doesn't. Even in modern times, people are still dying from entirely treatable diseases with the full development of medical science. If a person is doomed to die of pneumonia, he will nevertheless be treated successfully every year by millions around the world. If destiny here can play a role, why can it not play the same role in astrology?

Modern science divides the world into two parts: known and unknown. What is unknown today is supposed to be known tomorrow. Everything will become understood one day over a period of time. But the learned, wise men said that certain aspects of life could not be remembered. These things are not part of the field of human knowledge. Some aspects of the future often fall within the same sector.

Whoever studies open-minded astrology can not dismiss it as anything without merit. It is an easy task for astrologers to correctly say such things about an individual being, including his physical characteristics, his illnesses, his personality, his overall success in life as regards his money or fame, the essence of his occupation, etc., simply by looking at his properly drawn horoscope. Astrologers tend to go awry in the matter of details and the timing of events. A fresh approach to the subject is needed. Brilliant minds should research it, address those phenomena, and misunderstandings that science has accumulated in the past. Only this subject can then regain its legitimate position as a serious and important knowledge branch.

Astrology and Mankind

The United States Culture Describes astrology in the belief that they influence the course of natural occurrences on the Earth and human affairs as a study of the positions and aspects of heavenly bodies. Astrology is focused on planetary observation. In ancient times too, the practice of astrology was prevalent.

Astrology history is really an essential part of civilization and went back to the beginning of mankind. Some of the world's famous civilizations have extensively used this field. For example, at some point in time, the ancient Chinese Culture, the Egyptian Culture, the ancient Indian civilization, and so on all practiced astrology.

The ancient Babylonians possibly used Astrology for the first time. The Babylonians were the first to name the Sun, Moon, and planets days of the week. They were also the first to establish the horoscope's twelve houses. Damascus and Baghdad were known in ancient times as centers of astronomy and astrology. Egypt has made a significant contribution to the development of astrology. Some astrological signs of the zodiac are believed to have originated in Egypt.

Ptolemy is the first Greek astronomer ever to write a book on astrology. He codified the astrology of the sun sign, which we now know. Ptolemy tried to predict celestial bodies ' locations in relation to each other and the Earth by observing their orbital motions. Astrology was part of astronomy during his time. Astronomy later became an exact science, and astrology remained an integral part of theology.

The five elements, metal, wood, water, fire, and Earth, are stressed in Chinese astrology. Even their zodiac signs differ from other forms of astrology.

India has a rich astrological history. Even in the Vedic times, astrology was practiced in India. Astrology is one of Vedanga's six disciplines. Ancient Hindu Scriptures also attach great importance to different aspects of celestial movements and their human impact. Many in India are still studying and practicing astrology.

In Indian Culture, it is considered vital. It is used to make marriage decisions, start new companies, and move into a new home, etc. The Hindus believe that karma causes human fortune or misfortune in life, and the planetary movements are thought to influence karma. Among the Hindus, Brahmins are regarded as the best astrological authorities.

In India, astrologers say it is a scientific way of predicting the future. They also club this field of study inside Hinduism parameters. Hindus believe in astrological predictions almost unanimously

This ancient Indian tradition is also governed by astrology. Hindus claim that the full wealth and benefits of the occupants depend on the Vastu principles during the construction of the building. Indian astrologers believe they can prove the predictions of astrology to be logical.

Horoscope is an astrology part. Even in the developed countries of the West, reading the horoscope every day has become a trend. The Western mind has always examined everything and tends to rely solely on scientific evidence.

This does not, however, discourage the West from becoming fascinated with their horoscopes. Finally, through astrology, the Western world has woken up to the opportunity to learn and change its future. More and more westerners have begun to believe that the powerful planets and stars could affect them.

Western scholars include in their work the subject of astrology. Astrology has never been studied and explored before the way it was done in the last couple of years. In this respect, Indian astrologers should advance and show the world the power of astrology.

CHAPTER TWO

Helpful Advice On How To Learn Astrology

Astrology is best learned by observing the actual astrological location of the planets and by recognizing the connection between symbolic manifestations of the celestial cycles and economic, ecological, and social developments worldwide.

Tip Number One Astrology: Follow current affairs.

You can sense the various positions of planets and understand the various ways these configurations manifest by observing up on modern astrological activities and improvements. There is a strong configuration, for example, that reflects revolutionary ideas and uprisings. The uprising in the Middle East started whenever the planets were reconciled and transferred to these locations. If you practice astrology, not only can you predict or understand world events by following the current locations of the planets, but you can also view how celestial cycles play out in private astrology charts.

Tip number two for astrology. Understand and observe the astrology map transits.

It is very essential to follow the astrological energies in relation to your personal chart in addition to following the current astrological movements of planets. In your astrology map, when the planet in a new position in the sky takes a numerical angle to the birthplace of a planet, then you are in astrology transit. You would be under Uranus to your Moon, for example, if you were born in Aries with your Sun and Uranus to Aries with the same degree as your Sun. Uranus binds the Sun in particular. That would suggest your own private "revolution" for progress in your life.

Tip number three of astrology: Find a good course of astrology or workshop of astrology.

There are many ways to research astrology, but it can be very complex and confusing if there is no framework of simple and effortless training of astrology. Although it takes some time, as in new lessons, to gain knowledge, the best way is to learn from a knowledgeable astrologer who makes complex concepts understandable. Find a course in astrology that focuses on the current principles of astrology and the astrological influences on your astrology table. Look for an astrologer who you like and an experienced astrology teacher. You can learn from someone you don't like, of course, but why? It is easier not to have a personality barrier between you and your subject.

Tip number four for astrology: Write down your life story.

The best way to learn astrology is perhaps to construct an autobiography of events in your life. Take your time to really remember important memories and every memory you can. You fell in love the first time, graduate college, the first career, all major changes in life, get married, have children, get divorced, have a wonderful or disastrous love affair, transfer, fly. Write down the event dates. Then you will do detective astrology work by discovering the transits or planetary influences at that time.

Astrology tip No-5: Go to conferences on astrology.

Nothing like going to conferences in astrology to taste the complexity and diversity of astrology. Look for regional and national conferences in the country or research astrology conferences all around the world if you have a big Jupiter, why not? It is fun to study astrology with astrologers of the same mind that you meet at conferences of astrology. In addition to astrology seminars, most conferences give astrology workshops before and after the conference.
Astrology is a fascinating subject and can be overwhelming when you start learning astrology. Do not let the complexity prevent you from learning this beautiful universe gift, which can help you and the world around you. Learn how to be a co-creator with the planets ' powerful forces. Practice astrology, master this elusive ancient art of mystical knowledge and insight and be your own astrologer.

Astrology - A Traditional Perspective

Modern and European Astrology began in Babylon around 200 BC and is known as Classical Astrology, the earlier period of Astrology in Europe from 1200 to 1700. During the time from 1200 to 1500, medieval astrology and from 1500 to 1700, Renaissance astrology was known.

Astrology was very persistent and thrived during the 2000 cycles from the Greeks to Renaissance until it became fashionable because of newfound philosophies and modern materialism at the end of the 17th and 18th centuries.

Modern astrology focussed not on psychology but on the outer planets. The research was not established until the end of the 20th century. Modern astrology, by using various techniques developed and transmitted by careful observation of the heavens and planets, could provide accurate and precise predictions of upcoming events.

The Planets were equated with gods, and celestial phenomena were observed as omens, where the majority of people regarded the heavens as signs and omens. Traditional astrology varies from modern astrology, which, in its latest form, is more important than forecasting events: character interpretation and psychological insight.

An increased interest in ancient sciences started around the 1900s again, and astrology was studied again. While modern astrology can be considered to be excellent on the strength of a character analysis, the accuracy in traditional astrology can not be predicted. Sun sign Astrology also gave a bad name to Astrology, because people do not believe that one-twelfth of a column can be equated to hundreds of people at a given time.

Astrology has therefore been regarded as cynical because most people treat it as a divertisement and don't know that a true natural chart can not only act as a valuable tool for predicting future events but also for finding fortuitous times. Even if they are open-minded, many people may still doubt the true validity of astrology. Nonetheless, many people who read a private chat will be shocked by its accuracy.

Modern astrology gives a good insight into a person's psyche, especially when someone has to advise themselves after a tragic personal event or needs personal counseling. However, are most people interested in learning about the development of their own personal psychological composition?

Traditional astrology was divided into four main types, first natural astrology, which looks at events based on the true birth chart, and forecasts them. Then there is Horary Astrology, which discusses a horoscope, asking a specific question at a certain time.

Next comes Electional Astrology, which looks astrologically at the best times and dates for a certain issue. Finally, Mundane Astrology uses a wide range of techniques to predict events at national or long-term levels, including weather forecasting.

A John Frawley lecture on traditional astrology stated that tradition does not consist in strict observance of certain rigid old rules but in understanding and maintaining the act's spirit, and in adapting it to modern astrology. William Lilly tried many "new" methods in his day, which led him to the correct results because of his systematic (Saturnine) philosophy. What an amazing affirmation of our diverse modern world's traditional approach.

Methods and Techniques of Medical Astrology

Health astrology is the astrology division which discusses the customer's potential and actual health and diseases. During times of major changes in life, people usually come to the astrologer.
However, to the astrologer, people come in the later stages of the disease, often after some type of operation and rich history of doctors.
When occurrences in the history of the disease correspond with certain astrological transits and forms, we will consider the astrological cause for the disease, make a prognosis of the length of the disease and decide on the appropriate therapy, etc. Often the opposite situation also happens: the consumer attends the normal astrological session, but the astrologer sees a risk in the horoscope well before the threat occurs and materializes.
Many standards are attached to the advice given by the medical astrologer. Is there an operation or not, is there chemotherapy or not, is there radiology or not?
The cruelest branch of astrology is medical astrology. If you can not encounter tough terminal pathologies, if you do not want to be

lethal about the consequences of your advice— better not. When you are not a professional medical doctor, you will need to study and read literature, consult with medical practitioners, gather information on the Internet, take part in forums, groups, community websites, etc.

The healing issues are very different from what astrologers do during teaching. In an ideal world, astrologers advise, and customers change behavior so that stars and planets send them the surplus energy. Medical astrologers may be practical and recommend that they wear such crystals, shades, aromatherapies, herbal remedies, etc. It is best that the medical astrologer and physician careers are not combined. Ideally, medical astrologers don't heal, and clients are not the patient unless a doctor or a certified homeopath is a medical astrologer. The medical astrologer should not be a healer either: he or she should only make a highly skilled prediction of malignancies that have manifest themselves as disease and will, unless nothing is done, remain manifest in that way, potentially with more serious consequences as the time goes by.

Medical astrologer applies both astrological techniques and methods by which the essence of the illness can be deduced. He or she must be a professional astrologer, monitor a wide range of astrological methods, and use them for the good of the client and his or her wellbeing. As he or she gives advice about cures, but in an ideal world he or she can not cure by itself, it should connect with doctors and healers, know their natal charts and decide by synastry who should see next. For practical reasons, however, it is best for the client to find his or her own medical doctors and healers to go to the astrologer when something goes wrong; otherwise, the astrologer can be accused of a deal he or she has sent to the client if anything goes wrong (and with people who are ill will always go wrong).

The graph helps us to decide the kind of treatments such as homeopathy, Bach herbal remedies, vibropathy, massage, classic medicine, treatment of spa, aromatherapy, crystal cures, Su Jok, etc. The signs show the twelve major systems in the human body, beginning with Aries that represents the head, all of them with Pisces ' sign, which governs the feet. The signs comprising the planets are identified, or will most likely be, by birth or advanced horoscopes. For each sign, there is a special kind of tissue salt; these are building materials for the human body that combine tissues, organ systems, organ systems, and the whole body. These salts can be used alone or combined in materials or homeopathic doses to improve your health greatly.

Similarly, a special type of food is best for each sign. Health astrologers are qualified to advise on nutrition and in many ways, improve the health of the consumer. Using the doctrine concept, i.e., to find parallels between the zodiac, the body, and the herbs, signs can also be connected and guided towards the aid of the person.

Horoscope degrees in Medical Astrology Each sign has 30 degrees, and each is connected to 1 part of the body. Each sign has 360 degrees. The earth in this degree is a predisposition to disease— the degree tells us which part of the body is the problem, while the planet indicates which form of the disease. Likewise, midpoints and degrees can be linked.

The planets, asteroids, and Uranian planets are sources of energy in the horoscope, and each is unique. For instance, Mars energy is firelike; it fires the body's fires (which result in high temperatures) and thus cleanses them. Neptune is known as bacteria, while Pluto is known as unidentified bacteria and so on. The asteroids, especially the large ones, like Ceres, Juno, and others, act similarly. The Uranian planets can also be used in medical astrology. There are 8 "Uranian" planets, but the effect can be felt very strongly on the map. There are no observational details. Some of the planets had strong medical connotations so that the reputation of medical astrology research will rise to 90%.

Medical Astrology Houses
Of the 12 houses in astrology, five are more important than the others:
- First house -- the physicality of body,
- 6th house -- diseases,

- 8th house -- support others from, death, sex, terminal states, karma, cancer,
- 12th house – hospitals, isolation, and auto-immunity, psychic problems, monasteries.

Nevertheless, in medical astrology, each house will have its own particular meaning:

- No. One -- consciousness, face, brain insults, brain tumors, etc
- No. Two -- electrolytes, blood, food intake, hormones, diabetes, hypophysis.
- No. Three -- speech problems, the lungs,
- No. Four -- producing food for mother, others, milk; inheritance, genetics,
- No. Five -- infarction of myocardium, heart,
- No. Six -- meals, day to day habits, personal hygiene, diseases,
- No. Seven -- spine, the balance of the body, death through brain problems,
- No. Eight -- hypophysis, Expelling of the processed foods, kidneys, adrenal cortex,
- No. Nine -- cerebral hemisphere, the upper part of the brain, Neptune rules over the right hemisphere, Jupiter rules over the left;
- No. Ten -- metabolism,
- No. Eleven -- hemorrhagia, circulation,
- No. Twelve -- thymus, autoimmune diseases, liver, immunity in general.

Medical astrology is the astrological industry that addresses the customer's possible and actual health and diseases. In times of great life changes, people usually come to the astrologer.

Nevertheless, people come into the progressive stages of the illness to the medical astrologer often after surgery and rich history of coping with physicians.

If

Incidents throughout the history of illness correspond with these kin ds of astrological transitions., we could find the astrological cause of disease, predict the course and duration of the disease and decide on the required treatment, and so on. Often the opposite occurs: the client attends the normal astrological meeting, but the astrologer sees a risk in the horoscope well before the illness has manifestly materialized.

Most requirements are attached to the professional astrologer's advice. Whether or not there is surgery, chemotherapy, radiology, or not...

The cruelest branch of astrology is medical astrology. You don't do it if you cannot reach difficult terminal pathologies if you don't want to take a deadly responsibility for the consequences of your advice. You must prepare well and read literature, consult medical doctors, collect information on the Internet, participate in forums, groups, membership websites, etc. if you are not a doctor by profession.

Curing issues are quite different from what astrologers do normally when studying. Astrologers advise in the ideal world change customers ' conduct, so that planets and stars send them the excess energy. Medical astrologers could be more practical and recommend the use of certain crystals, colors, aromatherapy, herbal remedies, etc. It is best not to combine the occupations of professional astrologers and physicians. Ideally, medical astrologers do not cure, and the patient is not unless the medical astrologer is a doctor or, preferably, a professional homeopath. Neither should a medical astrologer be a healer; he or she should only give a highly skilled prognosis of malefic influences which, as time progresses, have already been shown as a disease and will continue-except where nothing is done-to be shown in this manner.

Medical astrologer applies both astrological techniques and processes, from which the essence of the illness can be deduced. He or she must be a professional astrologer in particular and must order and use a wide range of astrological methods for customers and their wellbeing. Since he or she provides healing suggestion, but could not heal on its own, he or she is the ideal world should be linked to healers and doctors, should know his or her birth charts, and decide who the patient should be next through synastry. Nonetheless, for practical reasons, it is better if the client chooses his own physicians and healers to accompany the astrologer. Otherwise, the astrologer can be accused of a bargain with the physician he has sent to if something goes wrong (and with the sick people it will always do).

The chart allows you to determine the type of therapy, such as vibropathy, homeopathy, classical medicine, massage, aromatherapy, spas, Su Jok, crystal cure, etc.

The Signs are the twelve large structures of the human body, all through the signs of the fishes, which govern the feet. The signs which contain planets will distinguish, or most probably be, by birth or through advanced horoscopes. A special tissue salt exists for each sign; those are the building materials for the human body, which contains skin, organs, organ systems, and the whole body. Using these salts alone or mixing them in substance or homeopathic doses will enhance one's health.

Similarly, a special type of food is best for each sign. Medical astrologers will be qualified to provide food advice and will improve the health of their customers in many ways. Using the theory of doctrines, i.e., the identity of the herbs, body, and zodiac, the signs can also be connected with herbs and prescribed for the help of the patient.

Medical Astrology Horoscope degrees Each sign has 30 levels, and each of these is linked to one part of the body. The world to this degree is prone to disease— the extent which tells us which part of the body is in doubt, while the earth is going to show what disease it is going to be. Similarly, midpoints and degrees can be connected.

Asteroids, Medical Astrological Planets, and Uranian Planets The planets are energy sources in the horoscope, each special. For example, Mars ' energy is firelike; it flames fires in the body (which lead to high temperatures) and cleanses it. Neptune stands for medicinally recognized bacteria, while Pluto stands for unidentified bacteria, and so forth. The asteroids, in particular, the large ones, such as Juno, Ceres, and others, are also interested. The Uranian planets can also be used in scientific astrology. There are 8 "Uranian" planets that do not have observational information, but whose influence can be felt very strongly on the map. Some of these planets have clear medical connotations, so the validity of medical astrology research can be improved to 90 percent.

We can only alert the client about cancer or some other such serious disease when we see a concentration of nearly similar transits. Since the transits and solar charts can be determined in advance, we can tell the customer precisely when his troubles will begin and when they will end.

Sometimes a similar predisposition from various configurations occurs. If there is a Uranus square to the Ascending, but Pluto squares that same Ascendant, the combination of action will appear twice. Now it only takes a Mars transit to empower one of these configurations, or Mars is in the Uranus / Pluto midpoint on the solar return chart.

Diagnosis of disease on the basis of transits progresses, solar and synastry charts In native astrology, we would need only a natural chart and transits in 90 percent of sessions there's simply no time to delve into all the charts that can support. Nevertheless, it is a standard in medical astrology to use many other forms of charts. There must be three independent disease confirmations, regardless of the diagram we see. In the case of medical astrology, searching for clues to the graph is often a detective work before you find the constellation that was involved when the symptoms started. By linking real-life events with their astrological roots, you can predict how and with confidence the disease will evolve.

The long transits of malefic planets produce all manner of health problems, while the progressive horoscope gives the best view of customer living in the long term. We always use solar charts in medical astrology because we see strong accents which may not last for a very long time, but sometimes leave the sequel for the rest of the client's lives.

It's also critical for whom you stay. The people with whom the customer lives share his or her resources. Sometimes they just cure by being there; others only sicker the consumer. The nation where the consumer lives also have its own horoscope, and this can also be taken into consideration.

Auxiliary Methods of Arabic Medical Astrology consist of two important points, one of which is subtracted, the third. There are approximately 500 Arab pieces, some of which relate directly to health. Pars Fortunae is the most prominent Arab element and blends Sun, Moon, and Ascendant influences.

Each house has its own set of Arabic parts. The sixth house, for example, has two Arab sections, of interest to astrology: Bad fortune, incurable diseases, and sin(Asc+Mars-Saturn), Curable diseases (Asc+Mars-Mercury) and the sixth house includes parts of the vanquished, which have nothing to do with health, and for the servants and prisoners of war.

The number of Arab house parts varies from house no. 7 to house no. 8— 5, etc.

Quite often, hourly astrology produces loads of information. Instead of the birth chart and the charts derived from it, we erect the chart for the time we ask the question about the disease in horary astrology. Reading a schedule diagram is different from reading a natal and all other diagrams, so do not use it unless you know what you are doing. Nonetheless, it is useful to learn scheduling astrology, since it often provides a direct look at the real situation, the course of the disease, possible operations, and deaths, etc. We should only do this if we know for sure when the disease starts. It also has its own rules.

Electional astrology attempts to find out when an action should commence. In medical astrology, such diagrams could be studied to find out when the therapy prescribed is supposed to begin, when the doctor must come, and so on.

The importance of medical astrology in conventional healing medicine is a well-established patient's status at the time of calculation and knows statistically if the prediction is good or bad. However, the future of the patient is never discussed and is almost always used when something bad has already occurred. Medical astrology is the lack of a connection between the patient's documented diagnosis, his current therapy, and the disease's future development. Since astrological prognosis can be made in advance, something can also be done in advance. The normal follow-up in medical astrology is homeopathy and other energy healing methods, because the treatment of energy "spends," however, the energy that planets and stars give us through the astral body. Medical astrology has the greatest advantage: that it helps us not only to foresee that techniques and remedies will cure but also to avoid certain techniques and remedies and to take and apply some other method of cure.

The Careers In Astronomy

Astrology is the process by which a person's character and future can be decided by aligning the stars and planets. Astrology is not working and can not predict events or characteristics of the future. Eastern astrology is event-oriented, and they will tell you with much greater precision what happened in the past and what will happen in the future. Horoscopic astrology is most widely used to examine people's birth charts to interpret the attributes, psychological traits, and to some degree, destiny.

The astrology of the Arab period is the direct predecessor of today's Western astrology. In fact, our astrology may succeed that third stream of ancient astrology. This form of astrology, developed by the Greeks and based on certain basic ideas that were developed in Babylon, is also referred to as' judicial' or' genethlial.' This is the sort of astrology that most of us now know whether we are faithful or not. The problem of why people believe in astrology is more fascinating than the horoscope info. Psychologists have demonstrated that customers are content with astrological predictions for as long as possible procedures are vaguely individualized.

The best way to understand astrology is to learn how it started. There is no question that astrology is the oldest and most common of all pseudosciences at the same time. In fact, astrology is used to improve our knowledge of our universe. In the past 30 years, this psychological approach has grown significantly as astrologers are improving their advice. Astrology is a magical thought that gave us creationism and most alternative methods of medicine. This is in accordance with scientific reasoning and compares the practitioner with the Enlightenment tradition.

Astrology is pseudoscience because, usually, people believe in it for illegal purposes. He doesn't give any examples. The analysis of the relation between the astronomical positions of planets and events on earth is, to put it simply, astrology. Astrologers believe that at the time of a person's childbirth, the sun, moon, and planets have a direct influence on the character of that person. Astrology is a magnificent mix of science, art, and craft. The best part of it is that he can never embrace his entire knowledge, no matter how much one learns.

Astrology is believed to affect or associate the locations of certain celestial bodies with the personality trait of an individual. Those who studied Astrology used celestial object observation and a diagram of their movements in the past. Prior astrology knowledge is not necessary. From the very beginning, the four levels all possible astrological knowledge shall be included in the study for your own successful practice. Astrology is called because it comes from the stars; it's called because theology comes from God. It's called theology. Astrologically, to live is to eat the tree of knowledge of good and evil with pleasing concupiscence and to bring death to themselves.

A comprehensive astrology bibliography is beyond the scope of this FAQ, but certain books were included. The interested reader should visit a well-stocked library. Since heavens were never meant for these purposes, however, astrology is a dangerous and unlawful practice. Stars have been created to keep the calendar and to declare God's glory. Glory. The lessons are for anyone who wants to learn how astrology is done and how astrology is done. They are especially for skeptics because science requires that a subject's knowledge be evaluated.

Because if astronomy is studying the motions of heavenly bodies, the results of these movements are studied in astrology. The astronomers of the ancient world focused on a division of the cosmos through which the superior and eternal bodies of the celestial worlds governed the earthly or sub-Mundial sphere, where all was death and transition. But astrology isn't just love and money anymore. Many other questions are answered by astrology. The art of professional astrology is to help others to find what they are called to do.

Shamanic Astrology practitioners are trained in the unhelpful awareness of the night sky and in the sacred patterns, phases, and movements in the universe. Astrology is also an art form—one for simple sketches and complex portraits of men, families, businesses, nations, and more. As the studies of ancient Egypt also show, astrology can clearly have spiritual and religious undertones. Astrology is unscientific due to the fact that constellations are recessive or changing. Precession was not known to the early astronomers and thus was not taken into account in their system.

Although entertaining, astrology with the Sun Sign is a quite superficial and slightly helpful application off a complex old science dating back thousands of years. Learn how astrology can inform your choices and increase your own knowledge — ancient practice and study of the stars and planets in astrology. His history goes back to the time of Babylon. Such a template is astrology.

Wholistic Astrology is a way to interpret a horoscope so that all aspects are taken into account. We can see trends such as career, finance, and social needs in external areas. This is why the "study of signs" is known as astrology. Without an effort to overcome the impetus of any force or motivation for intervention, the signs indicate what the patterns and certain causes are likely to be, and in any case, astrology shows. There's a certain astrology today, but it's not true "traditional astrology." Were you aware that in the early history of man, astrology was considered science?

Astrology is a true science of human experience rather than a stupid old idea, superstition or pseudoscience. Its symbols allow room for human behavior vagaries, which can never be reduced to simple and absolute formulas. Maybe there is hostility because astrology remains a living practice, a true competitor of popular respect and support. I hope that common rivalry will die between historians and social scientists and that this powerful custom and ideology will be recognized. This means that astrology is significantly more accurate to predict human behavior or events than mere chance. Most satisfied customers assume that their horoscope represents them correctly and that their astrologer has provided them with advice that's good.

Astrology were harmless, and it's fun. Regardless of its former glories, it now seems a five-and-one look at the cosmos. Perhaps the oldest topic and also in a way the most neglected is astrology. It's the oldest because astrology existed as far back as we were able to investigate human history. Rather, they want to provide anecdotal proof-stories tell how accurate astrology is. In real science, anecdotal evidence wasn't acceptable because it is all other negative interactions people and people have are too easy to miss are not good at remembering and reporting experiences accurately.

Astrology is predicated on an individual's birth charts. At birth, the position of the Sun, Moon, and planets is shown on the zodiac. In addition, astrology is not a fast study. Traditionalists used to say that it takes about 30 years for a participant to pass around Saturn. Vedic astrology is part of a comprehensive, integrated system of learning which can be enhanced by contact with his "sister" sciences. The Vedic Astrology system is kind because not only is one person told what might occur, but a list of potential remedies or corrective action is presented to offset the amount and quality of karmas that come back to them, as shown in the chart of birth.

CHAPTER THREE

The Art of Astrology

The art of astrology was based on the notion that the relationship between the position of the planets and the nature of the person who was born at the same time exists. The foundation of this idea is the fundamental idea that the Universe and all its components are not separate but inherently linked in a single whole. What happens in a very large, macrocosm, or Earth also happens in a very small microcosm or human being simultaneous.

It's not so much that now the planets influence the individual, as people generally believe in astrology, although the Sun and Moon definitely do. Therefore, the position of the planets and the essence of individuals are a reflection and a manifestation of the same universal force acting on them. So when the process is known, what the location of the planets can see will tell us something about the existence of the person Birthed in the same moment as well. A simple analogy is how we tell the time using clocks. We can read the time on a clock and know much about what will happen in the world at that moment without actually having to witness it.

The full art of astrology has several essential components. This needs time and place for an occurrence that is normally a person's birth. When this event takes place, Astrology then considers the position of the planets in the sky, the signs, the houses, and the aspects (or links) between the planets.

Astrology's first part is The Planets. In all, ten planetary bodies are commonly accepted, with some new ones still discussed by astrologers. The Mercury, Sun, Mars, Venus, Saturn, Jupiter, Neptune, Uranus, and Pluto. They're all here. The Earth is also an essential part of astrology because it is used to draw up that sign and houses we will address later.

Throughout astrological thinking, there is no coincidence or pure chance of the planets, but there are the underlying purpose and importance of the Universe. Each celestial body reflects particular energy in the world, some of which would call it angelic power. This is supported by many years of observation, literature, mythology, and even common words in our language.

For example, Mars is often known as a god of war and energy and battle. People would call upon this God to inspire victory for them. The red color of the world represents power, sexuality, and inspiration. We derive terms such as martial from which war, discipline, and military order have been linked. Mercury was, on the other hand, known as a communicator and trickster in Roman mythology, because he could move so much faster than anyone else. He is often portrayed on his feet with wings. Mercury was the gods ' envoy. Mercury is the fastest planet in our Universe to orbit the Sun. The metal is used to say the temperature because it adjusts very rapidly and receptively. This is also where we can change the word mercurial meaning. It is also called

Quicksilver, which reinforces the idea of pace and transition. Jupiter gave rise to Jovial's terms. It is a huge planet with many moon orbits, much like a king or queen with many subjects. It was always considered a vast, inspiring, optimistic, fortunate force in mythology. In reality, the Earth has been saved several times from meteors, drawn by Jupiter, and absorbed on its surface.

We understand the different ideas of all planets, but how does this affect us, individuals? The Universe is a whole and not separate, as we said, so as the planets embody such energy forces, the individual also has these forces in his nature. Some of us, like Jupiter, are larger than life and inspirational, others like Mercury, many major athletes, and warriors, or even despots, as embodied in the Martian theory. Of course, in reality, we all have these principles and the principles of all the other planets within ourselves, but as we will see next, they are in slightly different forms.

So if each one of us has the same planetary forces within us, why are we so different, and why are we expressing these forces differently?

According to astrology, it is about where the planets are at birth in the Zodiac. This brings us to the second area of astrology—the signs.

The planets are traveling along a fixed path with the stars as far backdrop along the night sky since the stars are farther than the planets. These star clusters along the path of the planets contain twelve equally large sets of stars known as zodiac signs. From the end of March, Taurus, signs are Aries, Mercury, Gemini, Virgo, Leo, Scorpio, Libra, Capricorn, Sagittarius, Sun and Aquarius. Although they don't correspond exactly with the constellations named in the sky. The Zodiac is the background or screen to see the planets. For example, at the time of someone's birth, Mars could have been in the constellation of Aries. This essentially means that the backdrop of the stars behind Mars, from the viewpoint of the Earth, would be that of the Aries part of the Zodiac. In the same way, each planet would have a star background when someone was born, and each planet could lie in any of the twelve zodiacal signs. Conventional astrology only includes the constellation in which the Sun lies when you are born. I.e., She is a Leo would mean the Sun is laying before the constellation of Leo at the time of her birth even if we didn't advise you to see!

What are the Zodiacal signs all about? The zodiacal constellations are like a filter that colors and affects the energies represented by a planet and are expressed in some way just as the planets represent various forces.

For instance, Aries is the Zodiac's first sign. It is related to the spring and rebirth season after the long, sleeping winter. New life is to be seen everywhere, optimism after the bleak time still exists. Aries is about new starts with vivid, free-flowing heat, and it is the first of the signs of flame. It's very much about innocence and childhood and a little naivety as the first sign of the Zodiac. It's the start of an adventure. It is conveyed mainly through practice. But if we look at cancer, it's a whole different message. This is a water sign for the family, the past, the home, and the nursing family, and expresses itself mainly in feelings and emotions.

Now, if we take the planet Mars, which we mentioned before, when the planets are described, this is the strength of personal energy or will and the ability to hold your position and strive for what you want in life. If Mars is present in Aries at the time of the birth of a child, the flow of energy is represented by practice. as you will see in an athlete, military commander, or a person with such a temper., they would be competitive and uninhibited. When we discovered Mars in cancer, however, the energy would be emotionally conveyed. It is less apparent and more subdued, and the energy will psychological overreaction or psychological manipulation, or surface if only a friend or a family member is threatened.

Each of the ten planets may lie in such a specific sign of the Zodiac. However, there is a wide, wide range of combinations. Due to this fact and the connection between planetary positions and peoples, one can see one of the main reasons why so many different personalities inhabit our planet. Astrology, in turn, does not believe that personalities are formed exclusively through the growing process; it believes that the fundamental components of a person are already there waiting for their expression at birth.

Besides this astrology, Houses has the idea. This will be the third area of art used in astrology. We said before how much the planetary energy is processed by a sign-in, which they are. However, the position of the house adds to that by saying in what areas of life these energies are mainly expressed. The houses are between one and twelve. In the Ascendant, which is the eastern horizon of the chart, the first house begins. The place of the Ascendant depends on the person's location at birth. As you go around the chart, the number of the house goes up to the twelfth and final house.

The first house and the Ascendant or rising sign deal much with the man, his worldview and way of speech and his own personality; the fourth house, the lower point of the map, is a person root and family; in contrast to the Ascendant, the descendant is the descendant that is the beginning of the seventh house and has to do with the person's meeting and relationship with others. The tenth house is about the profession and public attention. The twelfth house is about surrendering all things to the universality. The trip around the house is basically a journey from the individual's self-awakening to experiences in the world to lead ultimately to the collective consciousness and end of the person.

When we add to the previous information that we had about the house of a planet, which was the celestial energies filtered with its symbol, we can now tell where those energies primarily manifest themselves in life. It can be expressed in, for example, the field of the individual or the family, the workplace, or relationships or many other areas.

An example of the planetary sign and house all working together is a man saying his Mars in the Seventh House in Aries. Uninhibited (Aries) force (Mars) transmitted by sex (Seventh House). Sounds interesting! Sounds interesting!

We should note the final area of astrology is the relations between the planets. Some planets were seen as connected if the location where they are located is at a certain angle from another planet when the chart is drawn as a circle. The planets have various possible relations, such as conjunction (next to each other), a trine (120 degrees), a square (90 degrees), and an opposition (180 degrees each other). There are several possible connections between them. These are symbolic numbers because the 360-degree ring is split into one, two, three, or four sections. The conjunction and trine (the divisible circle of one and three) are easier, and the opposition and the square (the divisible circle of two and four) are more difficult.

A conjunction of two planets would mean that the two energies would be harmonious and indivisible. For example, a person connecting Mercury with Mars would have his personal energy inherently linked to his communicative abilities. You may well have a witty, strong tongue. A square of the same two planets would mean that the planetary energy is associated, but in a more difficult way, requiring some sort of tension, the single one might have a sharp and vital tongue. They'd have to work on this during their lives.

As you can see from all this data, every chart is special, since we are essentially unique as people and why the art of astrology is so challenging and fascinating.

Know the Different Types of Astrology Services

Most of us still feel bad for things that are not happening, and something or another that isn't healthy for us. We wonder why we have such things. I know a friend of mine who had an acute disease. Her parents almost sold all of the hospital bills they had to pay. She's good today but often remembers the days of her hospital and asks me why she and her family had such bad luck.

My best friend's dad is an astrologer, and because of flaws in our horoscope, he says bad luck comes to us. However, his father says that astrology can solve all types of problems, whether financial, personal, marriage, or work-related. Astrology was a science that involves the study of the Sun, moon, and star positions at birth. An astrologer studies the positions closely and predicts your future on the same basis.

Different Astrology forms
Indian Astrology: Jyotishi or Moon Astrology is also recognized. Indian astrology is also known as Vedic astrology, as it came from the Vedas. Astrology in India includes 12 zodiac signs: Aries, Taurus, Gemini, Cancer, Virgo, Leo, Libra, Scorpio, Sagittarius, Capricorn, Aquarius, and Pisces.

In the Vedas, the five elements that are water, fire, air, earth, and sky are listed. An Indian astrologer takes all these five elements into account when studying a horoscope. Your astrologer will follow a constellation-based calendar in the center with the moon to predict your future. It is because the moon rules the mind and emotions of the human being.

Western Astrology: Unlike its Indian counterpart, Western Astrology revolves around the movement of the Sun. Eastern astrology suits Tetrabiblos from Ptolemy. This type of astrology represents 13 constellations from the zodiac. Ophiuchus is a sign in western astrology as well as the 12 zodiac signs.

Tropical astrology: if you predict the future of a person from the Sun and from other planets based on the locations of the Earth, it's tropical astrology.

Arab and Persian Astrology: In ancient Mesopotamia, this type of astrology first came into existence.
According to Arab astrology, at the time of their birth, each man or woman is born with 12 weapons. These weapons are available in three sets of four weapons each. They help a person fight the disadvantages in his or her life. But a weapon can not determine our destiny in advance. On the other hand, you can change your destiny and grow in life by changing weapons.

Relationships, medical astrology, Nadi astrology, and financial are the other types of astrology.
You can visit an astrologer when you face something bad or think someone was cursing you. He understands your problems and helps you overcome your problems. Many people have evolved in their lives by easily going to a good astrologer to overcome their financial, interpersonal, marriage, and other problems. He will have complete control over you and your partner and heal every misfortune in your lives to bring peace.

How to Get the Best From Your Astrologer

If you are consulting an astrologer your first time, you probably don't know exactly what to expect from an Interpretation. You may be nervous and careful about what might be revealed during the session. Recall that awful episode in the 8th grade? Aware of new experiences is a totally natural reaction. Your friends might have been reading before and can certainly tell long stories of their experiences.

But what do you expect from the astrologer? Here are some things to consider if you want to get the most out of your first meeting with your astrologist.

Be honest about your birthday. Your astrologer asks for your birthday to create a custom chart that is unique to you based on your time. 5 p.m. birth times are highly suspect because 4:55 p.m. was more probable.

The ideal time of conception is when the infant takes his first breath. The kid inhales the universe's potentials at this precise time. It is vital that those who expect or plan a child in the future get at least the minute, if not the second, of birth. One day, children will look for an astrologer, and it's important to know their correct birth date. If you do nothing else for your baby, get the time to be born.

Sometimes you can pick up your Mother's birth time, and some of the birth certificates have or a baby book reference. Just don't guess if you don't know for sure. You might think that you have to have a birth date for your astrologer to do your chart at any moment, or that they are both incorrect.

Your Mother may not really remember when you were born. You might think, "but why can't you remember Mum? Why didn't you pay attention?" Actually, there's a great deal going on during a child's birth, so if time isn't noticed and written down, then it's memorable. Being in a workstation of unfamiliar nurses, you have just met to take care of your person's most intimate details is a very stressful time.

Your astrologer would like to hear, "My mother thinks I was born sometime after lunch, but before dinner." This information enables your astrologer to adapt his or her interpretations accordingly. When you give "After lunch" a birth time, your astrologer will compensate for the time short and build your chart accordingly. You and your astrologer benefit from this training. You get a better reading, and your astrologer can interpret you better. That might seem to be the same thing, but it isn't. Your reading is important, and your astrologer is likely to be knowledgeable, compassionate, and informative.

Get to the point Usual one-hour session begins the face-to-face interaction between the client and the astrologer. This can be the one and a half hour mark and, in some situations, even two hours. Nonetheless, usually, one hour is the information you as a customer can understand and learn during your first meeting.

Your astrologer will ask if anything specific to the initial reading needs to be focussed on, and this is your opportunity to take advantage of your meeting. If you really want to take a closer look at your love life, say so when you book your appointment. You might also be distracted and not listen to all the pressing career problems that your astrologer explains in the future, because they know what happens to you by means of transits and other predictive techniques. You may be worried about your love issues and don't care about dull things like work. Don't wait until you leave the office to say, "Will I abandon my boyfriend?" If you are immediately concerned, it makes sense first of all, preferably when making your reservation. You might think your astrologer already knows, but not all of us are mental readers.

Term This is a really common courtesy. Tell your astrologer and make an appointment. Nobody appreciates being ambushed with your pressing problems on a Saturday afternoon. Your astrologer will draw up your own charts and diagrams carefully when holding a potential meeting. You should consider all the existing planetary conditions and the possible impact on your life with respect. You may prepare yourself with meditation or breathing techniques, which will lead to a confident and meaningful consultation.

Consider your astrologer's gift to you For your astrologer, and it's very often psychically drying to give yourself during the consultation, especially when difficult issues arise during the session. One troublesome place of my heart is sorrow. The death of a loved one can cause sadness and relief. In anybody's life, grief is not an easy time. For the astrologer to help you navigate these dark days, weeks, or months, you must psychically give yourself the gift.

Are you a regular client? The serial client One who goes from one practicing practitioner to the next looking for answers that appear so unclear? It's no problem to hear a second opinion, and you certainly have to find an astrologer you identify with. That being said, please stop moving your last astrologer from your mouth to your new astrologer in the first paragraph. He or she is instantly concerned about you and can only guess your next remarks in the office of your potential advisor.

Talk to your astrologer Many consumers prefer not to know if they consult an astrologer. There are many ways of reasoning here. Astrologers understand that the best part of bravery is discretion. We understand that some things are best left unmentioned and you are in the right place if you are discreet. There is no astrologer I know who will discuss the maps, information, or problems of their client freely among other astrologers.

If you can speak honestly about your astrologer, then your friends and family can be more comfortable to refer to them. It's good for business and good for astrology by singing their loves enthusiastically (which is what most practitioners want).

It's time to step up and advise those of you who enjoy your astrologer. Tell your friends about your faith. Explain how helpful it was to collaborate with your astrologer. You don't have to get into your life's nitty-gritty details. Ask interested persons you know when they call for an appointment that you mention your name, trust your astrologer, and appreciates your appointments.

Can't get on yet?

In the unlikely event, you are unhappy with your astrologer's service, and you have to tell him directly. There is no need to be disrespectful or mean, but just clarify where you think he or she was incorrect and give them a chance to look at their work, and the astrologer will approach it again if it's your appropriate task. You give the astrologer an opportunity to re-evaluate his research by bringing your questions to his notice. Nobody tries to do that. It's best to split ways if you really think you can't maintain your marriage.

We all live in our own charts. It takes effort to get along in life. If you have found an astrologer who is in touch with you and your rhythms, keep them close to each other. You are one of the lucky ones who will enrich your life with astrology. The fact that you read this chapter shows that you have hope and trust in the future of astrology. You make an important customer, but the payback is the huge advantage astrology can offer you and your life.

What You Need To Understand About Astrology

Astrology is said to be the science that teaches us how to create horoscopes and use the positions of celestial bodies to observe and understand human life on Earth, at least what is reported on a leading website in astrology. I do not see how an analogy can be drawn between astrology and modern science. Science and astrology are two fields that are very distinct and founded on very different principles. Science is based on the principles of experimentation, analysis, and inference. Theoretical or statistical evidence must always be included in scientific principles. Although astrology has well-defined concepts of its own, they are very different from science.

Given what many astrologers may say, astrology is not restricted, and we have to understand what astrology is before we could use proclamation science. Astrology (Vedic), the product of divine inspiration, is believed to have been given by the Goddess of richness, Mahalakshmi, to the Hindu sage, "Bhrigu." This knowledge was documented in old sacred texts, of which only remains. Astrology is not a flawless science and just as good as an astrologer. His expertise dictates how correct the findings are and largely depends on his depth of knowledge, level of experience (the quality of predictions made), and experience. Nevertheless, it would still make sense to suppose that even an astrologer, who has been successful in all accounts, cannot claim to have complete knowledge of astrology as his or her knowledge cannot exceed that contained in the existing texts because they are themselves incomplete.

As explained on the leading website in Astrology, science and astrology are based on diametrically different points of view. Science still grapples with compelling questions about the Universe, the creation of the Universe, the possibility of parallel universes, an infinite fraction of a second after the Big Bang and time.

So, what was there before time began? If the Universe has been expanding ever since its formation, to what does it expand? The information is so small that it sounds absurd to these questions. Vedic astrology, on the other hand, stems from a belief system based on the principle that the Hindu scriptures can provide or with their aid, an explanation for everything that happens. Many Vedic scholars believe that what scientists today discover has always been known by the sages. For example,' Rahu' and' Ketu' twin Vedic planets are special to Vedic astrology. It is said to represent a legendary serpent whose head is' Rahu' and the tail ' Ketu.' These two planets are considered malignant and devour other energy forms such as eclipsing or weakening the Sun and Moon. The color is black in' Rahu' and grey in' Ketu.' The resemblance between' Rahu' and' Ketu' is very striking, and the black hole is known to be a white nain on the opposite end of a black hole. The relevance of the number' 108,' which is the number of beads in the Hindu rosary, is another example that can also be found on the astrology website. Although these beads of prayer were made during the ancient Vedic period, we now know that Figure ' 108,' because the distance between the Earth and the Sun is approximately 108 times the Sun's diameter, is particularly relevant. The diameter of the Sun is about 108 times the diameter of the Earth and of the Moon, approximately 108 times the diameter of the Moon. Have the ancient Hindu sages been able, long before telescopes existed, to determine these celestial measures with such precision?

Of course, none of the above is empirical, but there is a question of whether science is sufficiently advanced to clarify astrology. In my view, a scientist would first have to be able to understand and learn the concepts of astrology and practice astrology in order to explain or refute astrology. I hope that he or she would then realize that astrological predictions are not simplistic in nature. All are not black and white, as there are real shades of gray in science.

In addition to the use of Vedic astrology as a way of predicting the future, Vedic astrology also enables remedial measures by using gemstones, talismans, prayer rituals, Mantras chants, etc. A parallel Universe of constellations, stars, planets, etc. exists in human body, according to the ancient Vedic writings. This Universe clearly does not exist in the same physical form that we learn from astronomy. This life can be felt, however, by the awakening of the' Kundalini,' or' Sleeping Serpent,' which is a magnificent flowing thread through the spinal cord. Nine stars, twelve zodiacs, and 28 constellations are known by Vedic astrology. The chief astrologer of the above-mentioned website for leading astrology Pandit Sarvesh Nagarvedic explains that the nine Vedic planets are granted semiagod status, but not all those celestial corpses are strong and depend on offerings made for strength on Earth. If we on Earth pray for or please the energy of a planet, through the acquisition of gem, we tap into the power of the Sun, existing in our own parallel Universe. Therefore, the planets are easily rewarded and respond by offering their blessings to their adorers.

So, what does it all mean? Do the same forces exist in the heavens or within us that control our lives through astrology? "As above, so inside," the answer would seem. Astrological factors are not far removed objects, which function in isolation, they are also part of the Universe, and we have the means to improve or reduce them, as we wish. It doesn't mean that we can totally alter fate, so we have the ability to change the position of the planets in our horoscopes, which is naturally impossible. What we must say is that, through astrology, everyone is going through good times and bad times. The fundamental principle of astrology is that events and deeds (karam) are above all. As Christ, astrology supports those who sustain themselves, but we are able to change the power of astrological powers by using our knowledge of astrology so that we can go beyond good times and reduce the negative impact of bad times.

CHAPTER FOUR

Meanings of Astrological Planets

When an astrologer speaks of the planets in your chart, they refer to the Sun, Moon, Mercury, Venus, Mars, Jupiter, Uranus, Neptun, and Pluto, but not to astronomy as defining planets for simplicity. The Sun is a star, the Moon is an earth satellite, and the status of a dwarf planet is demoted by Pluto. History and legends have survived and evolved over thousands of years, and the importance of astrological planets is derived. The planets symbolize different parts of our mental makeup.

The Sun is the center of the solar system, and it takes a lot of weight to interpret personality on the chart. Astrology of sun signs is very common, and most people are aware of their sun signs. The Sun is a good part of what you are going to do or aspire to do in your life. It will also show your natural tendencies to get what you want. For example, if your Sun is in Aries, you will only go for it, and if your Sun is in Capricorn, you will think about what is good or bad, what is going to or may not happen, and plot a course to do what you want.

Emotions are the main astrological meaning of the Moon. The Moon shows how we react to the world. It symbolized your family and home environment in the early stages. The Moon is what you like. You need to have to be safe and thorough. What is your Moon's sign and home, and how it interacts with other planets, reveal your deepest secrets and emotional needs.

Mercury is called a winged messenger; communication is the astrological meaning of Mercury. What Mercury sign and house are in your chart shows how you communicate, whether it is easy for you to express yourself or if your thoughts and feelings are difficult for you to transmit to others.

Venus is commonly known as the love planet, but Venus is more about what we love. Venus is where our time and money are spent. You are drawn to quality products if your Venus is in Sagittarius, and you would spend money on a great trip with an art object which is nice to look at. Naturally, Venus is about relations and the person with whom we want to be. When Venus is on the astrology map, you should know what kind of relationships you are going to have.

Mars is symbolic of the internal motivating force. A solid Mars shows itself as someone with a high sex drive and a competitive edge in life. Knowing the importance of Mars will remind you how easy or difficult it is to inspire you to achieve your objectives. A weak Mars may indicate that you start a project or want the fuel to complete the trip.

Jupiter is known in astrology as the great beneficent (with Venus as the least profitable), which means that Jupiter brings good things. The planet of expansion, protection, chance, and blessings is Jupiter. The downside of Jupiter is that we can feel so good with what happens that we never think that something bad will come from what we do. One can be caught off balance, believing that the lucky streak never ends.

Saturn has the reputation of not the most flattering astrology. Saturn is the master of jobs, hard work, hardship, commitment, and can not do anything. It is true that we reap what we sow under Saturn. You can achieve great things by having a strong Saturn in your chart. You will be able to stay with something and continue to work through the challenges. A weak Saturn can mean that you give up or even don't try.

For Uranus, the astrological cliché is: assume the unexpected. Uranus is the world that shakes life in a new way. You should expect to do things differently anywhere Uranus is in your table. For instance, Uranus is in your 11th house of friendships, and you can eclectically mix friends and find friendships with people who have something else to bring to the table. Uranus has been in the same sign for seven years. Therefore, the sign-in will be the same for a large group of people, but the house in which it resides and the connection it creates with your personal planets special to you.

Neptune's common astrological meaning is a creative, dreamy, spiritual seeker, eluding, and able to see what you want to see and refuse to accept. In your astrology chart, a strong Neptune implies that you are a dreamer. You have the opportunity to see what might be a great artist. If an artist looks at a piece of clay, he can see no clay but a magnificent sculpture. You see the best in people in life. A powerful Neptune in your chart may mean that people are dropped for this.

Pluto may be reduced to the rank of a dwarf but bears a big box. Death and rebirth and regeneration are astrological concepts of Pluto. You will experience many changes in your chart as you have a strong Pluto. Metaphorically speaking, there would be many rebirths and deaths. It is vital to have various careers, marry and revamp your personality completely as you undergo a number of transitions and transformations in life.

The importance of astrological planets is a complex topic, and the scope of signs and meanings is worthy of several books each. The astrological planets in your chart of astrology are a way to understand your life and how to handle tough or complicated times. A symbolic understanding of the planets helps us to understand why we are the way we are and unravel the mysteries of life.

Astrology Horoscope Chart

Have you ever wondered why the planet appears to have all the luck? Were they lucky born? If not, what did they have to do to enjoy such a lucky overflow of their loved ones or people with whom they are so close?

Believe it or not, they had nothing drastic to do. Many of them might have been born in "lucky" waves, but most of them didn't seem to find luck after happiness either in matters of the heart or financial matters. Nevertheless, their regular act of reading a horoscope chart is common to these men.

It is by reading the respective horoscopes for the day that this "lucky" party will find out if the day is a good day for the company, dating and making life-changing decisions for others.

Horoscopes answer questions like: Is it a good day to ask someone you want? Is it a good day to invest in a new company? Is it a good day to find a business partner? Is the future partner a good company partner for your zodiac? Will your potential date be a good sexual partner tonight?

Such charts will also answer personal questions such as: Will you marry on the 15th or 18th? Should you build a north or south facing home? Would your family be spared tragedy if you live in a house that has a so-called "lucky" lot?

You will find answers to these questions by reading an astrology horoscope map. There are people you know who always seem to be fortunate in every aspect of their lives. This is because you take into account what your respective horoscopes tell you. You don't follow exactly or literally what the diagrams say, and you use what it means as a reference for your next step because its zodiac signs mean something to them. For you, your zodiac signs influence your daily life, your future, and your destiny. It forms part of who you are and what you accomplish in your life.

For these reasons, they find horoscopes important and have done a regular reading of a horoscope chart for astrology, if only to make the best out of every business deal every evening and every important decision in their lives.

Now you know the secret of this "lucky" party. Would you like to be as fortunate as they? Check a horoscope astrology chart now - and for the rest of your life so that you're never lucky!

Vedic Astrology and Western Astrology

Vedic astrology is rooted in old times, more specifically supported by the Vedas, ancient Hindu spiritual texts, and probably the old text written about the world from about 5000 to 8,000 years ago. West astrology is said to have been developed by the Greeks and Babylonians around 2000 to 3000 years ago.

The relationship between the earth and Sun is based on Western Astrology. This philosophy is based on the belief that since the Sun is the core of the Earth, the Sun is more important than any other spiritual entity on this planet. West Astrology makes astrological predictions based on the relationship between the Sun and the Earth's tropics, Tropic of Cancer and Tropic of Capricorn. The date of 22 March is said to be the same day and night. This date marks the start of the spring, as well. Modern astrology regards this date as the start of the year, as opposed to January 01, the Roman date of the beginning of the year. As the first date at the beginning of the year, the Western astrology states that Aries is the sign from this time of year and accompanied by other signs.

Vedic astrology was very different from Western astrology or Indian astrology. Vedic astrology has no norm for reflecting the start and end of a year. Vedic astrology is focused on the alignment and interconnection between stars and planets. It does not only depend on the relationship between the sun and the earth because of the rotational and progressive existence of the earth which results in a change of its equinoxes by about fifty seconds in a year (time of equilibrium between day and night), which results in a shift of one day every seventy-tree years. This relationship is obviously influenced by this situation. The signs must be changed one day to preserve the principle of astrology. This aspect is far more precise and accurate than western astrology in Vedic astrology.

Vedic astrology, in its function of astrology, is comparatively deeper, broader, and more accurate than Western astrology. Western astrology focuses more on the psychological features of an individual and on predicting future events less or almost negligible. Vedic astrology is, however, also about stressing the psychological aspects of a person, but also about predicting the events of the coming time. It also provides a clearer view of the possible Karmic patterns of a person, i.e., whether he is interested in Paap (sins) or Punya (virtues). Vedic astrology also tells you intimately about the various situations that may occur at different times in the life of a person.

Astrological Choices - Sidereal or Tropical Systems

Astrologers don't always keep it simple, like most other human efforts. There are so many charting options, so many strategies and animal hypotheses that it is hard to get through the maze of possibilities. Both systems have their followers among the people who believe in astrology, and both have their detractors. We we got a problem here? Was one device right and not the other? Are both right? Are both right? It should help to better define the difference between the sidereal and the tropical systems.

Astrology, as we know it today, is created from a melting pot of astrological practices from throughout the world, from ancient times to modern times. Everything was kept, little information was ever removed from the boat, whether or not it hurt, but everything discovered by new experience was added. In some way, astrology can be found on every inhabitable continent of the Earth, and elsewhere, it could be buried under tons of ice and waste or lost to volcanic disasters, tsunamis, or earth movement to mention some causes of lost data.

Publishing itself isn't that old when it comes to the world's human occupation. Most of the information has been transmitted orally over the centuries and generations and has not all been translated correctly, correctly or accurately to date. Some may be incorrect, incomplete, re-translated, edited, or lost. There's a great deal of work, but try to imagine that such knowledge has been thoroughly transmitted over the ages and under all conditions by selfless beings. In my view, this is not remotely possible, especially when people are involved. We can be highly eager and incredibly destructive. That being said, I could be convinced that if a large tablet appears somewhere carved in lightning by a supreme deity, shielded from the risk of defilement, change, decay, erosion, and so on.

There are many astrology outlets, and they are quite special. Everyone was assumed to be equal by those who followed the process, and some of them are in disagreement. What was ideal for a riverbank society was not necessarily relevant to the conditions of blizzards in the Arctic region or the Middle East deserts. Depending on which sky view is used, two basic camps in astrology are popular. Both camps start with Aries in the zodiac circle and end with Pisces. Even ancient astrology, it was not always the case, but it is true today.

Many claims that the stars in the sky are "fixed" in association with each other and that astrology should be based on the celestial calculation of fixed stars and constellations. The sidereal astrology mainly uses Jyotish (Hindu) Eastern Astrologers and a minority of western astrologers. This system recognizes and retains an ancient system of constellational astrology, the Fixed Zodiac, which matches the zodiacal constellations.

Western Astrology uses a different base to measure the Earth's orientation in our solar system and our obvious seasons. It is the Vernal Equinox that is random as our Sun— the nucleus of our solar system—reachesoo Aries every year on or about the 21st March. The signs pass through the zodiac and end with Fish, just like in the fixed system, to complete one complete circle. Notice the difference on the start date, about 24 days difference. This seasonal system is known as Tropical Astrology, and this system is observed by most western astrologers (as do I).

Once these two systems coincided in about 290 AD, they moved away slowly but surely with the current separation at about 24 degrees in the intermediate years. Just before this joining, astrology itself underwent a serious transformation since the information known as astrology was seriously investigated and codified into a combined body of information due in large part to the influence of Ptolemy. The bulk of western astrological information used today stems from this compendium of information, which was then generated and codified. Of course, time and experience have improved or changed these techniques, but little old material has again been discarded, as more data is added to the body of knowledge. A new way is underway to study the knowledge of our astrological ancestors to develop classical astrology. Most famous astrologers, authors, and educators are researching these old and new laws and endorsing them.

Sidereal and Tropical systems have come down as reliable information systems over the years, but in design and application, they are very different. There are strong supporters, some of whom are confused by the use of the "other" method. As always, all systems rely on the exactness of the work carried out, the abilities of the astrologer, and the knowledge studied. My good friend is a very good Vedic astrologer in what he is doing. Every year the whole nation of India is read for the year to come. This works for you. Since India has a population of over one billion, you can't argue with this kind of success. But the readings for the sidereal system of my Vedic friend and my Tropical system practice are very different. Each person can contribute to an understanding of his or her life and experience but will adopt completely different approaches. My Vedic friend also read me with his system, and my experience worked in his interpretation. Again, you can't argue successfully.

No rules say we can't have more than one system. There's no reason to think that one is right in the end, and the other is wrong in the end. Every system has its own value. Your choice of the graph will depend on who you are and what you want to learn. Acceptance of the technology and information depends on your early stages and practice. Any logic and explanation that is' natural' can resonate with you more quickly and easily. It's not because one system is perfect; it's just about what runs best for you.

Marilyn Muir, author of "Hope and Change Presidents: Bringing hope into our future by getting into our astrological past." Based on groundbreaking research by respected astrologer Marilyn Muir, this book presents these four presidents ' extraordinary parallels in their aquatic links to the USA and in their character and inspiration cultures.

Non-technically, the author explains how his sky maps synchronize with the important events of the lives of Presidents Jefferson, Lincoln, and Kennedy, who all held office at deep points in our nation's history. Ms. Muir reaches deep into the past of the USA to forecast the future of our nation. Demonstrated by careful astrological research on how the nation not only suffered deep defeats under each of the watches of these Presidents, it also achieved higher and more prosperous points.

CHAPTER FIVE

Significance of Colors in Astrological Remedies

The visible light of seven wavelengths is reflected in indigo, violet, brown, blue, white, orange, and red (VIBGYOR). Such colors come from the Sun and fly with varying energy intensities at different wavelengths.

The visible light is the source of the biosphere's life and responsible for all the biogeochemical cycles of the earth's surroundings, which sustain plants and animals, including human life. The main energy source is the Sun, where the light waves come from.

The value of colors has recently been recorded by scientific research. Nevertheless, before the development of modern science, its significance was understood to the people. In India, Vedic astrology was established. Developments took place in the Greek Empire, Egypt, Babylon, and also in the Mayan civilizations. The importance of color for astrological remedies has been stressed in all astrological treaties.

The fundamental theme of research in Vedic Astrology is the role of Navgrahas (nine planets) in a horoscope that is said to guide the whole life of the indigenous from birth to death and beyond. The nine planets often emit or reflect different colored rays. A single world is characterized by reflected and released light rays. Works on these topics are also available in the astrological literature of Egypt, Greece, and Babylon.

The Sun's hue is a combination of orange and red. It is generally considered to be red in color, however. The Moon is pale white, but the red-orange rays of the Sun are reflected. Mars is orange, but it also represents the Sun's yellow rays. Mercury is black, reflecting green rays. Jupiter is orange-yellow but mainly reflects the spectral blue rays. Venus is considered pure white but also reflects indigo spectrum rays. Saturn is black and reflects the Sun's violet rays.

In Vedic astrology, the two shadow planets Rahu and Ketu were also assigned colors. Rahu is considered to be black and Ketu to be green.

Color consistency in astrological remedies:-We also find in astrological predictions ' lucky number' and' lucky colors.' Everywhere, the role of color is rightly emphasized. Astrologers employ different ways to resolve the strengthening of vulnerable planets in order to balance an individual's life. The means can be meditation, tantra, gem-treatment, puja (rehung), daan (charity), etc.

While various mantras support various planets, hundreds of tantra systems use different colors in fruits, flowers, leaves, roots, grains, pulses, oily seeds, cloths, woods, coal, etc. Lal-Kitab, a treatise on astrology, provides a detailed description of these remedies. The puja system developed in Vedic times suggests using white rice, green feeds for the promotion of different planets and deities, red and red vermillion, yellow and red fabric, white sandalwood, red sandalwood, and flowers of varying colors. There is a section below.

Sun: Since the color of the Sun is red, red flowers or Safran-colored objects should be used to enhance the Sun in a person's horoscope. The preferred stone is red ruby. This color is energy and power. It also demonstrates vitality and creativity. Excess red, however, is harmful. The weight of the gemstone must, therefore, be carefully measured. This color is not recommended for people with heart difficulties.

Moon: Pale white. Moon: pale white. Each color includes all seven spectrum colors and has cleaning properties. This affects the cycle of thought and contributes to morality and spirituality. But excess white is not good, too. The astrological methods for Moon strengthening in the horoscope include white flowers such as jasmine, white lotus, lily, curd, milk, white sandalwood, rice flour, etc.

Mars: The Mars red color radiates somewhat yellowish rays. The distinction between Sun red and Mars red is that Sun's red refers to royalty, while Mars ' red refers to aggression. Mars redness includes the RBC (red blood cells). Mars red deficiency can cause blood-related problems, while red excess can cause accidents and over-aggression. Red or yellow is recommended for the treatment of Mars-related problems. The recommended gems are pink and red coral. Red glass, Ashwagandha (winter cherry), turmeric and onions that correspond with its fiery existence are herbs and grains prescribed.

Mercury: The color of this green planet is peace, harmony, and hope. It has the ability to soothe agitated nerves and mind. This color is, therefore, good for people with heart problems. This is also perfect for women who are pregnant. Over-greening can lead to lethargy. Because Lord Vishnu is symbolized by Mercury, basil leaves of green color (tulsi) are recommended to deal with problems associated with Mercury. Other items include bhringaraj (Eclipta Alba), flowers of passion, zizyph, mint, sage, etc. The gemstone is compatible with the green emerald.

Jupiter: Jupiter's hue is bright yellow or yellowish. Such two shades usually have positive effects. Therefore, this is a beneficial planet. The light warms and energizes the nervous system. The yellowness stimulates the mind. Ashwagandha and other yellow flowers are compatible elements for the treatment of Jupiter-related problems. Often recommended are noodles like almonds, walnuts, and cashews. The gemstone that is compatible with Jupiter is yellow Saphir and yellow topaz.

Venus: the color is pure white, a combination of all spectrum colors. The lunar is pale white, but the lunar white of Venus. The white color results are the same as in Moon, but Moon is simplicity, while Venus is complexity. Roses, jasmine, saffron, lily, lotus, white muscle (Adscendens Asparagus), Amalaki (Officinalis Emblica), Aloe Vera(Aloe gel), etc. are suitable components for Venus-related problems. Diamond is the compatible gemstone. We also prescribe white zirconium and quartz crystal.

Saturn: Saturn's color is red. The lack of light causes this color. The rays released by Saturn are black. Black is an irritated person's calming color and is also known for its protective properties. There are also negative qualities, such as resistance, obstruction, opposition, and hostility. Black excess is a cause of depression. In general, the compatible elements of Saturn are black including, urad, black sesame, Ozokerite(shilajit), comfrey seed, Triphala (including haritaki, bibhitaki, and Amalaki), iron, etc. It is a blue sapphire compatible gemstone that is very likely to be recommended due to the fiery nature of the earth.

Rahu: This shadow world is called smoky or painted black. Camphor, eucalyptus, bayberry, lotus, sandalwood, etc. are compatible treatment elements. The suggested gemstone for Rahu-related matters is Gomedha (hessonite garnet).

Ketu: Usually, this shadow planet is known to be colored black. The brown color is not the spectrum's original hue. Ketu problems include bayberry, juniper, passion flowers, wild ginger, skullcap, bhringaraj, and many more. The gemstone recommended is the cat's eye (family chrysoberyl).

The Astrological Horoscope Forecast - The Best Predictions

A friend of mine, too, will inquire about her horoscope when she sees me reading the newspaper. Horoscopes usually talk about your wealth, love life, or day's fortune. It also includes your moods and sometimes your lucky number or what you can not do to avoid problems or bad luck during the day. This is why many people look every day at their horoscopes to find out what their daily or weekly future is. Typically horoscopes are posted in newspapers, magazines, and books. But what are horoscopes, and when did they begin? Who started it? Who started it? Okay, let's try to know the horoscope context.

Let us try to know the context of the horoscope of astrology. The ancient Greeks used horoscopes, astrology, and the position of the moon, sun, and star predicted and predetermined the life of the person. Astrology is the Greek name meaning "star science." We claimed that the life of the individual and the events of the future could depend on the position of the sun or planets. The farmers were also previously dependent on the constellations ' positions. During this time, the planters used the signs of the stars to decide when to plant and when to harvest their crops effectively.

There is no formal education to provide reliable information during that period. People looked at the stars in the sky to find answers to specific constant questions about their continuing life. In reality, we are still facing problems and can not find solutions today. Some people go to astrologers to know their solutions to the problem, or many business people would ask for their future. It was China that started to research and use astrology in agriculture and to decide the best seasons and months for the different planting cycles.

In 500 BC, the philosopher Plato was interested in astrology and studied it even more. Due to Plato's study of astrology, the interest in astrology remained alive. Galileo Galilei, who was the first person to use the telescope, continued his research. When Christians had a powerful voice that had been secretly concealed by the science of astrology. The Astrologer William Lilly renamed astrology "Christian Astrology" with the aim of avoiding the Church's wrath and making it more acceptable in 1600. He published his own "American Astrology" magazine, which was significant for the popularization in horoscopes of astrology, as we know them today.

Besides, the Greek one also had its own horoscope system, but when Greece used the constellation, the Chinese used signs of animals such as rats, ox-tippers, birds, dragons, cats, rabbits, etc. The Chinese also used different methods. The use of animals depends on the date of birth of your data. A horoscope was a diagram that shows the aspects of stars and planets at a specific point and predicts the future of not the individual, but also of a geographical region or even of the world.

Throughout time, horoscopes in astrology have been used to determine when future wars will take place. Miss Nancy Reagan hired an astrologer to protect President Reagan, as an attempt was made to murder him. The astrologer predetermined the time to sign key documents, the right time to visit places, the correct time to hold meetings and conferences. Well indeed, we may say they were accurate forecasts because President Reagan remained alive until his two appointed as President of the United States were done. Horoscopes of astrology are enjoyable, fascinating, and definitely accurate.

The Best Predictions

The astrological horoscope has long caught the interest of the people. It was researched in detail, and incredible attempts were made to find fresh and appalling findings. Many people walk for life, and business uses the horoscope to guide their lives.

If you do not know the astrological horoscope, then the information you get from all the signs and symbols the astrologer uses to interpenetrate the horoscope can be fascinating and quite mysterious.

You will read the past, predict the future, and also show your personality traits with the astrological horoscope. Astrology can be very accurate in predicting an occurrence or in determining what kind of path you will pursue.

When it comes to fate, astrology is by far the highest and should be taken seriously. An astrologer will warn you of the periods when you have to pay attention and when opportunities are open. You will benefit greatly from the availability of resources like that.

Astrological Horoscope and Your Destiny

You know you can use astrology to set your goals to help you build the future for yourself. You can see that the horoscope of astrology is like a roadmap you can use to create your own destiny.

You can see what is going on when the transiting planet triggers some of your natal planets by having your own personal horoscope. This is a very powerful knowledge that is available to you. You should make this work to your benefit because it will tell you when it's time to act and when to sit and wait.

Astrology can help you to set the goals for your life here. Setting goals is like building your own future, and you will definitely be a winner when you combine it with astrology. Once you know what astrology can offer you, it will be much easier for you to devote yourself to your goal.

Astrology is a great help in forecasting your future, but it only predicts the kind of energy with which you have to work, and you can make the most of what the astrological planets have ever to offer you with some creativity and imagination.

You can build your own future by setting goals, and when you have written down and often read your goals, you can set the law and the law of attraction into motion and activate it by focusing on your goal.

Your dream goal, which you write down at first, is not only written down in the stars but maybe a little overwhelming for you at first, and you may find it difficult to modify your goals. What you should do is set yourself a few achievable goals that lead to the big objective. You will be shocked by how well it feels when you see the effects of your efforts.

When breaking down the changes you will make in order to achieve your goals, and you will be shocked what a difference your life will create. You will notice after a while that some of the more disagreeable thoughts and situations you have in your life are no longer happening to you.

Following the advice, you can get the best out of the energy that astrological planets send you, and you don't have to feel that you are victims of some of the negative astrological aspects of your chart, because you are working with the law of attraction.

Do You Believe in Astrology & Horoscopes?

For generations, people have been intrigued by the subject of astrology and horoscopes. There is a mystery, and it is never certain that one should believe in the forecasts or not. Quite often, as they seem to know about your life and where you are, they seem to reveal the truth.

A story tells the stars and planets. And there are those who believe that as the earth moves and the various constellations move into the planetary atmosphere, it affects the result of our future. The transition can be projected so that the future can be prepared too.

As with any predictions, you can usually change the result simply by doing something else than you would do. If an astrologer announced that your relationship with a partner would end in a certain location on a certain night, it would be clear to prevent it. Or perhaps at another time, you would go there. Perhaps you'd like to meet him somewhere else. Whether it's all in your mind or not, the forecast won't occur. You can even believe it in your own head so much that you can actually avoid it.

However, it's more involved sometimes than that. And there are other constellations as well as the moon and the planets to be thought with. After all, there is a great deal going on all at once in this big universe. But is the subject of astrological prediction real?

There are horoscopes in the newspaper that seems to be far from the mark. This can easily convince a person that horoscopes are simply not believable. But it may only be because they're so wide. How can one Scorpio horoscope be the same for any Scorpio that day? Looking at it like that, it seems quite absurd.

But when you go to an astronomer, and she examines all the evidence of your birthday, a very different set of predictions emerges. These are designed to reflect your date of birth and time.

When you were born, the stars and planets were in a certain region of the universe. During your entire lifetime, the astrologer will tell you about things. If they are generally true, it's hard to doubt her future predictions without having admitted anything to her beforehand.

In order to make sure the astrologers are genuine, take a visit. Have her set up your astrological chart, and if you are somewhat uncomfortable with the whole future, just give her one to two predictions in the future. That's after she tells you, of course, what your life has been and what your successes have been. The topic of astrology/horoscopes can change your mind.

CHAPTER SIX

What is Real Astrology?

The Random House Unconsolidated dictionary defines a Horoscope as a heavenly diagram showing planets and zodiac signs relative positions, for use in birth calculations, forecasting events in the life of a person, etc. The dictionary also describes the Horoscope as a prediction of future events or feedback on future behavior.

The American Heritage Dictionary defines the Horoscope as an astrological projection, based on a diagram of the position of the planets and stars at a particular moment.
The word Horoscope comes from the Greek name, "see the hours." The Horoscope is also classified as an astrology chart, Astro chart, birth chart,celestial map, map of the sky, star chart, cosmograms, vita sphere, revolutionary chart, circle, or just the chart. The Horoscope forms the foundation of the astrological horoscope rituals. In the jargon of laymen, Horoscope is an astrologer's interpretation of the chart via a system called astrology of the sun signs. Nowadays, according to zodiacal signs, most newspapers and magazines display regular horoscopy. It is increasingly popular among the masses by offering them insights into their lives and by looking into their future in immediately. But many astrologers find these as meaningless because horoscope is highly personalized and the interpretation by a single planetary position is difficult to generalize to thousands of readers. An horoscope diagram derives astrological interpretations. The Earth is in the center of the diagram and is surrounded by planets. To order to build a horoscope, an astrologer must have an exact time and place for the birth of

the subject or the initiation of an event. Then the time is translated into GMT. To order to show which planets over the horizon are visible, the astrologer uses the time difference between GMT and local time at the place of birth. A table of houses is then used to divide the Horoscope into 12 divisions around the ecliptic globe. In addition to these rooms, astrologers must also understand the relative or aspects angles between planet to create a horoscope. The Indian and Chinese zodiac signs are very different from the astrological signs accepted in the West. West astrological signs, like Taurus, Aries, Cancer, Gemini, Virgos, Leo, Scorpio, Libra, Capricorn, Sagittarius, Pisces, and Aquarius have been divided into 12 zodiac signs. This distinction is rendered according to the birth date of the subjects. For example, the Leo zodiac sign is given to people born between the dates of July 24 and August 23. The horoscopes in the newspapers and magazines are not so accurate. Nevertheless, people from every corner of life and every age appear obsessed with it. It has become part of many routines every day in the morning. In a country like India, horoscope research astrological consultations are a must on many important occasions. This refers to all the major events of daily life, such as the birth of a child, the start of a new business, marriage, career etc. Indians assume that your Horoscope will influence your personal or business life. Horoscope consultations are, therefore, a must before such important events occur. With the aid of certain procedures, any faults can be repaired. Horoscopes are also important for selecting the right match for a man or woman. If the bride's horoscopes and the bride suit, the pair are assumed to have a happy married life. A few documents are necessary for matrimonial matching. The bride's and the bride's horoscopes are both dated of birth and time of birth and place of birth. If there is no horoscope, then the bride and bride's names should be taken. Horoscopes for predictions, health, life, family, marriage, jobs, education, divorce, babies, business partnerships and legal cases, etc.

Sagittarius Moon Phase Astrological Horoscope

Astrology is all about the relationship of Earth with planets and all celestial bodies above and how they impact us and our climate here on Earth through their motion and interactions. The Planet symbolizes some force or energy, like each of the 12 zodiac signs, constellations, which consist of 12 bodies or groups of celestial beings around the Planet. It's Aries, Sagittarius, Capricorn, Waterfowl, Leo, Virgo, Libra, Scorpio and Pisces. Your astrological chart: at the time of your birth your astrological chart is like a photograph of the universe. Everything in the sky above and beneath the horizon is intended to influence the individual born' under.' The sun, the moon, the planets and the constellations (or sets of stars) most of the astrologers deal mainly with their sky location- their relation to each other, their position, or angles to you. Some astrologers will include fixed stars while compiling an astrological chart and some will still include asteroids. There will never be two astrological charts close. Your own private astrologer chart or any other' drawn' astrological chart is just as special as your fingerprints. Your Star Sign: when you refer to your' sign,' it refers to which of the twelve constellations or groups of stars that surround the Earth the sun is passing through at the very time of their birth (without knowing it). True Horoscopes: What you could call' true' astrology goes far beyond your sunlight or horoscopes, which so frequently occur in journals and magazines all around the world. Such horoscopes are far too generalized and fantastic for anyone's real use, and the great majority have reached a point of pure titillation, perhaps with some' real' or even useful astrological facts. Although the subject is generally written by true astrologers as "horoscopes," the subject is a serious injustice as most horoscopes (but not all) are now written simply for the big money that the mass media is willing to pay just the signs of the stars for this entertainment.

Astrology Horoscope

You'll have a great working week due to an increase in the production of jobs. You must be more interested in social matters because the contacts you make will help you to gain self-confidence. Your social status has risen to a level where people know who you are and where you are in the vanguard of your success.

You would become a person who gets real attention and will be valued and rewarded for your success in your work. It is time for you to move on and become the aggressive person at work, and let others around you know that you are the one who pushes the company forward. Your coworkers will do everything they can to keep up with you, and because of your mindset, they will be more successful. You need to use your colleagues to your advantage because they are ready to lift you to a major promotion.

The real thing you're going to come out like never before. You will take advantage of your positive approach to your workplace and family. Your family is at the heart of your life, so make sure you do not forget everything they do for you. You will have a special relationship with your wife that revives the love you once lost.

Aquarius Snake Horoscope

The snake is the most snappy of all animals, based on astrology horoscope map, so those who were born under a serpent sign will bear the characteristics of a mysterious, charming, and wise human. The typical long-term tendency of a person born under the Aquarius snake horoscope is more likely to become an intelligent financial consultant or a businessman itself. Or perhaps someone who is always at the forefront of government, wheeling, and trade. A theologian, a prophet, a priest, or a philosopher, is characterized by someone who uses more his intellect than his brawn. He or she has a fine lifestyle-clothing, accessories, music, books, fine dining, socializing, all good in life. He or she often dislikes ludicrous debates, and this is induced by his knowledge and enjoyment of all academic subjects and his natural grace and panache. The smart conversation is what fascinates, and they fully want to communicate. As they are after depth, not quantity, the only downside is that when the conversations are repetitive and only about one subject, they lose fascination and interest easily. We enjoy daring non-cyclical tete-a-tete, in short. Focus is lacking when an idea is monotonous and uninteresting due to the delivery period or the way it is delivered. Aquarius snake horoscope also says that those born under the snake sign have the uncanny ability to judge a person or situation correctly, with the inclusion of what may happen in the future if a certain situation is pursued. They have the ability to determine the right course and decision, and they follow it tenaciously and vigorously. The negative aspect of this is that they rarely hear anybody else's feedback and suggestions, and this challenge often results in unnecessary trouble. All of these sign data can be found in the horoscope map of astrology.

In general, the aquarium snake horoscope reveals that snake people act fast when decisions are made quickly. Time is hardly wasted because, with this inherent belief, they move quickly and decide what to do in a jiffy.

However, the aquarium snake Horoscope shows that life for the snake people is not all-powerful and full of activity. You do know how to enjoy the hunky-dory times and relax. But be sure sooner or later, your sense of consciousness and intellect will come to life when even a single match of idea has been created. This type of Horoscope is only one facet of the many in a horoscope chart in astrology.

Understand What You Can Learn Through Astrology & Horoscopes

Astrology/horoscopes are designed to map the planets and the moon and sun. This map is called an astrological diagram. Astrological charts that can provide information about life and death are of interest in many cultures. In order to determine the exact position of the planets, the moon, and the sun in the astrological chart, the person concerned would need to know the date, time, and location of birth.

The sun and the moon are often called planets in astrology, but we know that this is not technically correct. Saturn, Venus, Jupiter, Mars, Neptune, Uranus, Mercury, and Pluto are the other celestial bodies included. The Earth is not included as this is the point we look from in the world to the heavens.

Each astrological diagram consists of 12 houses. These are a specific aspect of life, such as employment, romance, or family. Since only ten planets are used to assemble a diagram, two are empty. These should reflect the aspects of our lives, on which the universe does not feel that we need to concentrate your energies; perhaps in a previous incarnation, you have already mastered those issues.

The location of the sun at birth decides your sign of the sky. The positions of the other planets are measured according to their influence on the sun sign. The moon sign and its positioning are also taken into account in a reading.

A qualified astrologer may paint a clear picture of the life and personality of an individual by simply interpreting the details in an astrological diagram. It is often said that with time, the information gained from a diagram may not be as exact as other astrological phenomena can play an important role in the events.

If you have ever wondered why in life, you always seem to be making the wrong decision, then perhaps by reading your horoscope, you will find the answers. You can even use astrology to understand better whether your profession is the right one and whether a relationship is going to succeed or not.

It's not so hard to read your soul together with your partner and find out whether they are truly your soul mate or whether you will always be arguing and disagreeing. An Aquarius, for example, is thought to be a good fit for a Libra, but not a Girl. You can do so online if you are interested in having your birth chart produced or in getting an up-to-date reading from an expert. You don't have to see an astrologer any more. All can now be achieved from the safety and security of your own home.

CHAPTER SEVEN

Looking Into Astrology & Horoscopes
Advice For Virgo

Not all belief in astrology/horoscopes. However, some interesting information is available. While some of it might seem generalized, personality characteristics can be surprisingly accurate. Here are some information and advice for Virgo that may be interesting for you.

Often, virgins are described as the brain. They're thinking. They're thinking. You love to analyze things. It is difficult for a Virgo to grasp a twist. Throughout their lives, they seek peace and harmony. Tell a Virgo if you want to know something. They usually have good memories.

Virgos can remember remarkable information from their infancy. Sometimes they bring these childhood memories to adulthood with them. Sometimes this can cause problems. To let go of a positive word of advice to those born under the sign of Virgo.

It's hard for Virgos to let go. You must note that the past is gone. They can't do anything about it. You have to cut your losses and continue to do so at some point.

Sometimes this cerebral approach can be harmful to you. Sometimes, after someone else has given up, you can have a friendship. You don't want the person yet. You simply can't understand why they left you. You must know why. Why? This state of mind is perfect for you to seek knowledge. Nonetheless, relationships can get you into trouble.

You are often called calm under pressure. People might think you're easy to go. That could be the case. Yet, dear Virgo, you tend to hold things in too much. Instead of dealing with things, you suppress. Everybody does this, but you are more likely to react like this.

Sometimes it can be disruptive to love and work. Long-term elimination brings a sudden break. For a long time, you will deal with things very well. You then reach a point where you can't take it anymore. You will burst for no obvious reason. Perhaps you don't know the reason, yourself.

You can feel much better a few minutes later. The problem is that you can hurt the feelings of someone. This person could be very dear to you. Most Virgos would do well in their basement or garage to have a punching bag. Go out there regularly and put the bag into a presentation. You might be surprised at how fine you sound, then.

The good word of Virgo's suggestion is to do it. Sometimes you just have to do that. Don't talk about the circumstances. This only increases your natural tendency to keep things in place. Remember the old adage of long study and incorrect study. Dear Virgo, this can benefit you in many ways.

You may fear impetuousness. This is not possible for you. You are so cool. You are too cool. You're organized too. You have to let yourself go and sometimes enjoy yourself. This person will teach you how to have fun if you have an Aries friend. A friend of Aries or a friend of mine can also help.

Summary Are you looking for Virgos advice on astrology/horoscopes? You're cool under the flames. You might be too cool sometimes. You have to blow off steam every now and then. Keep your house with a punching bag. Cut it loose every now and then. They'll show you how to have fun if you have an Aries friend. Listen to them. Listen to them. A friend or colleague of Aries can also help.

Pisces Moon Phase Astrological Horoscope

This week, your high energy level will make you more creative. You will have more responsibilities in having new workers you train. You will be asked to be a leader when you participate in meetings this week. Fellow workers should follow your advice and benefit from your leadership. You will have many problems at work and be responsible for taking steps to address these problems responsively.

Your business will keep you busy, so that your affairs at home are difficult to manage. Make sure you keep the attention of your parents, even if you don't have it. It is important that you maintain positive relationships and make time for your loved ones. You can get family members from other parts of the country who need to be informed of family issues. They are going to inspire you and help you with your company.

Financially, with your earnings high, you will have a fantastic week that encourages you to try new things. Maintain cash flow is the most important thing to remember. You will have some opportunities to invest in property and find each other

Free Astrological Readings

Learning free astrology is a very interesting topic with which many people engage. Free astrological readings could help an individual to gain a broader understanding of himself and the things around him each day. Today, people are even looking for the help of a psychic counselor to explain each sign's different types and significance. The biggest advantage of having free astrology readings is that you don't have to expend lot-the readings are free, and you can refer to them whenever you want. The study of astrology refers to the understanding of the various zodiac signs, star signs, sun signs, and many other astrological signs, all of which play a major part in the self-discovery of each person.

You could still learn a great deal about yourself and several experiences you have had by understanding your astrological signs in free websites of astrology. By constantly referring to free astrological reading, you would gain a deeper view of yourself, of astrology as knowledge, as well as of the many signs you come from. Free astrological readings send you the daily dose of your horoscope and the horoscope of any other person you would like to know about. And whether you're preparing for a specific day, month, or year, free astrology lectures will help you better prepare for the future. The free reading of astrology consists of a day to day guide and helpful advice on every day to help you with some guidance from the mental counselor.

More and more people find that free astrology readings in their daily lives are accurate and useful. If you are a person with a strong spiritual perspective in life, you will certainly benefit from exploring the field of astrology. If you ask for free advice on astrology, most of it is also spiritually inclined. You can also seek advice from your psychic counselors on issues related to your love life. Indeed, most free websites in Astrology today give free advice on love and relationships to people signing up or logging on the sites. It takes only a few clicks, but the benefits are overwhelmingly inspiring and advantageous. Readings and guidance on free astrology are really helpful in making your life a little easier.

If you are unsatisfied with the readings from the websites, no harm is done to you. It is your duty to believe and act on the results of astrological research. And as it's free, you're not going to lose anything.

Pointers For Free Astrology Reading

Free astrology has affected many people's lives and continues to play a role. We can never see how profoundly free astrology had consequences in people's daily activities. Since the world started to revolve and people have gone around the planet, people have turned towards the stars for answers. The reality that whenever anything good happens to us, we look to heaven and thank God, and when the exact thing happens, we also look to heaven and ask God why. Some people say the interpretation of signs in the sky has helped them reach decisions that change a life, and those people thank the sky for that. Nearly all races, Indians, Americans, Asians, Eastern Europeans, and others practiced astrology.

Astrology is based on the core belief that positions between celestial bodies will disclose the correct information about a person's temperament, business, and other issues. The astrologer is the individual who practices astrology. We believe the movements of the sun, the starts, and the moon are very close to our everyday lives, and therefore, we view them and publish them as horoscopes. And, moreover, these movements of the heavenly bodies reveal not only future predictions but also retell past events. And free astrology is usually linked to superstition. Actually, the National Science Foundation's faith in astrology is supposed to be pseudoscientific. And before, between astronomy and astrology, there was only a thin section. However, astronomy has gone through the years and is known in a scientific way to be the empirical study of celestial bodies and is completely devoid of any link with astrology.
"I'm looking up, and I'm looking down." So Tycho Brahe summed up his astrology research. At some point, astrologers were even confused about the correlation between the stars and the events on earth. Several astrologers have argued that

the heavenly bodies are the origin of events, and they are not foreboders of events. When used for forecasting, Free Astrology has two primary methods. Astrological transits refer to observations of celestial bodies, while forecasts are based on astrological progressions. There are several practices used by today's astrologers.

CHAPTER EIGHT

Free Astrology - Know Your Future and Be Ready For It

Most people have a desire to know about the future, and astrology is a branch of research that can help a person to do this. Astrology consists essentially of a group of traditions, systems, and beliefs in which the celestial objects may use the relative positions of people and events to understand and interpret them. The internet is something beautiful place where you can find a solution for almost everything, all the knowledge you want about astrology or anything else you want on the net. For those who are genuinely interested in astrology and would like to know the whole thing, you can find the free guidelines for astrology. Some sites offer free tips and guides for anyone who wants to know more about the subject.

Some of these free astrology websites have various interactive features that can even support a beginner. You can apply your charts, and these places can read you free of charge. All you need to do is check and sign in for those websites, and you can apply an interactive feature on the website to your horoscope. There are also many other apps on a page that provide free astrology to people who are genuinely interested in everything. There are today several places where you can make your own birth chart, and based on it, daily forecasts on several things can be sent to you. You need only find a site, log in, and you can access all the free information you want about astrology.

At some time, when there were many bad things to it, astrology was not so common, but it was revived soon. Nowadays, progress in science and technology has made many things possible for us. And it has become pretty simple to learn about your future and predict things through free astrology. There are several websites that provide all those who are genuinely interested in astrology with free information on astrology, numerology, tarot card information, and other things. Indeed, today, various forms of divination are so popular that several people come up with online sites to inform people and discuss them.

There's many astrology software that could also help you read your birth chart on the market. If you have a computer at home, you only need to buy the software, download it and learn how to use it. You don't even need the support of a professional or an expert to help you know the astrology field. The different functions of the software are very simple to operate, and as all things are explained in detail, you can do this easily. You can now easily explore and see what the future has for you.

Free Astrology - Know Your Future and Be Ready For It

Man might have reached the moon, but most people still believe what their stars must say on this earth. The study of stars and planets to predict the future is known as astrology, and this is an important part of many people's lives. It goes to the extent that after reading the horoscopes in daily newspapers, thousands of people start their day. Everyone looks for answers to hundreds of questions about his life's problems. Astrology has several branches, and one of these is Indian astrology.

Most astrologers offer free services, and the reason for which the majority of people use astrology, problems, and their solutions, is free astrology. The predictions are based on the analysis of birth charts, sun signs, and astrological studies. The remedies suggested by the study are based on the same. Free astrology also provides matching and important information about gemstones and their effect on a person's life. Everyone can choose free astrology every day, monthly and weekly, and know what the stars have to say.

As we all know, the signs of the sun are based on a person's date and place of birth. The position of stars and planets, in accordance with the principles of astrology, is responsible for changing the lives and occurrences of certain events. The difficulties of life and happiness depend on the location of his stars and planets. Astrology does not change the future but remedies the problems that will happen in the future or that are currently happening. This helps to reduce the brutality of evil events.

Throughout India, people keep their babies ' names as per their birth charts. This is done to ensure the child has good luck in the next few years of his life. Everyone can opt for free astrological horoscope services that are available free of charge on the Web to solve problems in their lives. Expert services for a nominal fee are also available. You may take the help of a specialist in astrology to receive the birth charts. The birth charts can then be used to match and name your son. Astrology is an immense topic, and it is impossible to know how it works without the intricacies being known.

Psychic Insights for the Astrological Signs

2016 Astrological Sign Psychic Horoscopes Read your Aries Sun, Moon, and Rising Signs: You've got your very best thoughts yet. People have more trust in you... By their contracts, commitments, and opportunities, they show this to you. This is a time of collaboration, new companies, and new partnerships with people who are really doing their job. You get the assistance you need. It's a much stronger year than last year.

Taurus: This year, things happen quickly. You decide quickly. You change locations or change your job at the start of the year, or you are at your second home. You're ready to go at the start of the year after a sluggish lead last month or two. You could set up a new business. Things are very well thought out; you've already made tough decisions, and now you implement them and establish yourself, and do what signs on earth do well: stabilize yourself.

Gemini: The concept of correctness... Being in the right place and acting on your right destiny this year remains at the forefront. It's like you've taken a player... You understand what's right for you, and you are implementing it much more powerfully. Moon, the planet of prosperity and wellbeing, have a strong influence and make the right choice for your future. You get much more right about your life, and you can be confident: you have made important basic, right choices.

Cancer: It's a year when things come to their heads. This can be a little overwhelming, and because of changes that seem or are happening to you, you can expect some conflict. But some things need to be done. It's like the world is rotating directly in front of you, and you will obey their shifts and decisions. The unexpected can happen, but everything is meant to happen, and the first step is to recognize changing circumstances that may be difficult at first to understand.

You have the chance to raise your revenue, be part of a team or institution that gives you more money and be happier!

Leo: It's all because of inner accomplishment in which you gain a lot more control. You want a better working mind and inner peace. It's a year that you struggle with resistance, and it's a deeper passion for life, love for yourself, and love for others that you can push through resistance. You may resist getting what you really want, but you will continue to make the important choices that lead to your own achievement.

Virgo: Life in 2016 is much clearer for you. Maybe you're engaged! You make the right connections and very good relationships. Everything you really start works! It's a great year for a new company to launch. You know where you belong, you know with whom you belong, and you know what you do. The Sun is laughing at Virgos!

Libra: That's quite a sales year, but it must be because both of you want to move forward... Perhaps you want to travel, or learn more about the material world, what you want. You are aware of how to get it: you need to connect to a certain company, but it looks like that connection is made, and in 2016 or before the end of the year, you are better able to do so financially.

Scorpio: It looks like a creative year! This would be a year when you could get pregnant, and the time would be good if you wanted. Recently you have disengaged or left circumstances to do more than you want. You are freer and financially better coordinated and are more imaginative and articulate in physical terms. You may have a huge project which starts later in the year, maybe in October. It could be set up a lot when you have to brace yourself for it in concrete steps.

Sagittarius: You can get out of any situation. See all as a work in progress: your wellbeing, your relationships, and your financial goals. This is a year when you do not take big moves, but your job is just to keep things moving. You might still be worried, but for nothing. An even pace is the best way to get the work done. It's a whole year more even.

Capricorn: You will give a lot this year to get what you want. Fortunately, you feel strong. You feel strong. There is another way of coping with emotionally strong circumstances. This won't be your fault; it's just what's going to happen. This is a good year because you are especially strong in mind, body, and spirit. At the beginning of the year, things aren't very simple how to get where financially you want, but give it more time... April is more telling.

Aquarius: At the start of the year, you are quite busy. You may have been given a big task that makes the holiday feel like a break. It's a year in which you don't have to think too much. You're really busy doing your part and inspiring in something creating. It seems like you have the luxury of being fully involved in your dreams and potential and not so concerned about instability but concentrated on the hopeful future.

Pisces: This year, you're thinking a lot. You move forward, you advance your projects, but you also move partnerships forward and get used to a new order with partnerships. It's a less emotional year. Things have changed; this year, things are different... You are moving towards a different destiny and more supportive partnerships than in the past. This is a year that is much more balanced, but perhaps more sober as you move into a new sense of settling.

The Great Astrological End-Time

The Future is upon us, a result of great end-time astrology that affects mankind today. Global warming is a fact now. Since 1970, catastrophic climate changes have intensified, including earthquakes and volcanoes. At the same time, we have also seen a growing rise during depression and suicide. And that we are moving for a Sixth Large Extinction of about every earthly life.

Virgo and Pisces are astrological signs across the zodiac, forming an axis that activates the end-time energies. Virgo governs decay and death, and fish dissolves, which brings a value of dramatic change to the periods occupied by these symptoms. The table is cleaned and washed to make room for a new festival.

There are 12 ages (my terminology) in every age, and 12 stages in every age. We are at the beginning of the fish era from 1980 to 2160. This is a doubly powerful lake of breakdown and disintegration that adds a lot to the value of the end times of this period.

Our history has acquired a definite end-time flavor since the Pisces (1965 to 1980) of the Aquarius (1800 to 1980) age of the Pisces. Since 1965, poisonous chemical and nuclear waste came to the headlines. A sudden increase in the extinction of species became a major concern. Throughout Europe and America, international and domestic violence erupted. Welfare has grown dramatically, and inflation has started to tear our lives ' economic fabric. The rate of depression and suicide began to rise. And today, these trends continue. The weather conditions began to change after 1970, and the frequency and intensity of earthquakes and volcanoes began to increase. Global warming is now a scientific fact with catastrophic future projections in the next century. And many scientists are claiming that a sixth major extinction event has just taken place that will impact any life on earth.

We can look at history to take a look at it. The Virgo epoch of the last two centuries has a history of social and political division that has led to periods of feudal isolation. The Virgo period of the Aries era, from 1080 until 900 BCE, saw the internal fragmentation of the Egyptian Empire, the break-up of the First Assyrian Empire into the warring feudal state cities, and the creation of the feudalist, Greek, city-states as the Greeks migrated to their present country.

The same division of society has taken place in the Virgo age of the Pisces Period, from 900 to 1080 CE. In a system known as manorialism, Europe has disintegrated into small, fragmented cities and manors. Three separate Caliphates divided the Islamic empire. In China, the Tang Dynasty became a fragmented feudal system where local warlords ruled in the emperor's name. The Mayans in Central America disappeared suddenly and mysteriously after 900 CE.

The Fish Age also shows a history of social and political chaos and disintegration. A time of extreme domestic violence and social breakdown occurred during the Fish age of the Age of Aries 180-0 BCE, in the Latin Republic of Rome after 200 BCE. The number of slaves imported into the city increased enormously. Citizens have been forced out of their employment, and a huge welfare state has been created. Gladiatorial games were created to keep citizens and the streets busy. On the outskirts of the town, large slum tenements have been built to house the poor. The city was divided by a growing split between rich and poor as the middle class disintegrated into poverty. As greed substituted civil duty, politics became a path to wealth and energy. Similar trends in the social breakdown and internal conflict were also observed in China between 200 and 0 BCE in the Early Han Dynasty.

The beginnings of these same trends are easy to see in our modern world in recent decades. The programs of benefit and entitlement have become a necessary part of the political landscape. Global warming and climate change are markers of what is dramatic today.

Is that something to think about? The smaller Virgo and Pisces periods establish socially and politically disintegrating times. The longer ages are times of big end-times. Virgo's Age

12,960 to 10,800 BCE is in the zodiac opposite to our present fish age. Around 10,000 BCE reveals that large animals were extinguished globally massively, the Pleistocene extinction, likely due to some sort of celestial cataclysm. This is very near the end of the Virgin Period, as close as possible to this end-time period.

Beresovka mammoth was found in the mouth and stomach frozen with fresh, undigested butter cups. In order to prevent food from continued digestion, the mammoth would almost immediately have been frozen to -150 degrees Fahrenheit. Temperate trees frozen with fruit still on the branches are also found in Siberia. The Alaskan muck pits show several thousands of large animals killed, immediately frozen, ripped apart and mixed with the broken bark of trees, as though they were all suddenly tossed down in a single cosmic event by a supernatural force, mashing them all.

A sudden rise in the world's oceans also occurred at about 10,000 BCE. Since the 1950s, numerous reports have been made of discovering in the Caribbean megalithic underwater stone walls, stone roads, and temples. More recently, a town was discovered in the Indian Ocean off the coast of Northern India at less than 100 feet of water. A recent NASA satellite photo shows a man-made stone bridge or a route from south India to Sri Lanka. All of them were above water before 10,000 BCE.

Over 500 myths and stories worldwide remember at least one such tragic universe in the past that ended the disaster. A few remember more than one such devastation. The ancient Egyptians, who gave us ideas about Atlantis, claim that the process of end-time catastrophe is continually repeating. This is consistent with the discoveries of this astrological end-time cycle.

Now that we have been in the Pisces era since 1980, it all could get worse. The twice-strong astrological force of the destruction of fish and of the disintegration and death of

Virgo threatens apocalypse right now before the promised Golden Age of Aquarius, Christ the Millennium. So, how do we survive as a species in the next age?

The astrology which says we are in trouble also tells us to use the best astrological energy. This means embracing the highest energies of the fish, deepening the spirituality of the fish. Fish govern spirituality. The planet Venus is exalted in Pisces, giving the religions of this era the enhanced impulse to devotion and expressing to everyone around us selfless and compassionate love, with no judgment. We meditate or pray, the mental technique of the Virgin, which enables us to overcome fear, and that enables our private energies to align ourselves with the divine forces of the Fish and God or Goddess. The expression of those energies in our lives strengthens the community and allows us to channel the effects of these periods towards our own ends.

Although the aquarium age is still a good way away, fish rule contact with other worlds, higher worlds. After the Pisces' spiritual journey will enable us now, without waiting for the Golden Age of Aquarius, to contact him and create the sky. Fish rules dreams. Dreams. They should choose to dream of a new world free from inequality, violence, and misery and free of catastrophic prophecy, or at least of more damaging prophetic aspects. Meditation and meditation to fulfill our goals help the powers in the utopia of Aquarius. Through Aquarius, the planet Mercury, the mind is exalted. Through positive thoughts and affirmations, our hope, our dreams, and our aspirations are embodied, and a new utopia is formed all Aquarius qualities.

CHAPTER NINE

Astrological Signs - A Deeper and Broader View

The night sky is visibly overflowing with pins of light, which are thought to be stars but can be galaxies, stellar kindergartens, or universes, and stars of all sizes, shape, and categories. Thousands and trillions of cosmic worlds exist. When you find yourself in a very dark night near the Earth's Equator, our own galaxy stars are so dense that it seems as if they were spilled milk across the night sky-our Milky Way Galaxy. Of course, all these natural wonders surround us during the day, but the brightness of the Sun is blurred. It is the night sky that allows us to see our universe unimpeded. There will always be more because the distances are so vast than we can ever see or understand. So is the world.

Through the years, people in sky clusters have found stories and photos, and we call them constellations. There are over 50 such constellations, depending on the reference you quote and the national system you use. Each constellation has its own myth and starry members. Twelve constellations are on the way to the planets orbiting our local Sun-the ecliptic, the ecliptic path. The ecliptic is the emphasis through the twelve constellations which we call the zodiac (circle of animals), and the large constellations on either side of this gigantic sky road. The constellations are not nearby. They are "out there," gigantic 30-degree parts of that circular path, at celestial distances. The planets that all are (close to) our solar system fly along this route, and we name the signs across the regions of space. The energy reflected by the earth seems to take on the new coloring or effect of this symbol as they pass through the twelve signs.

Think of bright white light (the planet and its energy) and put a red lens between it and the viewer. A red light would be seen by the observer. The light itself would not change; only the perception of the observer would change. If the red lens is removed and a blue lens is placed between that light and that observer, the observer will see that light source as blue; the light source itself will stay the same (the power of the planet) only in the observatory's perception. As a particular zodiacal sign moves through the earth and its power and experiment, it seems to be formed or affected by this large area of space. Our perception and influence of this energy are all that is actually altered.

The ego is an ego without regard to the interpretation or coloring of a symbol. Rising ego, positive or self-deprecating, it is still ego. All these expressions are still mechanisms of the ego. Mannerisms and conduct (ego-related) are tangibly modified, and the influence of the sign gives the modification. The nearest (planet) is modified (influenced) by the cosmic (sign) as each planet moves through specific areas of the sky. The signs and their symbolism and features allow us to read the story of a person in relation to the various functions that planets serve. The Sun is the ego and the personality. The Moon represents the nesting emotions. Mercury is, to name a few, the mind, training, and communication. This chapter, however, is about the signs.

Mythology If you're a mythology researcher, you have tons of material to know the signs from. Every legend or story has to do with human behavior and experience. No matter the source of legend that you choose, the stories, such as wisdom, strength, fearlessness, warriors, healers, mother and father characters, etc., are paralleled. That legend tells its own story, but each legend has to do with humanity, and that is why there is a common ground for learning and applying it. If a myth is about wisdom (or its lack), it will focus your attention on this Quality when you read a wheel. Who knows who fits all of these mythological possibilities or part of them?

Philosophy and psychology If you are theoretical or psychological students, regardless of their origin, you know that they are human nature studies and their powers, strengths, and weaknesses. Carl Yung, an eminent psychologist, and psychiatrist called astrology and used it extensively in his research. You may apply your psychological or theoretical interpretation by defining the basic premise of a symbol. What is the core of the sign's lesson? For example, the Aries sign can be brave and straightforward, but it is foolish at times. That hint will open up several possibilities of human experience in your conscious knowledge of philosophy or psychology. Who knows who suits these theoretical or emotional possibilities in whole or in part?

Symbology is among my favorite tools. The sign symbol opens a mental book about this sign in an astrologer's mind. Eleven of these constellations are depicted by the glyphs of humans or animals. The only non-human or animal sign is the Libra symbol, with the justice scale as a reference. For example, what would Libra experience or have as an inherent quality in its life? To some extent, Libra must see all sides, weigh and measure, know that any action results in identifying a few qualities or experiences. Spend time with each symbol or glyph as they help you understand the symbol and its past. Who do you know fits in whole or in part with the symbology of any sign?

Activity mode What exactly is an activity mode? Others take direct steps, others build up or create or weigh the advantages and disadvantages, and others talk or teach and change, adapt and adapt to the circumstances. The cardinal signs: Aries, Jupiter, Libra, and Capricorn are those who tend to act. There are set indicators for people who tend to create or construct and join into value systems: Taurus, Leo, Scorpio, and Aquarius. The mutable signs of these signs are those who tend to talk, teach or alter, adapt, and respond to the situation: Gemini, Virgo, Sagittarius, and Pisces. Regardless of the planet's power, the sign's impact reflects one of the three general features. Who do you know well defines this style of activity?

Inherent Quality What is an inherent quality of a person? One value could be charismatic and creative. This is true for some, but not for all. Another could be terrestrial and very basic, sustainable in nature. Other people could be emotional, instinctive, or imaginative. Perhaps one could be mental, social, and friendship. These are all characteristics "want to have" in humans, and we can share many of them but are not always dominant or apparent in a number of compositions. Three signs express each Quality. The performance of the fire signs is dynamic and charismatic: Aries, Leo and Sagittarius. The Quality of earth signs is fundamental and durable: Taurus, Virgo, and Capricorn. The Quality of water signs is emotional, instinctive, or imaginative: cancer, Scorpio, and fishes. The Quality of air signs are intellectual, social, and relational: Gemini, Libra, and Aquarius. Who do you know that these qualities are expressed dominantly or constructively?

Astrological Signs Through The Seasons

One of the ways we need to create a better understanding of the complexities underlying each one of the astrological signs would be to look straight at the immediate cyclical process, which is taking place in nature. Through looking at the cycle of birth, death, and rebirth that takes place in the course of a year, we can become more associated with seasonal changes and also discover hints of the essential functions or "work" of every astrological sign. We will begin with Aries in the Spring and walk through each astrological sign to see how they fit into a larger ensemble. Through recognizing the values of each symbol, we can understand how each of them is an integral part of the broader system.

Aries-Initiation-Germinations-Emancipation

The seedlings break up out of the seed after sowing and germination and enter the soil through emancipation. The Aries principle stands for the catalytic process and for actions of initiation and innovation. It's not necessarily the task of Aries to do! The task of Aries is to take action using their natural leadership and delegation skills in new and innovative ways to empower others to get involved.

Taurus-Fertilization

The outward drive to creation and prosperity now present in Aries gives way to the methodical and pragmatic forming of the new life while creating a safe foundation for future growth. The Taurus theory requires realistic forming and meaning creation. They have the job of defining and codifying their values, what they own, in order that they are able to actualize their potential and leave an inspiring legacy to other Gemini— Dissemination. The Gemini theory is motivated by the importance of linking entities to each other in order to make ever more connections. The job is to encounter a variety of emotions, thoughts, and meetings so that structures or concepts of information can be developed and then spread to others.

Cancer-Assimilation

The sun is at its zenith at the summer solstice. The budding plant has taken nourishment from the atmosphere and starts to manifest a recognizable shape. The Cancer theory requires the assimilation of observations of specific personal eating experiences from the outside world. Their task is to create a safe and stable sense of belonging for themselves and others based on their experiences of a positive family image or centered on the awareness that they belong to a larger spiritual family.

Leo— Fruition — Cultivation— Production— Upgrading—— Fruits are ripe and ready for grazing in the summer heat. The Leo theory concerns the maturation and transmission of creative energies. We are to tap into the beauty and fiery spirit of the divine child within and to serve as role models for other people in how to allow this power to spill forth to bear fruit.

Virgo-Discrimination

Reaping in Leo now reaches full harvest in Virgo; harvesting is ground using the discriminatory faculty to clean, accurate, and carefully do so. The Virgo theory requires the study and enhancement of Leo's creative output by means of discernment and performance. Their task is to use the descriptive capacity and discipleship of the spirit to strengthen and refine the external body to become a cleansed vessel for the Holy Spirit.

Libra-Resolution-Equilibrium-Completion

The autumn equinox marks the start of fall, triggering a natural balance. The drop of the leaves starts with the creation of fresh humus, which eventually restores the soil, which is exhausted by the growth of the years. Equanimity, justice, and meditation are associated with the Libra principle. Their mission is to be peace-makers; to cultivate a social consciousness, which is just for everyone, and to reflect and reflect on the harmony and beauty, the light and the dark, of ties.

This cycle refers to the beginning of an internal turning time of nature when external things gradually die, and life returns to the planet. The outer forms have died to leave only naked trees and bushes above the barren Earth, from which life will grow once again. The Scorpio theory involves the fall into darkness, turning the ego and becoming a dominant bearer of light. Their task is to play a role in other people's highest use of passion and power.

Sagittarius-Diversification-Expansion
Despite the deterioration and rebirth in Scorpio, the Earth now teams with new life; earthworms break down the material that has decayed and fill the Earth with new energy. The Earth expands simple materials into complex, life-changing nutrients. The Sagittarius theory extends the concrete spirit (knowledge) by demonstrating how the perception of diversity (sapidity) generates meaning. Their task is to codify their religious and philosophical knowledge through role models and dogmatic teachers of universal wisdom.

In the winter solstice, little is left above ground during nature, and every living being has to conserve and maintain its power to survive the cold winter. In this period of shorter days, the Earth endures patiently, awaiting the emergence of new forms. The Capricorn principle shows how self-confidence and power and authority consolidation lead to mastery. Their job is to be positive models of performance and the right use of power and authority.

After the survival in Capricorn, much of the life energy of nature is still buried under the surface. In the aquarium process, we see the removal of nature from its superfluous forms. Everything that is no longer useful or that has not passed the winter test is discontinued. The Aquarius principle concerns the breakdown and reform of collective values. Their job should be visionaries, humanitarian activists who have joined the next collective wave of the future and are committed to being at the forefront of human emancipation.

Pisces-Integration

The composting soil is ready for spring planting at the final stage of life. The disintegration of Aquarius comes to a logical conclusion in the complete destruction of the form. The Pisces principle involves abandoning the personal sense of "I" in order to allow integration into the whole. The task of fish is to teach us the value of surrender and to support us in opening our consciousness so that our perception of separateness can transcend.

Astrology in a Holographic Universe

Amongst others, the physicist David Bohm thinks we can live in a universe that is just a holographic projection of a reality that exists beyond our universe. This idea actually supports the Vedic idea of Maya or illusion is what we see, and the shamanic or pagan idea of living in a dream world, a reality that exists outside our dream. At present, the holographic projections are a movie and static, nothing like the real and solid universe we see around us, living, breathing, and loving. A complex holographic system would have to allow for the development of our world, as we understand it, which is archetypal, perhaps even mythological.

When we live in a holographic universe, we must ask ourselves what kind of mechanism is required for that universe to exist. This method was the zodiac, the universal mythological holy circle of animals or animating concepts. I tell this because we may be living in a dodecahedral universe with twelve sides.

For some occasions, many have found that the cosmic microwave background radiation from the Big Bang on the left has tiny peaks around large areas of the heavens. A smooth and circular universe that expands will give us a smooth context.

In 2003, Jean Pierre-Luminet, a French astronomer from the Paris Observatory, reported in the Nature news journal, together with an international group of astronomers, his observations that the universe could be finite, around 30 billion light-years long, and contain 12 slightly curved pentagonal sides, just as much as a soccer ball. This is important. With 12 hands, our universe might easily have strong astrological qualities and connections. It may be that our universe is built on the intelligence of some sort that incorporates certain important astrological laws into it.

Besides space with a possible astrological structure, time reveals similar astrological links. Astrological ages are generally accurate enough to suggest an astrological model that guides the history of man over long periods. The zodiac views itself in this light as a fitting tool for defining a holographic world like ourselves. It is interested in spatial structure and shown in time and astrological structure.

It looks like that. As a final planet, we should conclude that there is a space reserved for the formation of a physical universe, maybe within a much larger area of godlike or celestial life for the sake of this exercise. A mental zodiac serving as a conceptual model for physical development is put in place. From this metaverse, a beam of light Mother / Father, with information about both reality and manifestation, descends to a point at the edge of this zodiac. The light then splits into two beams, a beam of Mother and a beam of Daddy. The mother beam is mirrored from the Father beam at a 90-degree angle. A light with information and knowledge of the Goddess circles the zodiac. The Mother Beam has twelve equal parts. One of these twelve rays is then mirrored and disseminated into the middle of the zodiac in each of the twelve astrological frames. Through window gives this light necessary for a physical universe living qualities.

Two parts of the astrological zodiac are important to this concept. Originally, the twelve astrological signs governed the seven initial planets. In ancient times, the Taurus sign was usually positioned on the Ascendant, the site of the first building. This put the seven planets in the middle of the zodiac in a vertical line. The planet Saturn rules at the top of the circle the signs Aquarius and Capricorn. The Midheaven lies among them. The next two signs are regulated by the planet Jupiter, the Poison the left, and the Sagittarius on the right. Jupiter lies in this middle hierarchy just below Saturn. The planet Mars, the next one in the solar system in line with Jupiter, rules the Aries signs to the left and Scorpio to the right. Mars lies in the middle below Jupiter. Venus then appears, Taurus to the left and Libra to the right.

The planet Mercury rules Gemini on the left and Virgo on the right on the fifth level below this axis. Mercury often rules division as a quality, which results in a multitude of expressions in this position of the archetypal explosion of creation. Under this, each sign the luminaries, the Moon and the Sun express the creative quality of full and manifest division into a feminine and male living, yin and yang. On the left, the Moon governs Cancer, and on the right, the Sun rules Leo. The IC, the zodiac's foundation, lies between them.

The Father's light begins to descend into the middle of the imaginative astrologic model along this imaginary axis. As it does this, one-seventh of its beam is spread out into the design matrix in each planetary projection center to mix with the twelve incoming Mother beams. It creates a complex Moorish pattern of creative potential. The Mother's twelve energies mix with the Father's seven energies, creating circular wave patterns that contain the qualities and awareness of Mother twelve and of the Father seven.

What is required now for these to manifest is a third Child beam to illuminate the moray pattern. The Father's beam comes down to the bottom of the Mundi axis, animating the Moon and the Sun. Those two symbols symbolize women and men in nature, yin, and yang. Through the animating gates of Cancer and Leo, the Mother beam comes together with the Father light. Male and female were born archetypally. We were Hero Twins, Apollo, the Greek sun god, and his Mother Artemis, the Moon goddess.

A third light beam, representing the divine boy, is produced. Moon and Sun emanate from each of the seven planetary projector centers by this Child beam back up the global axis. The light then extends into the moray cycle, which enlightens the pattern, and our world appears in a solid and tangible form, moving, breathing, and loving.

As men and women, we are manifestly the Hero Twins. We are the Moon and Sun manifested in the bodies of men. One important aspect of the concept of the holographic universe is that people in our world are co-creators. Based on our cognitive expectations, we create happiness or sorrow. We are the third creative beam, according to the scientists and others who take this opportunity. Yet our journey back up the imaginative axis is full of barriers. This is the legendary journey of the Heroes.

In the East, this astrological fact is the religious concept of humans with seven chakra centers around our spinal axis. Each of the seven chakras refers to each of the twelve gates ' seven planetary rulers. Those who attribute this view relate that the chakras, the projector centers, are hindered by different mental attitudes and fears so that we find it very difficult to convey a more caring world from our higher points of interest. Right now, we tend to project quite well across our two lower chakras. Such centers are centers for survival and suffering, self-expression and control, Cancer, and Leo.

We meditate and indulge in spiritual practices to purify our backbone and gain access to our superior projector centers. As we learn to do this more purely, we gain the capacity to send out new third beam energies into the creative matrix, which will illuminate the moray pattern with higher creative energies. Once we have access to the heart center, which is ruled by the love planet Venus, we will then build a world of love, mercy, prosperity, and happiness. The two bottom survival centers will be turned into project beams that encourage adventure, Cancer, and Leo, working together with Mercury on chakra three and Venus on chakra 4.

CHAPTER TEN

Astrology For Love

Anyone would be fascinated to know who would be their potential partner. Most of us have actually thought about what our future partners would look like and what their personalities would be. And our expectations and aspires are affected by our climate, our peers and their success in their ties ("Sigh, I hope my partner will be just like the other one that is my best friend" or "Oh my goodness, I hope my future fiancé won't be like my best partner), the movies we watch, the television shows that we're recorded.
The fact which astrology may have played and would still play an important role in defining people's lives cannot be disregarded. The celestial bodies are always used to define a person's future and what he or she should do to boost his or her life chances. Even the most cynical of all of us have looked at the daily horoscope at some point in their lives to see what is on their lips in the crazy world of love. Astrologers and star readers destroy in the romance universe by reading

what the celestials claim in relationships about the future of an individual. Most people begin by going to daily newspapers not to read the current events but to see what is open to them in the tunnel of love with their daily dose of love astrology. And millions of dates have been calculated and canceled due to the accuracy of love astrology consulted.

Love astrology allows you to understand yourself better and to justify why you are doing what you are doing. And it also determines for you the best social partner by matching your zodiac signs with others and finding compatibility.

-Zodiac sign has its own unique personalities and underlying behavior, and there are specific zodiacal signs which are somewhat in contrast to others, but which also fill the gaps and make them a perfect match. And this is what astrology of love hopes to achieve by giving you advice about how to respond to specific situations in life-based on the motions of the star and other celestial corpses.

Compatibility is based on animal zodiac signs for Chinese astrology depending on the year, month, and day of birth. All species have their own basic features and personalities, and these are the targets of searching for someone to balance these inherent features.

Astrology and Love - When Opposite Star Signs Attract

I will concentrate in this chapter on the compatibility of two opposing star signs. These are the six pair of signs on each other's opposite sides, and they are the following:

- Aries and Libra
- Taurus, Scorpio
- Gemini, Sagittarius
- Cancer, and Capricorn
- Leo and Aquarius
- Virgo and Pisces

and I think of Bonnie and Clyde, the Gangster couple of the 1930s who were just not able to get enough of one other when talking about opposite star signs.

Clyde Barrow's been an Aries. He was a man of action who totally ignored the law. The reverse symbol was Bonnie Parker, a Libra. There are often libraries living in them, and ideas can be valuable to them. In the case of Bonnie Parker, she was a very verbal girl who loved to write poetry. Yet she had to meet an Aries lover-although this culmination was the death penalty, it resulted in a hail of bullets.

The searching for credibility is part of the interpersonal dynamics between two opposing symbols. We know who we are, and this is just half the story—we have to find out what we are not to find completion.

A friendship with opposite signals can be highly satisfying from a positive point of view. There will be much fun, and it will be a long time before they get sick of each other.

The relationship between Gemini Angelina Jolie and Sagittarian Brad Pitt is a possible example. Despite media speculations, something obviously keeps them together, and maybe it is connected to a shared versatility.

That takes me to the cardinal, set, and mutable astrological' qualities' or' modes.'

The signs are Ario, Mercury, Libra, and Capricorn; the signs are Taurus, Leo, Scorpio, and Aquarius; the signs are Mutable: Gemini, Virgo, Sagittarius, and Pisces. Cardinal Signs paid the project a great premium. Fixed signs find stability to be necessary. Mutable signs consider variety to be life's spice.

And if two signs are opposite each other, they will have the same value, by default. Gemini and Sagittarius are both Cardinal, Cancer, and Capricorn. Which means which opposite signs will have a similar way of dealing with the world at some point.

Marie and Pierre Curie were an example of a successfully fixed pair, who had opposite star signs. She was a Scorpio and a Taurus, who, together with Henri Becquerel, were both super successful scientists who were awarded a Nobel Prize for Physics.

Marie and Pierre Curie have taken advantage of their Fixed signs. They worked on their research work and went on until they discovered what they needed. In fact, they have spent ages looking for radium through loads of pitchblende.

But if there is no common goal for a Scorpio-Taurus pair, the fixity could be a problem. There is a danger that every individual is enshrined in its particular world view, and a compromise, if not impossible, can become difficult.

Generally, the relation between two opposite signs is very strong, and a magnetic attraction appears to occur. Nonetheless, it's a tough partnership, and if it succeeds in the long term, both parties will demonstrate maturity and integrity.

CONCLUSION

Astrology was everyone's favorite discussion point. People have caste the entire system completely and say that it is useless, while others have devoted their whole lives almost entirely to the fulfillment of astrology. For years, free astrology has been around. People looked at the stars and talked about fates from time immemorial. There are so many things that make astrology so difficult to reflect on without getting into its depths.

A professional astrologer must be a competent mathematician and an astronomer who can predict star movement. Now the two sciences are not in the weakest sense of the word mean or base. A lot of knowledge is needed to learn and practice astrology. Free astrology is not as free, as you might think, in terms of its value. The horoscope is calculated, yes, calculated by my friends. The date of birth and the place of birth are first recorded. Then the exact celestial positions at birth are identified, and a horoscope is prepared that shows how the life of the particular person is created.

Someone needs a lot of concentration and dedication to astrology. Free astrology can be used by people from different sources. Most online websites format horoscopes free of charge. These may not be too thorough, but they are good enough to give you a sense of what is coming for you and what lies ahead.

Free astrology will tell you precisely where and how your life will go, and what years will be difficult for you to take care of. It tells you what years are favorable for you so that you can risk things back in place with a little confidence and faith.

NUMEROLOGY

The Ultimate Guide for Beginners on How to Master the Secret Meaning of Numbers, Uncover How Zodiac Signs Influence Yourself and Your Relationship and Unlock Your Destiny

By Jade K. star

INTRODUCTION

Have you ever wondered what life's meaning?
Have we all planned our lives for us from the start?
Who made us? Who or what formed us?
Some assume that numerology is the solution to all these questions.
And for what is numerology?

Some examples: Numerology for name Numerology for horoscopes Numerology for love Compatibility Numerology for future planning Numerology for decision-making and choice.

So how does it work and what is numerology?

Numerology is a symbolic language-the meaning of numbers.

The study of these numbers helps to identify and reflect characteristics, talents, motivations, and the way people live.

For more than ten thousand years, numerology has been used to accurately disclose the secrets of wealth, love, success, and happiness hidden within yourself. Starting with your name and birthday, numerology will help you understand who you really are, why you're here, and what you can know. Through observing the trends of monthly and annual growth cycles, numerology will help you plan your future and take a more active role in your life. All the numerologist you need is your full name and date of birth. The numbers in your name are assigned to the letters. The numerologist then applies the numbers to your birth date in a variety of variations to calculate the leading figures. The main numbers are interpreted, and the personal characteristics are described in detail. Find out more about yourself will allow you to develop in ways that might previously seem impossible. Numerology helps you make the most of your strengths and tackle your limitations more effectively. The precision in numerology is impressive in its depth of detail, and its completeness comparable to astrological analysis.

Provide immediate insights into any past or present relationship and consider your lover's deepest emotional needs. Relationships are a compatibility testing ground 24/7; take advantage of the attraction power between numbers. Is your husband's boyfriend material? Is your girlfriend going to make a wife compatible? Figure out what every number of birth really needs and gives the three males just like the three females in a relation? Do heroic action marches affect your personality in one of 18 comprehensives, gender-specific profiles of every birth number? Or does Jupiter test your attitude nicely? Learn how planets impact you by your number, is the girlfriend of Pisces 6 as married as the female virgin 6? See how your birth number blends your power with your sun sign in one of 108 different birth signs with birth numbers, which of the most enthusiastic are birth numbers?? Who's got hot tempers?

The benefit of using numerology and human attributes-as we do in numerology-is that they are mixed normal and inherently. Nothing is arbitrary in joining number 1 with originality or inventiveness, because 1 means the beginning, origin, first, birth regardless of the language in which the number is used. In numerology, you will also find that every single-digit number has a meaning that easily relates to the rhythm of things with our perspective.

CHAPTER ONE

What Is Numerology?

Numerology is the information branch that encompasses the supernatural sense of numbers. Modern numerology is art characterized by and involves aspects gathered across history from a myriad of different cultures and guidance from different ages and civilizations. The revered Greek thinker and mathematician Pythagoras is perhaps one of the best-known proponents of numerology, and many claim that he is the art's founder. Nevertheless, this ignores the fact that the old Babylonians and the ancient Hebrew Kaballah practiced numerology and astrology, numerology has many variants which are still practiced. Just as no form of astrology can really be defined as definitive, no way of numerology can be determined.

Numerology, it may be argued, is the most intuitive and straightforward of the many arts of divination, and everything really needed is a date of birth and a complete name for any person in order to delve into the significance of the numbers and secrets associated with them.

Numerological charts consist of eleven numbers 1 to 9, 11 and 22—for example, when the numbers from a person's name produce a number that is not listed in 11, then the numbers are broken down until they are finished. (The figures are broken down). A number is assigned to each letter of the alphabet.

- 1 - A, J and S

- 2 - B, K, and T

- 3 - C, L, and U

- 4 - D, M, and V

- 5 - E, N, and W

- 6 - F, O, and X

- 7 - G, Y, and P

- 8 - H, Q, and Z

- 9 - I and R

Simply put, you should give your full birth name (not your married name if different and you did not change it for any other reasons) and your day of birth date/month/year, in order to find what you commonly call your destiny number.

For an instant, if we looked at a totally fictional character named JONATHAN GOLD HAWKINS, who was born on 16 November 1959, it would collapse as follows.

J (1) O (6) N (5) A (1) T (2) H (8) A (1) N (5) G (7) O (6) L (3) D (4) H (8) A (1) W (5) K (2) I (9) N (5) S (1)

From the name alone, you would subsequently add the numbers together.

$1 + 6 + 5 + 1 + 2 + 8 + 1 + 5 + 7 + 6 + 3 + 4 + 8 + 1 + 5 + 2 + 9 + 5 + 1$

This equals 80, which would, therefore, be represented as 8 + 0 = 8.

However, adding his birth date $1 + 6 + 1 + 1 + 1 + 9 + 5 + 9 = 36$ to the 80 from his name would give you a total of 126 which would be resolved further to $1 + 2 + 6$, hence reaching a destiny number of 9.

But, what about the numbers 11 and 22? Well, these are often referred to as the' master numbers,' and these versions are believed to be highly charged and represent 11= 2 (1+ 1) and22= 4 (2 + 2) and are considered to have a performance and a learning potential.

From the destination number (sometimes referred to as the' life way number'), a trained numerologist might calculate the characteristics for which you were born and decide how it would enable you to live.

People with a destiny number one are said to be predominantly assertive dominant souls who can lead them to success. These are individuals who know something very well what these want, and while they make loyal friends, they can also be very egoistic about success. We face challenges and often with joy as we flourish here. These are also very good at promoting life changes, and when any change starts, these are usually found to lead the charge. They're charming and charismatic, but they aren't particularly good team players, because they're not intrinsic in Alpha.

Those with a' Two' destiny are the celestial negotiators of the world. They listen to their universe, absorb information, digest what is wrong, and serve as a mediator to build harmony. You are spiritual idealists, and if you accept that and encourage your own instincts to grow, you will begin to unravel all the complexities and the many questions life throws. They are gentle peacemakers who are able to understand each counterpart they meet in conflict and demonstrate an unbiased attitude because they care for others by trying to make everyone feel valued.

Those who come under the amount of destinies ' Three' are the world's innovative communicators who find their place through their initial ingenious creative talents. We are bright, imaginative people who thrive on hope and beauty. They aren't the most practical people, but when they have the opportunity to shine through acting, writing, or speaking publicly, they can reach a dazzling level of personal success. They are charismatic hedonists. They often discover that living for today is a way to cause problems tomorrow, but the attitude is' Tomorrow is for tomorrow, today is for life.' In order to align with a widespread expression and perhaps one which has formed a sense of cliché, they are the lives and souls from all sides, but most importantly, they do not fear the light of day, and they are so in love with social interaction and talking.

The' Four' way of life is the journey of practical thinkers and planners. People with this number as their fate number are trustworthy societies. We excellently plan, build, and objectively work on ideas and projects that are idealist, but also profoundly grounded and rational. We are happiest when we present the abstract concepts of imaginative people and make an abstract reality. Their dedication to task completion can sometimes be seen as a stubborn will, but in fact, it is only the pure expression of intention and instinct. You can see where others talk and know the best way of turning details into tangible results. We have professional credentials that are solely based on common sense and perfectionism.

Those who are on the five paths of life are the forward-looking social innovators, imbued with sincere sympathy and empathy, giving them a freedom of thought and a moral attitude that simply seeks to create a world of equality, justice, and harmony. Whether this world is within its own domain or on a broader global scale depends on its circumstances and impact, but the results are virtually identical. We have a comprehensive view of the community's needs and recognize where these needs may not be met. They think creatively, show an adventurous flair with their ideas, and know-how to communicate and inspire them. These are charismatic and convincing facilitators with continuously active minds, which can sometimes make it hard to stick to routines or ideas and sometimes make them seem wicked. The strength of their compassion and love ensures, however, that nothing is ever really forgotten, and they always think and intend a better world.

Those who come under' Six' are the natural parents of society, and they are people who seek to take care of and support those who fall into their domain. They prefer to join committees or teams and, of course, step up to the top of this company, not because of a real competitive push for influence, but because they have a genuine want/desire to be careful leaders of any group of people. They are idealists who long for a definite role in life and feel unhappy if they don't think that they serve any purpose. Like those who follow the way of life 5, they are simply the purest of humanists, but they have a realism that may sometimes be missed by the forward-looking innovators of the way of life 5. They want to accept responsibility because responsibility makes them feel useful, and they care for, warm, and loving caregivers in this role.

The' Seven' way of life is full of life investigators who observe, investigate, and evaluate the issues that affect them. We are swift and detailed thinkers who carry insightful judgments to events or individuals and appear to be extremely comprehensive with all they do. We usually can't see that not everybody can do this and that those who work differently can be stubborn and unforgiving. But this toughness is short-lived as they continue to be loving beings who eventually strive to achieve harmony and peace. Their keen insight means they are often the first in all groups to recognize deceit and uncertainty within others, and this tends to indicate that they have not so many friends (their quest for peace and quiet means they don't bother dealing with deceitful people). It is difficult for them to open up to others because they know that they evaluate unconsciously how they tick others and are uncomfortable with somebody doing the same to them, but they are not entirely closed books. Confidence and honesty make them respond, and once they feel comfortable with you, the chilly outside (born out of insecurity) will melt away until they stay in the heart of the people on their way to life 7.

Life Path' eight' has given world leaders the opportunity to organize and lead; they are ambitious, self-led leaders who were born. We are driven people who, if they are not careful, end up living with nothing but work and determination that leads them, but who are able to harness their other strengths which allow them to assess others correctly and see where they can fit most effectively. They are incredibly accurate. We may be discounted by their conviction that they have to fulfill their goals to complete them and to advance their life. They are often brave, inspiring people, but tend to be more aspiring to the material than to the spiritual in life.

Ultimately, the emotional heart of the universe is those who walk along life path' Nine.' They are compassionate, generous, dramatic humanitarians, and while people on the 5th path of life see injustice on a large scale, they are in individuals on the 9th path. They have empathy for the needy, sometimes to the detriment of themselves, as they may be seen to take care of themselves just a little too much. Their position as the highest single-digit means that they have been chosen as the universal carer and do so with honor and courage. You have no benefit in life and can show so much kindness that it can be detrimental to them again. It is the most selfless approach but has many moral and karmic rewards.

Naturally, life paths are simply templates and do not precisely determine who we are, and people with numerology expertise consider other factors when determining your precise location in life. Unlike astrologers and astrological charts, numerologists and numerologist charts are capable of acting as instruments to tell you fate.

Does Numerology Really Work?

While numerology is probably the least known or understood in the metaphysical sciences, it enjoys a considerable recovery at present. Does this revival because of current global problems challenge our society, and can numerology help solve issues that many feel threatened by??

Numerology is based on the fundamental terms on the premise that everything in the world comprises and is influenced by numbers. Numerology is well established in civilizational eons, and numerology is considered to be probably the oldest science known to man. The analysis of numbers was thought to be highly crucial in early Hebrew history. The Hebrew alphabet letters are based on numbers. The relationship between the message and the number was said to be interlinked to the cosmic forces. Later in the Middle Ages, numerical mysticism originated from Merkabah's teachings, which were a branch of Jewry. Then Gematria, the mysterious mathematical interpretation of the scriptures, was established by the German cabalists in the 13th century.

Evidence also exists concerning the use of numerology in China, Rome, Japan, and Greece thousands of years ago. The ancient Greeks have provided us with an abundance of technological and scientific information, which is becoming even more critical as time goes on; we are crediting for the modern versions of the numerology with the Greek philosopher Pythagoras. It's true that Pythagoras not invent numerology, but numerology was taken to the different level through his theories. This is why Pythagoras is credited as the founder of numerology.

Many mystics and writers also contributed their understanding from the beginning of the twentieth century to shape what is now modern numerology.

.But, none of this answers the question-" Does that really work? "Note, you live in a society where you have to deal with others irrespective of what kind of job. Others could be your boss, friends, colleagues, other employees, government officials, partners, business partners, and your family. The list is infinite. You may find it easy to deal with some people and difficult to deal with others. You have to deal with everyone and every situation differently so that what we all call a degree of comfort can be a catastrophe otherwise. Regardless of the reason for trying to influence someone, numerology can assist you figure out thing that makes someone lean to you. It really helps to check the statistics.

Businesses should deal with numerology efficiently. Choosing a business name is part of the essential aspects of starting a company. The name chosen is the logo and tag of your company, and this is an identity that needs to be clearly conveyed to your incoming customers. A company name has a strong force, which can create great success! Nevertheless, it can be the trigger for a persistent middle-of-the-road and quality battle. Whether you start a new business or have an established company, then you really should use the numbers to improve your company and eliminate disharmonious areas.

Yes, numerology works really. Using numerology in your daily life, you will resolve many of the challenges that are only as precise and measured as possible. Discover easy and fast ways to maximize energy and reduce stress! You will know some fantastic descriptions of your physical, cognitive, emotional, and intuitive abilities! Why not find out which of these are the worst and best and what they can do for you!

Uncover the secrets of your personality that you sometimes do not fully understand!

Why is numerology working? Numerology is, again, an ancient and robust science. The answer is simple. For over 4,000 years, some of the world's leading minds and mathematicians have created, refined, and strengthened it, and all the recent developments in both math and numerology, reading and calculation can be made for you that have never been possible before.

EXPLANATIONS ON NUMEROLOGY

Numerology is a science that reduces the energy of vibration in numerical equations. Both numbers can be reduced to one, but three, and 11, 22, and 33. We are of particular importance for other topics outside the context of this text. What about zero is the number used in numerology, the question is often asked? Many students of numerology believe that the number zero is a non-number and is the perfection of the gods. Moreover, all vibrational energy has zero within it so that it reaches a higher level of consciousness if it knows how. There is no correct definition of numerology. It's just like any hypothesis-a theory. Each theory builds on preceding structures. In first state numerology, self-awareness was obtained with gods, but the theory of health, wealth, and prediction was adopted in modern times.

Although many do use numerology solely for self-awareness purposes, you will find here a simplified version of the numbers in relation to self-consciousness and its corresponding alphabetic correlation.

- 0-Gods-It is a non-value number where everything begins and ends, reflecting the wisdom of Gods.

- 1–I am–Inspiration, autonomy, concepts, creativity, and development are the number one — the power to start something.

- 2-Sharing-Cooperation, contact, selection, responsiveness, decisions, and the very rhythm of your vibrational energy is number two.

- 3–Express–The third is self-expression, and enthusiasm, that fills a person. Mapping life and interaction with others 4-build-The fourth is a hard task to find yourself through routine and process logic. That's realistic.

- 5–Process of transformation and adaptability, allowing the opportunity for further choices, is number five. This is a number packed with power.

- 6–a comfort–The sixth is the nourishing one who expresses love and healing — a devotee, caring for oneself in order to share the energy.

- 7–search–The number seven is the one that reaches much further into its introspection theory. The analyzer is more like zero.

- 8 –collect–the number eight is the one who organizes their confidence and has a great deal of integrity and rational consistency within their own convictions. There's nothing black or white.

- 9-Feeling-Number nine is the one full of knowledge but who walks alone because of the lack of emotional weaknesses. This one does not come from introspection but from experience an abundance of information and awareness.

- 11-accept-The number 11 is the unrelenting dreamer. It cannot be based on earthly things — the big visionary.

- 22-Expand—The number 22 is the one who takes ideas and theories from others, testing them and extending them to change their own beliefs regularly.

- 33-We are one-the thirty-three number is one that doesn't actually know what they are or who they could be — a missing person who is always trying to get lost.

When a person studies each of the numbers and only then can he understand clearly what his own numerology diagram might mean.

One simple experiment is to take your name (that given when you were born) and to match every letter of your entire name, including first, middle and last names and its corresponding number in the above map. Take your names and add them together to give you a base count.

The first letter of your name is thought to be your foundation. It means that it is the harmonic sound experience of who you really are.

When you add and lower the letters of your first name, this number is considered to be the secret to your friendship with others.

Problem areas in your life are believed to be represented by any numbers that your name lacks. In the case above, 2, 3, and 8 are absent. Taking every number and looking at the diagram, one thinks that you can identify the issues that need to be addressed in your life.

If you only use your name's vowels (including y as a vowel), then the number will refer to who you are. There are many different numerological variations from various charts that correlate the numbers to letters, use your date of birth, and obtain additional supporting information from the change of name. Different books discuss profound differences in numerology and interpretations of the significance of the numbers. How you use the information is essential about numerology. It should be used as an instrument for self-awareness and self-growth. All other software must be used with the utmost caution.

Ancient Chaldean Numerology for True Meaning of Name

We're all curious about who we really are, why we do what we do and what the future might hold for us, particularly in view of the upcoming 2012' change' (a 25-year preparatory round that started in 1987), so possibly why visits to tarot readers, astrologers, and numerologists are becoming increasingly popular. While astronomers might be challenged whether or not Pluto is a planet and tarot readers might wonder whether reversed cards apply in a reading, numerologists do not all use the same system. Let's say you met one numerologist in Timbuktwo and a second numerologist in Timbukthree and used the same name and date and still got two completely different definitions of your lifetime and energy name, supposing that you would be more puzzled to emerge than you were.

So here's the thing. That's the thing. There are two numerology systems: one is the Pythagorian system or standard one that is commonly used today. And indeed, about six thousand years ago, around three thousand years ago (approximately three thousand years before the current system came to light), the numerology mother was born in Chaldean, hence the term Chaldean numerology. This system includes the meanings or vibrations of numbers with letter meanings or vibrations. The numerical value of each letter, unlike the conventional method, is more religious and shows partly by the number 9 considered' sacred' by ancient persons, which is reversed by application to any letter meaning. There are other discrepancies between the two modalities: it is enough to conclude that Chaldean numerology is the harder to cover a brain, but worthwhile because the outcome is far more accurate, descriptive, and meaningful.

One crucial fact is that the power of numbers, as well as letters, is scientifically known. The idea that we project our own energies or vibrations is nothing more hogwash than Einstein's relativity theory (E= mc2) is the hogwash. We all started with numbers (2 cells join together) and letters (Y and Z chromosomes). Yes, it was once believed that knowing the name of someone had control over them. This is true even in today's world. We give our names liberally to almost everybody who asks and, once the name is known, everyone can find it. If this happens, anyone who looks for our name has control over us. Identity theft comes to mind. So, if we are able so willing to give away the power of our titles, why should we not look closely at this power on earth ourselves? It's ours, after all, and probably the most valuable asset we have, but it often doesn't happen before possession is called into question. There is so much more to a name than is commonly accepted, and this is what Chaldean numerology means: revealing the truth about force in your name and providing instruments to use it.

Here's a quick reading that can be done by any of you. Add your month of birth to your birthday, like: I was born on the 10th of March, so my childbirth journey would be determined by the month of birth (03) and the day (10). Just decrease the double-digit number you come up with (four for me) and read the following short story and see how it relates to your own life. Your number will show the specific direction you are taking or how to get incorrect.

Often, in the middle of the forest, a caveman wakes up. He's got a bump on his face, and he doesn't have an idea of who he is. What he knows is he's trapped. He knows. By itself. By itself. One (1). And he's cold and hungry. He doesn't worry about looking for help, as far as he knows, nobody else is there. He has no memory and, thus, no reference point. So he follows his (natural) instinct to live and gathers some berries to eat and some large branches of the leaf which he uses to build a temporary shelter. Somewhere in the back of his mind is the notion that heating up a loose pile of brush and twigs brings two stones together. For a few minutes, he floods and hisses about his efforts, but continues until he achieves his target. When he sits before the warmth of the fire and eats more fruit, he pats the big stick next to him, which gives him protection if he needs to protect himself against unwanted intruders. He feels energetic, driven, and is busy planning the next day. He intends to explore the surroundings, gather more food, pursue one of those creatures whose eyes he sees reflected by the fire and perhaps a coat. But suddenly, his attention has been diverted by a new presence in the darkness that is beyond the light and rises up at his feet. He's unprepared for business and doesn't know how to react.

There's someone like him just outside the circle. A man has longer hair than he, which is quite impressive, but he is even more fascinated by the around globes in his head. In the near future, he has coaxed this creature into the light from darkness and settled next to it in the bed. Now he's no longer alone: there are now two (2). In the following days, they grow to look after each other. Each nurtures the other and becomes inseparable over time. She seems particularly happy: she sorts around the camp and helps prepare the food he's going to pick. She looks like she's going to be close to him; hold him and hug him. With her company, he feels relaxed and loves the gentleness of her voice, her eyes, and her hands. He is feeling home and safe with her and sharing their mutual happiness in the dark night in history's oldest dance. It's almost as if they've hunted for each other all of their lives.

A few months later, they are shocked and delighted when a miniature version of themselves emerges from her belly, almost like sorcery. (They had wondered why she had become so fat!... these are cavepeople, remember.) But, their euphoria soon diminished as they remembered the hard work they had done to care for this little bundle of joy. At conception, both of them are three (3) and a tiny version of the woman who has to be nurtured, adjusted, amused, burped, and comforted in a constant, ongoing band around the son. When the infant sleeps, their only respite. And that seems to be happening in 20 minutes. This is a brand new thing for both of them, and their minds are never finished. So much is to be thought about and done. Each one learns to give the other time to relax and think, or they will both burn out. It's a necessity.

A short time later, they start to clear a space in the woods next to a large rock by mutual decision. Use strong branches as spines, the hut or home began to be built using the stone and three long trees, deeply buried in the first holes as the four (4) corners of the tower. After bracing a number of smaller pieces of wood against this base, the whole structure is covered with broad leaves, moss, and branches. This method takes a lot of time and energy, but they are satisfied with the results as they knew that their child needed a proper and healthier place to live and raise and recognized that it was their responsibility. Now the family is grounded, and a schedule can be set up. Every parent has duties and responsibilities and is responsible for ensuring that the essential elements of life are upheld.

Now we'll go a few years quickly and concentrate on the son, who's now 14 (14/5), a teenager. All parents note that their child seems to have spent more time away from home (that has, of course, been restructured and expanded) than it really is. What the parents do not know is that the teenager has explored the city, visited neighboring villages (yes, the parents found other people like them and became part of a scattered community) and has even kissed a groove. Her friends (5 of them!) gave her funny smoking and drinking a liquid that has affected her body and mind in various ways. She is curious about everything, and she seems to have enhanced her senses: she reacts to something that promises excitement and adventure. She is bored with routine and home, looking for a change, independence, and challenges. Bevor, she understands the need for balance in her life; she needs to experience many different situations and circumstances.

Speed forward again, just a few months this time. We still focus on the young person who has run wild and experienced all kinds of things, some good stuff and some not so good. She recently saw that she is tired of everything and that she feels lonely, despite the people with whom she is surrounded. At 15 (6), in her honor and away from her home, she realizes that her heart feels empty and hungry at the same time. She wants to nurture, receive unconditionally, hugs, and affection, and knows that only one place and two people are able to fulfill her wish. She goes from party to home and is met with smiles and laughter and genuine love. For the first time over a long period, she feels at peace. She is really loved here, and she knows it and loves its brand newly. Her family is the foundation for her.

Following the troubled adventures of the teen, parents and children are in a quieter, more thoughtful phase. Although adolescents are young and still face many life lessons, their parents have encountered many scenarios and were thrown many rounded balls. People are getting older and spending more time their minds worrying about everything that has been and still has to be, including their passage through this lifetime. Throughout their natural developments, their minds are based on the reflection of the spirit: from the' other hand' of something conceivable to this life more than they can see. We understand the odd sense of unease which everyone has felt on various occasions (like when we stayed at home instead of a scheduled picnic and an enormous storm hit and inundated the lands around them) and wonder at its source. Every week on the 7th day, they sit on the bench they created, ponder and ruminate. Both are logical thinkers, but they are prone to mysticism, metaphysics, and invisibility. New ideas are considered and debated and shared, and parents understand that a new way of thinking needs to be opened to them.

The parents feel a new connection after this period of deep thought that goes beyond the material plane on earth. Each sees an absence of harmony in their life and seeks to strengthen and assist others. It is as if they have undergone a kind of transformation that has resulted in the development of personal power. We feel more in control of their lives, and more than we ever thought possible, they will concentrate and accomplish. We feel empathy for other people's problems and start supporting their neighbors and their society in places of need, but don't expect any reward. As a result, their own lives improve: they benefit in a way that they had neither expected material nor emotional. Within their culture, the family has a distinct reverence and thus provides a persuasive authority and control that they recognize but are careful not to misuse. The empathy they have learned to feel is the necessary element for regulating the power element attributed to the 8th level.

Now we come to the conclusion of the regular scale of numbers. The parents are now at the end of their earthly manifestations and are kind to all mankind and earthly creatures, thoughtful and genuine. Their lessons have been learned, and their expertise, which only years of experience can afford, is absorbed. They searched inside and are at ease with what they find. You respect the' intuition' tone and spend time creatively and consciously. (Their daughter has married and moved away for a long time now, busy with their own lives) They find joy in allowing their imagination to reign freely and often harvest the subtle energies of others, and, where necessary, they gladly share their love and help. You are planning and even anticipating your own departure from this' truth.' because deep in your souls, you know they just come back' home.' As such, these energies are correct nine. Compassionate, humble, wise, and sincere. In the last lesson, they understood that for a reason, everything happens, that all ideas are a lesson and that this« reality» is really a classroom, a place of learning, of liberation and of love: first the self, then, of course, others.

When you hit 11, 22, or 33, consider yourself a Master! Double digits have a vibration higher than single digits, or double digits have double strength. When the standard numerical scale of 1 to 9 can be interpreted as grammar and secondary school, instead master numbers are considered the equivalent of college or university. A master's number offers a chance of' higher education' literally. The Master Intuitive (11) represents a higher vibration of the original force (1), which translates into an unbelievably creative and profound ability to tap into insight and imagination. Number 22, the Master Architect or Builder, can also tap into the creativity and creative power of the 11 but can take them to the next level: a physical manifestation here on earth. Master number 33 is the highest frequency of devotion and self-sacrifice, perhaps to the detriment of your personal lives, to deliver to those in need. Master Healer number 44 also administers, although the 44 has a global scope that can sometimes offer humanity a significant healing potential.

Created with numerology simple

The numerological activity has its origins in a few areas, and the Hebrews also developed Chaldean numerology in Egypt, and Babylon and numerology were used in Rome, China, Japan, and Greece thousands of years ago.

Quick forward until the beginning of 1900, when Mrs. L. Dow Balliett, a respected Bible student, developed her own scheme of numbers. Ms. Balliett, widely recognized for introducing numerology studies to the western world, based her energies on making people see themselves as divine beings. Her efforts, together with those of Dr. Julia Seton, who is generally credited with coining "numerology," have brought this method to the forefront of culture.

What numbers are calculated: most regard the Life Path Number is the most critical number in the numerology map. This recognizes the innate talents and abilities with which we are born and reveals what we can do.

The amount of destiny is the sum of all of the letters in the birth name of a person and shows us what we want to do in our lives.

The number of souls is used to help communicate the intuition. It reflects the inner feelings, desires, motives, and various aspects of our spiritual forces and sensibilities. The meaning of the numbers that represent the vowels in your birth name is determined by adding.

The number of the individual determined by adding the values of the consonants in your name indicates how we are seen by others. That number gives us a valuable insight into which facets of our personalities must be "tweaked" so as to make first experiences more favorable.

The maturity number shows us how critical, rewarding, and satisfied we expect to enjoy our' golden years.' It is determined by adding our course of life and the amount of destiny.

The sum of the measured life path number shall add the numbers in your birthday: e.g., the 12 October 1975= 1+ 0 + 1 + 2 + 1 + 1 + 9 + 7 + 5= 26= 2 + 6= 8 Definition of the life path number. One (1)-Those with a life path number of 1 tend to be confident, self-starters who aspire to be the best to do anything they want. Competitive in nature, people with this life path number set high standards and can criticize those who do not meet expectations. A person with the Life Path number 1 should look for a profession that allows them to make full use of these talents; both entrepreneurship and government professions are a common career choice.

Two (2)-Those with Life Path No. 2 are generally described as peacemakers because they are frightened of conflict and confrontation and seek harmony in their surroundings. They are also accessible, patient, affectionate, compassionate, and comfortable to all sorts of people. Although these are all great qualities, it is essential for these people to remember that their pure nature will make others use them. Individuals with a life path number 2 will pursue a career that enables them to negotiate, analyze facts, and to act as supporters.

Three (3)— Those with a life path number three are imaginative, romantic, and enjoyable. By nature optimistic, a' 3' can have a strong sense of humor and prosper in searches that enable it to use its creativity. Consequently, people with life path number 3 are doing well in occupations involving publishing, speaking in public, acting, design, illustrating, and singing.

Four (4) –Life path numbers four are generally seen as stable and reliable. We are markedly truthful, respectful of authority, and appear to "follow the rules." Others, therefore, consider themselves lists holders, organizers and make sure that all project or initiative details are addressed. Career choices include anything in the fields of building, accounting, or bookkeeping.

Five (5)-Those with a Life Path Number of 5 can be quickly frustrated by daily routine and are often seeking improvement. Not surprisingly, they also thrive in environments that allow freedom, entertainment, adventure, and travel. Sometimes characterized as "the party's life," it is essential that 5s still participate in exciting activities. Otherwise, they risk turning to drugs, alcohol, gambling, or other stimulating vices. Popular career choices include marketing, interaction, advertising, new businesses, and sales.

Six (6)— Those with a life path number of 6 often have a nutritious spirit. They still try to strike the right balance between giving and receiving. Others often seek advice and advice at 6s because of their magnetic personality. Growing career choices include jobs in the service, pharmacy, and everything related to design, remodeling, and personal creation.

Seven (7)-People with a Life Path number of 7 tend to be unhappy with anything at their face value and feel compelled to observe and analyze virtually everything they meet. They can be seen as lonely and even enigmatic by others, thanks to their student nature. Common career choices include teaching, computer programming, and any occupation that requires a lot of study, deductive thinking, and technical skills.

Eight (8)–Those with Life Path number 8 are incredibly cost-effective, efficient, and productive. And they tend to like the more beautiful things of life, as you would imagine. Thanks to their addiction to material wealth, however, eight people tend to be employers and often take their job forward. Senior management, financial advisor, immobilizer broker, or any position of authority are common career choices.

Nine (9)-Those who have a life path number of 9 are considered natural leaders and are regarded as the responsible person even if they are not. Much of it is because of the humanitarian interests of the nine, and the bond between everything and everyone must be acknowledged. A person with this number of Life Path wants to treat others in the way he wishes to be handled. Popular career choices include business in the world, the arts, education, and health.

Numerology is a fascinating field of study to know more about yourself. You will be astonished at the precision of your numbers-try it.

Find your goal Numerology

For thousands of years, numerology has been used to decide certain things about a person. The Pythagoras was the first to discover that numbers have a vibration and that each number has a particular vibrational field. We thought we could build our lives by telling our parents our name with which we would like to be born and the specific birth date which we decide to come in. We have, therefore, learned the significance of the numbers and their impact on our lives. Numerology should also be used by our Spirit Guides to help us live by pointing out specific patterns of numbers to us as we go through our daily lives. Note that for some time now, the common language has been considered universal. This cannot be just a coincidence.

Upon finding a particularly fascinating truth about numbers, Pythagoreans became interested in mathematical mysticism. If a set of odd numbers beginning with number one is added, the result is always a square number.

Discoveries such as these led the Pythagoreans to conclude that "all is number," so that people can measure all things in the world in terms of numbers and proportions according to one interpretation. This is a good idea, and it has a good idea. Considerable impact on mathematics and science. Nevertheless, "all is number," according to another definition, implies that everything in the universe is numbered and can be reduced to a numerical value.

The Pythagoreans often defined numbers in terms of mathematics and geometry as a non-numerical function. Such features were more about instinct and mysticism than science or mathematics. Odd numbers, for example, are male and even women. The number one was innovative because multiple numbers can add any other number. Four of them were duality and were female, while three of them were male. As two and three, five represented marriages, and since this was in the middle of the numbers from one to nine, it was also justice.

The number of life paths: The way of life is the sum of a person's birth date. This number shows who you are at birth and the native traits you carry through life with you. The Life Path explains the essence of this life journey.

Speech Number: The expression or destiny number is a number derived from all the letters in your full name. This is how many talents and attitudes are described. You have to develop and use it in your lifetime. Sometimes this is called your potential or destiny. It may not be easy to live up to the qualities of that number, but it is your target. It is the intent of your life, the religious goal, and the area of your potential. Unlike your Life Path number, the term number reads more accurately as you MUST to accomplish your goal.

Soul Urge Number: The soul desires, or, as the heart's desire is sometimes called, is an essential influence in numerology. This consists of the vowels on your behalf.

This is the basic sense of numbers: descriptions from numerologists are relatively similar, this is an example of each number.

0—Infinite, Equality, Nevertheless, Boundless, True, Manifesto, Purity, Love, Omega, Possibility, First Cause, Unified Land, Origin, Space, Consciousness, Cosmic Egg, Creator, Universal, Unified Power.

1-Initiation, New, Self-reliant, Ambition, Leader, Will, Conscious mind, Action, Freedom, Originality.

2— Duality, Pole, Division, Choice, Cooperation, Gestation, Service, Support, Waiting, Patience, Harmony, Diplomacy, Psychic, Initiation, Adaptive, Partnership, Empathic, Comparison, Mediator, Receptive, Collecting, Helper, Memory, Reproduction, Pose and Negative Balancing.

3-Trinity, Demonstrated, Positive, Union of Divine and Man, Negative and Neutral, Attractive, Humorous, Friendly, Expressive, Friendship.

4-Practical, tidy, cautious, rational, hard-working, trustworthy, constructible, healthy, attentive, earthy, planning, material imaginative, green thumb, even-tempered.

5-Adventure, changes, autonomy, discovery, variety, sensuality, teacher of knowledge, creativity, childlike, fun.

6—Beauty, nourishing, harmony, love, wedding, family, accountability, understanding, sympathy, healing, empathy, perfectionist, order, duties, comfort, service.

#7-Philosopher, intelligent, looking for perfection, wise seeker, reserved, visionary, stoic, contemplative, aloof, introspective, philosophical thought, spiritual, religious, mystic, ethereal, exotic, rare, elusive, and otherworldly, mystery.

8-Performance, speed, energy, overseer, self-disciplined, control, achievement, authority, service provider, excellence, abundance, manager, psychology, businessman, product demonstrators.

9—Last, humanistic, imaginative, understanding, charitable, caring, sweet, loving, selfless, philanthropic, idealistic, spiritual healer.

Numerology was used for business decisions, advice on the relationship, the symbols of the Universe and Spirit Guides, unconscious dreams, karmic situations, what to overcome in that particular life, maturity, why to be, rational thinking. There are practically a number of things that make up who we are at all levels. You have to study and work a lot to find all this information yourself.

CHAPTER TWO

House Numerology

House Numerology is an ancient strategy used by people throughout each stage of their lives for thousands of years. It is still used today as a valuable instrument for all types of decision-making. One way to use numerology is not one you might have expected. The name is House Numerology when you plan to move-let numerology guide you when you choose your new home!

You want to start with the house number and add all the numbers together until a single-digit number is available. For instance, if the address of a house is 5712 Main Street, the 5 + 7 + 1 + 2 would be added to the total sum of 15. Then you add the 1 + 5 to give you a total of 6. Now that we have a single digit, this is the number "personality" of the room, if you like. This number can tell us a lot about what we can expect from the house and perhaps if it is the perfect house for you or if you're still looking. Let us now know more about the different personalities of the house.

1 Keyword: motivation, energy, productivity Great home for single moms, those who work mainly at home or who have a lot to do but maybe tend to be lazy. Select this home care if you're already high in energy and are working outside the house because even at home, you can find yourself working- which may be great for production but not so good if you want to spend time with your family.

2 Keywords: Warm, inviting, Cozy Wonderful choice for small and entertaining families or couples. The tenants and visitors of this house here will feel "at home." Once you enter this house for the first time, you can feel calm and serenity and recall your parent's or grandparents ' homes. The downside here could be a little too relaxed. You may be home, and people may wonder if you become anti-social with this numerological personality of your house!

3 Keywords: flowing energy, creativity, abundance. This home is ideal for artists, writers, and artisans. The occupants sense creative juices flowing continuously. You can have your best ideas in the tub, cooking dinner, or just relaxing on the sofa. If you don't know the arts or imagination, you might want to avoid this house because it can make you feel like you have a sudden surge of ideas, but you may be unable to find a new way of thinking. Think of "the block of the novel."

4 Keywords: health, security, grounding This is the type of house for a retired couple or single person trying to settle down in the world. This house is all about being safe, grounded, and long-term. People who live here tend to stay in a house like this for many years, but that is perfect for the above but isn't ideal for the growing family or for someone who wants to travel or who is willing to move in the near future as the house won't be appropriate for this ideal.

5 Keywords: Transform, Fly, Energetic Perfection for young couples who like to fly, or even families who want to have their children worldly or traveling. This house is the type of house to which you are not attached. You can leave and fly at

will with this house-numbering personality, and you know that your home is not so much a place you have been stuck down, but a place to relax and unwind between your journeys. If your job requires many adventures or even a long journey, you might not find this house the best choice.

6 Keywords: colorful, tidy, sexy. This house is particularly great for women because Venus is number 6, which of course, emotions sexiness! Living in this house would motivate you to stay brightly smooth, comfortable, and stylish. Bright, dynamic colors on the walls and a decorative flair ensure that this house looks and feels fantastic. Your friends are going to envy this kind of place! While this home is excellent for single ladies, it's also great for young couples or even families, especially if you stay in your mom's home. This house is not better for the elderly, because the house is so lively and "smart," and maybe flashy.

You could be advised to "act your age."

7 Keywords: scholarly, supervisor, successful people living here tend to be individuals or older couples or families. There is much success here, and this home is filled with books, classical music, and a traditional sense of style and elegance. Even small homes can be celebrated inside if this is their character. Guests in houses with this personality in house numerology can feel unwelcome; however, so be sure that you have a comfortable living space to stay when visiting you.

8 Keywords: Money, Prosperity, Conformity Similar to the personality of house 7, this house is also ideal for smaller or older singles or couples. People like the fruit of their labors in abundance both at home and abroad. If you're looking for a home that will keep your self-control and the feeling that you're financially successful, this is the home you want. This home is not suitable for raising families because money is more important, and things can be overlooked in life.

9 Keywords: Spirituality, Style, Comfort. This house is perfect for every type of family-it's lovely all around the home because it is best decorated with a classic traditional style. Those who are very religious by nature will be exceptionally good here and will be content and fulfilled at home. Comfort is essential, so make sure you have a lot of living space indoors and outdoors here to get the most out of this home. A small garden or patio area where you can enjoy nature is ideal. Anyone avoid this home if you're not spiritually opposed to anything dead. If you have closed this off in your life, you'll only feel uncomfortable living in this house.

Numerology Date Of Birth

The birth date numerology explains who you are, what you are doing well, and what your natural talents are. It also points out what we have to know and the challenges facing us. The birth number in a full numerology reading is just one piece of the puzzle.

To figure out your number, add all the numbers on the date of birth together, as in this example, until only one digit is left. The number of births doesn't stop you from being everything you want, which is a choice.

Originator 1 is first. It is natural to come up with new ideas and to introduce them. The fact that things are their own way is another attribute that makes them stubborn and arrogant. One is extremely honest and does well to master other skills in diplomacy. We like to take the lead and are often leaders or managers, as they are the strongest. Self-sufficient is definitely helpful for them. Lessons to learn: thoughts from others "could be as good or better and be open-minded.

#2 The Pacifier 2 were born negotiators who are well aware of the needs and moods of others and also think of others in their earlier lives. Of course, logical and very intuitive, they don't like to be alone.

#11/2 The intuitive 11 is the highest number 2 expression. Eleven have the inherent ability to adapt and to provide a spiritual vision of what is happening around them. Extremely idealistic in nature, they are often called dreamers. When they need a mediator, a harmonizer, or just a supportive ear, their fundamental understanding of both the earthly and the spiritual, and the strong desire to help others is often applied to them.

#3 Party life 3 is an idealist. They are incredibly creative, personal, beautiful, romantic, and relaxed. They initiate many things, but they don't always happen. You like others to be happy and do all they can to do that. They are extremely popular and idealist. You must learn to see the world more realistically.

#4 Sensitive and traditional are Conservatives 4. We like routine and order. They act only if they understand fully what is expected of them. You want to dirty your hands and work hard. They are drawn to the outside and have an affinity. They ready to wait and could be persistent and stubborn. You need to know how to be flexible and be careful to yourself.

Like the other two-digit master number 22, the Master Builder draws strength from the fact that they are in harmony with your spiritual side by carrying out your most mundane tasks. The physical world is essential and very coordinated and effective in the execution of their functions. They make significant leaders based on number 4 and the additional dimension of the spiritual part based on number 22 and have a solid foundation. We are trustworthy and idealistic and have great new ideas.

#5 The explorers are Conformist 5. A natural curiosity, danger, and excitement often end up in hot water. You need diversity, and you don't want to be in a rut. The whole world is their class, and in all circumstances, they see the opportunity to learn. The questions never come to an end.

They look carefully before taking action and ensure that they have all the facts before drawing conclusions.

#6 Romantic 6 are idealistic and need to be happy. To them, a healthy family relationship is essential. Your emotions influence your choices. You have a strong need to look after and help others. We are very patient and teach well. They like music or art. Loyal love make friends seriously. Six must learn to distinguish between what can and can not change.

#33/6 Compassionate 33 The love of beauty and balance is appreciated for years. They feel deep compassion for the world and must be protected against martyrdom, as they are overwhelmed by emotions. Also, don't sacrifice yourself for others. It may be more useful as a mentor to show others the way.

#7 Searchers are Intellectual 7. Sampling hidden information also makes it difficult for them to consider things at face value. Their decisions are not influenced by emotions. There is never a fast start, and your motto is slow and steady. We come from thinkers and are very well-informed and sometimes lonely. They are technically inclined and make great scientists reveal information. They like secrets. We like secrets. You live in your own world and should learn what is acceptable and what is not acceptable in the world as a whole.

#8 The problem solvers are Big Shot 8. We are competent, stubborn, and robust, and functional judgment and decisive. Their plans are high, and they like to live a good life. They're people to take responsibility. You look at people critically. We let you know that they are the boss in no uncertain terms. You must learn to base your decisions on your own needs, not what others want.

#9 Artist 9 is a natural artist. Artist 9 is unaffected. They are incredibly caring and generous and give their last dollar to help. We have no problem making friends with their charm, and nobody is new to them. They have so many different personalities that it is difficult for the people around them to understand them. They're like chameleons, they still shift and blend. They are incredibly fortunate, but can also suffer extremes in fortune and mood. You have to build a foundation of love to succeed.

Life Paths and Numerology

Someone ever came here to ask the old question, "What is your sign?" This classic collection line was used by entire generation of guys who were trying to take up girls-with dilute results. When women want the good coming back to them, or if you're a delicate man who wants to use a new product for an old cliché, try to ask them for the numerology equivalent of astrology signs,' What's your way?' Life Path-Your chief in numerology Your life path is your first number in numerology. It is determined by the addition of Fadic. This is the method of adding significant numbers together and increasing the result to a single digit.

There are (9) significant ways of life in which everybody works. In the path of life (2) and (22) in the path of life (4), there are also two sub-paths corresponding to the Master Numbers (11). Nevertheless, these are sub-categories of the main ways of life. The following is a brief description and a few famous people on every path of life.

Life Path the Leader's Path In this life, your goal is to be self-sufficient and to stand on your two feet. Such people are living to take action in their lives. These people are highly driven and concentrated, ambitious; they don't make advice well either. You must also battle to be a perfectionist and not accept flaws in your own work.

Lifeway Cooperator's Way In this life, your goal is to learn the ability to cooperate. These people are susceptible to others ' feelings. We are natural negotiators and always look for consensus in people's problems. They are honest and humble, and the people around them are always inspired. In competitive situations, these people have some issues and do not handle time pressure well.

Life Path Entertainer Path In this life, your goal is to entertain and make others happy. Such people seek love and attention and prefer to use their sharp wit and vivid imagination. Such people seem to live beautiful lives, have all the right moments, and have little effort to attract wealth and prosperity. They can't deal with boredom and fear that they're alone. They also tend to have problems dealing wisely with their funds.

Life Path The Builder's Path In this Life, your aim is to create a life-work based on your own work and sound work. They are meticulous planners, smart, practical, and willing to see the results of their own efforts. They are also highly conservative in thought and lack flexibility in thinking. People also fear new ideas that have not been tried.

Life Path The Seller's Path In this Life, you have the goal of creating freedom through the change in your lives and in your environment. Such people love change because of themselves. We are versatile, agile, multi-talented; in brief, we were born salespeople. Such individuals are thriving on competition and pressure to succeed. Taking risks and biodiversity can be issued for them.

In this life, your aimis to build balance and obligation both in your own lives and in those around you. We love beauty, harmony, and goodwill for themselves. You are trustworthy, honest, and seem to take responsibility for your life. We hate inequality, and we love fair play. We seem to get into their mates too much and think about trivial things too much.

Life Path Loner's Path In this life, your goal is to learn things through personal experience. Some people are individualistic and need time to stay healthy every day. We have great intuitive powers and high analytical abilities. These people are perfectionists and hate working on other people's plans. We also have trouble with taking advice from anyone and are strongly disliked by manual work.

Life Path the Warrior's Path In this life, your goal is to set small targets and then achieve them by battle. Such people love the power struggle that fulfills their lives. In pursuit of their objectives, they are strong, sturdy, and ruthless. The success of these people is not easy; they must achieve their goals by fighting. They're the business jungle beast. These people also have difficulties expressing their appreciation for their loved ones and managing their work and home life.

The Humanitarian's way of life In this life, your goal is to show the world compassion. Such people want to change the environment and better it for all. We are energetic and imaginative, as someone with such high goals would. These people are often drawn to leadership positions in significant causes or religious sects. They also tolerate other people's needs and wishes. Such individuals can also be warm if their goals are challenged or discouraged. They are usually not good people in detail.

Whatever the way of life in which you were born, all of them are equally valid, with lessons that should be followed and best learned. We all have talents and abilities, which we must learn to use to add meaning to our lives and make the world a better place.

Numerology and Relationships

More than 2000 years ago, in ancient times, mystics recognized that numbers represent both qualities and quantities.

Number mysticism, today is known as numerology, is one of the most popular forms of divination used to distinguish personality, compatibility, and timing.

To skeptics, we also do not think of the sort of numerology to which you are subjected by a cursory Internet search for numerology. Nobody's character is represented by a single number.

The collective power of everybody is symbolized by multiple factors in the native and the time maps.

Ideally, every root number one to nine and number clusters would be perfectly balanced in the graphs. But the over-balanced and under-balanced forms are far more common; this reality is the red flag of personality and challenging circumstances of life. Everyone has its own distinct, difficult parts in life to work through, so it goes through every lifetime until you get it right.

Associating birthdays with personality characteristics is a commonly used form of contemporary numerology, although multiple factors are preferred instead of just one. The energy of the other hundreds within personality and schedule charts supports or mitigates the symbolism of any single factor.

Single-factor reading safeguards include those uncommon individuals who can only use a handful or even a single factor, such as the day of birth, as a touchstone to reliably gather character, compatibility, and timing facts.

Identifying extreme over-balanced or under-balanced types of numbers helps to understand the associated energies and underlines the relationship styles of each radical number one to nine.

The number one is known for driving and performing as a very masculine number, and power squash romanticism. Since spending the whole day focused on his or her goals, no time remains for romance. Once you have a relationship, your partner will notice a lack of love and commitment from you. The one simply does not focus upon it and shows his love in other ways, like sharing the abundance he worked hard for.

Two of the root numbers are most considerate, thoughtful, and associated. You will have plenty of affection for both, but your hyper-sensitivity may be tired. For extreme cases, two of the figures are the most frustrating. But if you ever wanted someone to wear two different hats, to play two different roles as wife and mother or to be bi-sexual, both are perfect. Nobody beats two in a contest for the natural dual nature that can be constructive, favorable, or sinister, disgusting.

The three are distinguished by lively communication, laughter, and fun. He or she is manic-depressive and volatile, too, however. With three, you will have fun, but you can tire of his emotional ups and downs. As a musician or entertainer, Three is unsightly, however, the most superficial of all root numbers. Don't expect meaningful, in-depth talks with the three. Wait for a good time.

Four is the root number most accurate, and you may like he or she is also one of the more substantial numbers. Sometimes a bit crude, yet practical and efficient, four work is done. Job, family, and relationships are stable. Don't drive four as traditional as the root of all numbers to be unpredictable and adventurous. He or she is the rock on which people can rely, yet boredom and monotony are frequent.

Five are sexy, charismatic, unorthodox, and adventurous. Yet today he or she is here, and tomorrow he or she will be back. Those with more than five in their graphs were unhappy in conventional long-term ties. You need creativity Five are the least monogamous of all root figures, but he or she is a big love that can connect with almost everybody. A chameleon but a Zebra doesn't switch its colors, therefore don't expect the five to be the conventional romantic partner.

Six are the most based on conventional romantic partnerships. You can count on six to be loving and enticing matrimony until six get carried away by its fatal flaw and romantic idealism. "Our partnership should be like that...," the six said. Right, the marriage is the way it is, and you, Mr. Six, have to accept it. It's hard for six to allow what he or she can't change. The perfectly balanced sixth form is the recognition without the disapproval of how things are. Sadly, many more than six are over or less stable and just will not recognize what is partially symbolized by their misguided idealism in their partnership.

Seven are not geared towards relationships unless you make the connection of seven to heaven, the unseen spirits, and those on the other hand into consideration. You say to him or her, "Earth to seven!" and often it's appropriate. He or she is here physically, but in outer space, mentally. Seven avoids superficial little conversation. Only seven of your partners are healthy, as long as you don't try to encourage the seven to express themselves emotionally, you will have some intense, meaningful conversations. Repression is a common occurrence. It's not like seven don't like you, it's just like love and proximity to the seven is awkward.

Eight is the most real and financially inclined number of roots, so it makes sense that in eight, you can enjoy the more beautiful things in life. Eight also like status. Don't wait for a near romantic relationship. Eight can be difficult, and stuff in the bedroom may like rough. Divorce is typically costly for 8, so eight can be the greatest opportunists to marry well. Eight may be a bully, but the wise 8 is a master of balanced power and influence.

Nine is a stunning romantic partner, but he or she is generally uncertain. For example, your religious beliefs seem to be whatever you feel best at the moment. Nine have trouble with honesty sometimes, but his soul is more precious than it is. If you ever want a partner who is open to the idea of an open relationship, nine is your guy or your target. Nine have an abundance of unconditional love and make them a good father or wife. Nevertheless, drinking too much is popular among over-nine.

Number symbolism is a fun way to get to know people timing and character. It takes time to learn the fundamentals, like any other discipline, but once you do so, you have a piece of invaluable knowledge and understanding.

Numerology, Astrology, and Compatibility

Instead of considering astrological Sun signs, we believe that comprehensive astrology and numerology charts must be examined if the real personality, compatibility, and timing (prediction and forecasting) are to be taken into account.

In fact, a thorough analysis of handwriting carried out by an experienced professional offers much more insights into the unconscious, all of which cannot be contained in conventional psychological astrology.

You can assume that you are astrologically compatible with two seemingly gentle, compassionate people (both of them have abundant fish and cancer resources, for example).

Nevertheless, we find that you have very compact, short, extreme right slanted, straight, angular, heavy-pressure script, with rigid baselines and T-bars downwards. Plus, the detailed virtual charts contain bright patterns of over-balanced "8" and "1" energy. All of this, together with other substantiating data, alerts the researcher that he is a powerful abuser.

The full graphs of the other person contain, in part, a great deal of under-equilibrated "2" energy indicating dependency and self-determination. The script contains, in support of these ideas, martyrs and victim characteristics such as a small overall script length, light write-based, closely spaced words, overly rounded and immature-looking script, droopy-rhythm and connections between letters, pinned circle letters, short, weakly crossed letters T-bars, and x-forms, with letter x n

Unfortunately, a surface astrology interpretation will leave the opportunity for a highly toxic, if not harmful, match open.

Only about 100 years ago, psychology was not part of astrology. The 2000-year history of the study of astrology mainly involves forecasting rather than emotional character analysis.
Unfortunately, from our point of view, the majority of astrology in print or online today is basically new, emotional astrology and includes a superficial and twisted approach to science.

Astrology that is primarily only for amusement (although typically not viewed as such) includes, for example, Sun or Moon sign horoscope and readings by Astrologers who generally encourage falsehoods such as"... (numerology or) Astrology is not predestination, nor is it destination how things are happening is going to come up to you."

Some famous modern astrologers go so far offensively as to suggest escapism, good-wished thinking, and self-fulfilling prophecies. In response, some astrologers (like ourselves) say that it is possible to measure and outline personal fate (i.e., to impart a general inclination of destiny and, often, to be precise), to take responsibility for one's actions and life. Worse, they deny the existence of fate and also deny the reality that different degrees of inevitable (and measurable) hardship in people's lives have a divine purpose.

Truth is their numerology or astrology is not about fate or predestination. Doom and destiny are simply the original ancient numerology and predictive astrology.

It is curious that truly embracing karma and fate is directly related to taking responsibility for one's actions and how much of today's modern astrology provides a break from the harsh realities of life.

Checking Sun Signs, Moon Signs, or any other particular aspect without taking into account the different contents and trends of the maps is only an indicator of the ground. This teaches you almost nothing about the truth or the harmony of the personality with one another.

For instance, the Aquarius Sign is considered to be relatively harmonious with the Sagittarius Sign. When you pick ten Aquarius Sun Signs random and pair ten with Sagittarius Sun Signs, it is entirely possible that neither person will get along. It is also entirely possible that they all get along with each other.

The best romantic matches for the combination of the Libra Sun and Cancer Moon, for example, depend entirely on the health of the planets involved (stark or well or affecting trouble, like negative planets, wrongly predicted worlds, retrogrades, low house put, etc.), their rulers, their health and the rest of the several hundred aspects and trends.

For example, a person with a Libra Sun and Cancer Moon has excellent compatibility with an Aries Sun and the Capricorn Moon, both opposites.

Oppositions usually are deemed to entail poor compatibility, but sometimes very near resistance (opposing planets that are very close to the compatibilities chart for a degree or two) is more satisfying than a challenge, especially if the remaining composite contents are harmonious.

Oppositions are:

- Aries is against Libra.

- Taurus is against Scorpio.

- Gemini is against Sagittarius.

- Capricorn is opposed to cancer.

- Leo is against Aquarius.

- Virgo is against Pisces.

Junctions, the same combinations of symbols, reflect the intensification of the influence of the logo, which is positive and sometimes negative. It is generally a "hard" aspect, and not as easy as trines and sextiles to flow.

Although we feel that modern astrology emphasizes Ptolemaic aspects too much, it's good to understand them.

The fundamental aspects of Ptolemaic are oppositions (angle of 180 degrees), squares (corner of 90 degrees), junctions (angle of 0 degrees), trins (edge of 120), and sextiles (angle of60 degrees).

Square aspects are the mixture of signs with different elements (see below), like Taurus and Leo, usually suggesting stress and difficulty. Trine aspects are combinations of symptoms, such as Scorpio and Poissons (both water), which are the same element and are generally pleasant. Sextile features are combinations of signs that are compatible, but different, and generally favorable features, such as Virgin Cancer, or Leo with Libra.

Unless you embrace the simple method of examining the Sun and Moon signs only, which could better provide a glimpse, then the elementary combinations of signs for a necessary awareness should be tested.

Fire and air are harmonious on the ground, and earth and water are smooth. However, each component typically mixes well with itself (fire and flame, etc.).

- Leo, Aries, and Sagittarius are fire signs.

- Virgo, Taurus, and Capricorn were planetary signs.

- Libra, Gemini, and Aquarius are air signals.

- Scorpio, Cancer, and Pisces are water signs.

A surface approach includes Libra Sun, Cancer Moon, or water or Earth-Moon, compatibility with a Sun air or gas, but this is just the start.

If you need to go a bit deeper but still not undergo an extensive analysis, it is also helpful to consider the essence of this sign (Fixed, Cardinal or Mutable), as the male or female nature of the sign takes into account (Fire and air are males, and water is feminine).

We also strongly recommend understanding the personal timing of each person when it comes to compatibility.

Personal scheduling comprised of numerological and astrological cycling methods of the medium, short, and long-term continuous and noncontiguous cyclical timing regularly symbolically establishes or breaks relationships. The group cycles can be divided into groups that are the basis for the identification of patterns.

Two people may actually have nothing in stock, but their current personal time periods (some as short as a day, others as long as years) and the relationship changes, or even dissolve, when those time cycles shift.

Remember that we agree that it is possible to employ sun and Moon signs solely as spiritual touchstones for someone who possesses strong and stable psychic ability and a good general understanding of astrology.
But few have this ability in which you can read reliably and correctly without a comprehensive approach.

Finally, an astrologer will consider all the detailed diagrams, together with the thorough timing diagrams, and not only the Sun and Moon signals, if current compatibility really is to be discovered. Also, we found that if you want a high level of precision, you also have to take into consideration detailed numerology maps, along with handwriting assessments (subconscious biases and defenses, etc.).

A skeptical saying that"... do not believe in Astrology," to us, is reasonable and understandable when only Sun Sign Astrology, the basis for most astrological horoscopes today, is exposed.

Numerology Help You Avoid Superficiality

Since 1992, we have analyzed the quality of many ancient and most recent numerological sources. There is plenty of information; some decent, some bad, and the new student is easily misled, or even worse. We have acquired strong convictions through standardized tests as to which hypotheses and implementations are correct, and which are not. These are some common numerological errors for newbies, and you'll be ahead of the game if you stop them.

The decision to marry a specific day, for instance, is secondary, and often pointless, in the hope of good luck, compared to the charts of when the pair first meet, when they begin dating, and their unique personal timing.

The founder of modern Western numerology isn't Pythagoras. He is considered the father of a statistical theory based on modern Western numerology.

Personal years (a standard annual time period in modern numerology) begin on 1 January for everybody, not on a person's birthday, and end on 31 Dec for everyone. Peak Personal Year power is reached for everyone in September of every year. The energy of the Universal Year is starting and ending simultaneously and at peaks every September (e.g., the current Universal Year is 2007, which reduces to 9 by adding the 2, 0, and 7). Some cycles start on the birthday of the subject, and some don't. The Personal Year is not and is not clear through experience with a comprehensive approach, including many other timing considerations.

Any energy component of one digitology (negative or positive, balanced, or under-balanced) alone can be assisted or even mitigated adequately in the detailed diagrams by the other aspects ' energy. Therefore, it is unwise to concentrate on just one or even a few things to delineate or forecast. Some "numerologists," mainly those we heard in radio talk shows, make this mistake. There are hundreds of predictive measures in the detailed graphs, like phases in the cycles; only a few allow incorrect predictions. Surface interpretation is acceptable as an introduction to a more comprehensive analysis, but it only serves as little more than entertainment and potentially worse, it distorts science and opens the door for criticism (just as).

Fame, colossal money, lifetime happiness, incredible love, or anything else is not possible (no matter how much work you do on yourself, no matter how much you "integrate" your problems, and how motivated you get) if the detailed diagrams symbolically represent "what's" and "what will happen" if adequately interpreted. Those numerologists who deny this reality A) use a shallow numerological approach that disallows them an understanding of the workings of the destiny, B) refuse to accept fate because they fear C) choose to paint a flowery image with the intention of attracting a wider audience and therefore selling more books or services or D) refuse to acknowledge the cold and harsh realities Some people's lives include more obstacles and problems than rewards, some rewards rather than challenges and some harmony.

Being an "old soul" usually doesn't only "integrate" many of the challenges of life in earlier incarnations successfully, and it is more important to embody substantially more human experiences, including many trials and tribulations. An "old soul" is clearly known by its religious roots, which many master numbers, seven or nine, for example, symbolize in the simple numerology charts or in a very spiritually inclined ninth astrological room, or many other potential indicators. Many have successfully conquered life's challenges and continue to live a beautiful experience, but that doesn't mark them as "the old soul." In drug addicts, alcoholics and homeless people, most "old souls" can be found, as the powers of the "old soul" usually face a challenge.

The use of anything but the full, legal birth name (just as on the certificate of birth) in numerical analysis of the title just gives a personal reading of it. A human, who is an illusion, is not the subject's real, fundamental power. It is merely a "read picture" and is a bit like evaluating the signature alone compared to a good, extended sample of the script when examining the handwriting. Abbreviated or simplified names lead to additional readings, and the full information is far from a replacement.

The use, for the months (or days, etc.) of the year (for example, May= m/13/4+ a/1+ y/25/7= 12/3) as related to the delineation or timing will only provide a minor overview and is of relatively low importance for other monthly rounds and for the other comprehensive contents of the graphs. In truth, this dimension has been found to be relatively useless. Universal months (e.g., the first month of the year, 1 January of the year, 1 Universal month of 2007; 1 + 2007= 2008/10= 1) is, among other things, the fundamental foundations of discovering one's personal months.

Although the vibrations of the universes such as the Universal Month (see above) are vital and are used in calculation of personal waves, such as the Personal Month, the result is erroneous prediction is applied to a person's life (e.g. "as the Universal Month is seven months away, it is unwise to change jobs now" The individual's personal vibrations (personal days, months, years, etc.) are always more important in terms of time. For example, a 3 Universal Year vibration, which is very rewarding for one person, can also be a year of life-long challenges for the next person.

Carmic Debt Numbers (13, 14, 16, 19) don't always symbolize what you haven't done. They express what you have to handle because of abuse or neglect in previous lives of similar resources. Karmic debt numbers are not beneficial, and they are malicious. But it can be equalized in time by balancing the karma.

CHAPTER THREE

How to Woo the Numerology NUMBERS?

Sometimes you try to get somebody's attention romantically, and sometimes you try to make a good impression on it so that they get you for a job. With any reason you decide to have an emotional effect on someone, numerology can help you figure out what makes someone tick.

If you really want to meet someone, measure all the numbers that build him with desires and wishes. The following includes the Life Path Number (sum of the date of birth reduced into one digit), the Destiny Number (full name), the Soul Urge Number (vocals), and the Personality Number (consonants).

Life Path-Show your readiness to follow, not to be a leader. A gift of cash in his name always impresses a number 1.

Give your life for this person, no trouble. Express commitment, volunteer to be your personal support, and make sure you never challenge yourself anything. Never shine out this guy, or they will treat you as an enemy.

Make clear to him that you understand politics and individual needs and that your enemies or disbeliefs will not disturb him. Soul urge1 does not have to be condemned for "doing what they have to do." Number one Personality-Give them a flattering picture or any type of award or acknowledgment (faux or not), which recognizes them as number

Personality 1 enjoys money, spa trips, make-up, and shopping as gifts.

Nothing makes him happier than the proposal for marriage and the wedding ring on his lips.

Second luna, love and romance promises, and eternal faithfulness please this type. Signing long leases or long contracts in business makes this kind happy.

Teddy bears, photographs of you–anything that continually reminds you that despite your enormous insecurity, you always like a 2.

This type is highly rewarded with pregnancy as the child cementes their relationship. Children are the adhesive that keeps them together. You also enjoy all sorts of seduction–coffee, extended trips with only you and precious items, and accessories as gifts. Pulling on the heart is the key to winning over the personality of number 2.

Give it a long rope and the freedom to talk to anyone you want, or even to have affairs with.

musical instrument, a visit to a spa, clothes, or anything that makes them more entertaining. We like toys, too.

This person is probably most inspired by an exotic holiday. Giving them a picture of themselves (for example, a painted portrait) will also encourage them. It is also appreciated to show them in public.

This person considers himself very special and above the rules usually applied to any other number. Since they are so unique, they appreciate gifts and ideas that can't easily be imitated.

A lifetime promise to care for this person means most for him or her. They are also impressed by people who do not criticize them or who do not blame them for their situation. The best gift is money or a roof over their heads.

An offer of unconditional love is often expected either as a marriage or as a lifelong friendship. Financial assistance is always valued by 4.

They are usually delighted with any form of vacation or holiday or offer to clear the debts of number 4.

spa vacations, bill payments, and the basics they can't please a 4. Paying a dental bill or rent back would generally win a four face.

This person enjoys an exotic or extended holiday.

This person is most impressed by gifts such as luggage, air miles, and travel expenses.

This person will always be in love with the person who gives him or her full emotional and physical freedom.

A five sometimes can't hold anything for long, so that you have to keep things exciting and constantly to change to keep your attention. You love to go to movies, collect items and fly, of course —these things are your heart's key.

Marriage promises usually lead to sex. Old-style wining and dining draw most of them. In traditional ways, they like to be courted.

Give parents a gift or pay respect to the parents of the person (take them to dine) to hold them in the highest esteem.

Offer parents to get married or, if necessary, move the parents or their siblings.

This number is most impressive if you deliver family business jobs. They also enjoyed family-oriented gifts such as family portraits, kitchen renovations, and pools. Anything that will make an extended family happy.

A contribution to a significant cause or job impresses a 7. They are often broken, even if they are brilliant, so cash impresses them.

the ideal partner for seven men, including the planning, cleaning, and personal assistance, will take care of them everywhere. This should be achieved without emotional rewards being anticipated.

The individual acknowledges the gift of confidence because most of them know that they have difficulty dealing with emotional problems.

These people appreciate a formal, slightly distant companion who has a lot of taste and class.

The. The key to your heart is often to let this person show you well. In a person's life, you like to feel like a hero or rescuer.

They may not be more involved in gender and mental and philanthropic matters. We are very impressed with donations to charity on their behalf.

The person may not be so interested in material things as he or she typically can buy anything he or she wants. I like to have faith and to have a long line in a relationship to do what they like and see who they want. We are only impressed by very costly and exclusive gifts.

This individual appreciates spiritual values and enjoys gifts that accept themselves-self-help books, new age things, or religious artifacts.

Destiny number can be impressed by a charitable donation in his name for a good cause.

The very disorganized and flaky number particularly appreciates items that will keep them centered, such as paying the maid or shelves.

The Numbers Symbolic Meanings

Two steps or stages include understanding the significance of numbers and measuring the different meanings of personal numbers. This is the first time the symbolic significance of numbers is understood. Once you learn these nominal values, the numeroscope expressions can apply their meanings. These meanings can also be used in astrology, carto Mancy, and general metaphysics.

Through numerology, each point of the universe is granted access to information about all other aspects of space and time (past, present, and future), by the eternal mind or divine wisdom. This information is included in the numbers archetypes, which are only partially understandable to humans. Knowledge of the archetypes of numbers permits someone to align their will and ego with universe purposes. Understanding number archetypes can also allow one to participate and guide the processes of the universe or its existence.

Like the zodiac, each number symbolizes one step in the creation process. The first move is number one. The second step is expressed by the second step, and so on. For example, if the days are numbered three, you know that this day is the third step in any process that you are engaged in. If the address of a building you are in amounts to number five, you know it favors the fifth stage of any process. If you come across someone whose name is number eight, you know that this person's energies support the eighth step of any process.

Number Interpretation The following significances for numbers 1 through 10,0 and 11, 22, 33, and 44 are given together with personality characteristics and activities commonly associated with each number. The Pythagorean definitions and related geometric forms are provided, where appropriate. The stars, impulses, and elements of C are also talented. C. Zain's mystical psychology and the conflicts and personal power arising from the personality creation of Erik H. Erikson are included. Odd numbers are generally masculine, active, and positive. And woman, responsive and negative numbers.

Number 1— Object of Pythagorean numerology starts with number 1. Called a monad, one is shown by a dot. It is the source of all numbers, the source of everything. This symbolizes the fundamental state of freedom, indivisibility, and peace. Others claim it's both an odd number and an even number. The first is the number of Allah, the prime number of men, and the yang. It manifests the quantity of consciousness, light, ego, father, and authority as the active concept. The Pythagoreans saw 1 as excellent, desirable, necessary, and indivisible. The one is linked to the light, fire, red, and red-orange colors.

In any position in the numeroscope, the 1 marks the start of a new phase, beginnings generally, development, individuality, and selfhood. The 1 means the Sun and the energy impels in mystical psychology, the desire to survive, and be something. In the formation of identity, 1 represents the crisis of confidence vs. mistrust from which the power of hope comes.

Personality traits & behaviors 1 include imagination, desire, collective trust, bravery, autonomy, individualism, uniqueness, initiative, intolerance, aggressiveness, isolation, false pride, adventure, leadership, soleness, masculinity, newness, obstinacy, optimism.

Number 2— Polarity, Union Number 2 is referred to as a dyad and represents a line. This indicates the lack of initial cohesion. The 2 is duality, and the Pythagoreans thought 2 was an anomaly, the first woman, and an insufficient number. The 2 is the basis of matter, nature, and material evolution. The one was split into 2. A new relationship is now possible with the second. Anything external to the 1. was created. 2 is to shape dichotomies, to divide things into two classes, and to create life at the outset. Awareness of others creates tension and allows for union and partnership. The second is the first number of women, the number of polarities, pairs, spouses, opposites, and antithetic. The second is related to Earth, rain, oceans, and the orange light. Often 2 are blue connected.

2 indicates externalization, separation, stress, confrontation, alliance, relationship, collaboration, rhythm, connection, health, femininity, and motherhood. In esoteric psychology, the 2 means the moon and the household elements of race conservation. In the creation of identity, 2 reflects the freedom versus guilt and self-dubbing crisis from which the force will emerge.

Characteristics of personality and behaviors of 2 include uptake, adaptability, appeasement, attachment, awareness, balance, bonding, caution, conflict, kindness, malice, cooperation, cruelty, delusion, dependence, diplomacy, emotions, empathy, fitness, feelings, women, feminine nature, fluctuations, friendship, softness, home, instinct, intuition, hypersensitivity, marriage, etc.

Number 3— Synthesis Interaction Number 3 is considered a triad. It is represented by a plane, consists of unity and plurality, and restores peace to them. It's the first weird, masculine number. The fifth is the theory of spirit and the cycle of spiritual evolution through reconciling opposites by finding common elements or points of agreement. The 3 is the synthesis process. The 3 is the triune god present in most religions. The first is the argument, and the second is the antithesis, and the fifth is the description. The 3 harmonizes dichotomies and is considered a lucky number. It is warmth, joy, riches, flow, goodness, and rest. The 3 is related to Venus, love, harmony, equilibrium, intelligence, and yellow color.

When 3 is included in the numeroscope, it shows the potential for development, friendship, understanding, harmony, ease, and peace. 3 means Mercury and the theoretical components for proper change in mystical psychology. Through identity creation, the 3 reflects the initiative versus the crisis of remorse from which the power of intent emerges.

The following are personality and actions linked to 3: Animation, fashion, art, music, elegance, talent, charm, conceit, interaction, conversation, co-operation, imagination, culture, ease, power, excitement, entertainment, envy, equilibrium, expansion, expressiveness, extravagance, friendship, frivolous, joy, sadness, development, harmony, humor, and so on.

Number 4— Building, Development The tetrad is number 4. It is a solid and the first feminine rectangle. The 4 is justice, and it is firm, it is a perfect square. It also contains the number of elements, the seasons, the man's ages, lunar phases, and virtues. It represents the power in the material world to manifest ideas. It is said to be the origin of everything demonstrated. The four symbolized the planet, the universe, and every building in many ancient cultures. It consists of the number of foundations, solids, boom points, seasons, the (classical Greek) elements, winds, completion, solidarity, stability, balance, four kingdoms of matter (ancient Greek). The four of them are action, activity, energy, power, power, crises, sacrifice, the square, the cross and construction processes, and the production of solid concrete forms in the material world. It is the four roles of psychology in analytic (Jungian) psychology. The 4 is linked to Saturn and/or Mars, and the red, green, or brown colors.

Wherever the four are found in the numeroscope, it shows the activity and the dominant powers necessary to overcome obstacles, conflicts, and crises. There is a potential in the material world to manifest one's desires and/or to actualize essential relationships. The 4 means Venus and the social elements of the desire to link together in abstract psychology. To identity formation, the fourth signal the crisis of competence versus inferiority from which skill emerges.

The characteristics and behaviors related to 4 include: achievement, action, activity, aloofness, application, bitterness, construction, calmness, creativity, crisis, energy, concentrations, conflicts, conservation, building, engagement, decay, depth, determination, discipline, dullness, economy, efficiency, durability, following, shape, foundation, fundamentals, dull, goal-oriented

Number 5–Intelligence, originality Number 5 is the pentadium that represents man or man, and particularly those qualities that are most singularly human and that distinguish man from the other animal kingdoms, in imagination, in intelligence, in talents, and in self-expression. The five thus represent the quintessence, the humanity, the sorcerer, magic, the senses of (Western), and the elements of (Chinese). The 5 is the male marriage number because it adds the first female and the first male. It has the virtue of being incorruptible, as all multiples of five end in five. The 5 is connected to Mars and/or Uranus, the sky, and the light.

Wherever 5 is in the numeroscope, the existence of intellect, imagination, special abilities, unique nature, personal expression, and probably genius is indicated. In esoteric psychology, the 5 means Mars and the aggressive elements of defense and safety. The development of identity 5 signifies the crisis of identity versus role confusion, from which the power of fidelity arises.

Personality characteristics and comportments associated with 5 include: behavior, adaptability, adventure, adventure, belligerence, change, changeability, intellect independence, hurry, impulsiveness, uniqueness, awareness,t, conceit, courage, imagination, critique, experience, mobility, curiosity, discharge, business, expansion, instinct, innovation, irresponsibility, desire, magnetism, motion,

No. 6— Accountability, performance The hexad is number 6. The 6 is the number of female marriages because, by multiplication, it unifies 2 and 3. It is also the first perfect number and is a triangle area of 3-4-5. 6 is the advantage of activity and productivity. The Pythagoreans consider 6 to be the whole number as the number itself is multiplied (6x 6= 42~4+ 2= 6). The 6 was also a perfect number, since~1 + 2 +

3= 6. The 6 blends comfort, harmony, good luck, the 3's combination with polarity, and the number 2 knowledge. The six is a number three, effective, competitive, and efficient. It brings wealth, but commitment, productivity, and operation. 6 is also linked by numerologists to the human soul, harmony, creation, love, marriage, domestic happiness, and things of the heart. The 6 are connected to Jupiter, the Earth dimension, productivity, and the indigo color.

Wherever 6 is located in the numeroscope, the chances of success and prosperity through work are high. The 6 means Jupiter and the religious elements of the faith in leadership and tolerance in ésoteric psychology. In the creation of identity, the 6 represents the crisis of intimacy and alienation from which the power of love emerges.

The characteristics or actions of 6 include, elegance, pressures, carelessness, convenience, indulgence, conscientiousness, cautious attitudes, artistic, domesticity, education, legal, religious and/or spiritual interests, exaggeration, expansion, family, friendship, gossipy, peace, healing, integrity, hypocrisy, idealism, intrusion, happiness, justice

Number 7 –-The Pythagoreans are portrayed by the heptad and identified with the Greek maid goddess Athena, number 7. We saw 7 as a virgin number because they have no goods, and a ring can never be divided into 7 equal parts. The seven symbolizes the cosmic innovation cycle. It combines the divine trinity of the 3rd with the power of the 4th. The 7 is the level of creativity and the seven manifestations of God as manifest in the seven stars or angels. It reflects nature, divinity, and spiritual and destiny. It symbolizes occult mysteries, magic ceremonies, and mental and farsighted powers. The 7 is regarded as a difficult number to interpret correctly and accurately. The seventh is associated with Saturn, faith, dedication, energy, kingship, the earth aspect, and the purple color.

Wherever the 7 can be found in the numeroscope, religion and spirituality are likely to be prominent. The exoteric and/or esoteric aspects of religion can either be present. Odd and tragic incidents are also possible. To occult psychology, the 7 means Saturn, and the elements of protection, the ability to escape from enemies, and guarantee safety. In the formation of identity, 7 implies the generativity versus the stagnation crisis, from which the power of care emerges.

Personality features and behavior related to 7 include analytics, expressive, dreamy, efficiency, escape, precision, authority, bureaucracy, computation, confusion, conserve attitudes, contemplative, d fussy, impractical, intellectual snobbery, intelligence, introspection, intuition, inquiry, knowledge, lazy, lawful, religious, or spirit.

Number 8— Sacrifice / Power 8 is known as octal or goad. The first cube is 2x2x2=8. This is the first cube. Because it is 4 (action, movement, energy, and crisis), separated by 2 (outsourcing, division, stress, and conflict), the 8 symbolizes peak dynamic activity, the highest strength, and power point. It is regarded as a symbol of material success and worldly participation. The 8 are linked to the Sun and Uranus, habits, struggles, hard work, rose colors, and the intensity of transformation between red and violet.

Wherever the 8 is located in the numeroscope, it indicates the energy required to complete the description and structure. Sometimes the eight can be very challenging. It may feel exhilarating at other times when our consciousness flows through our work. The 8 is Uranus and the individualistic elements of abstract psychology and implies the ability to move from the past and to develop better ways. In the creation of personality, 8 means the crisis of dignity versus desperation from which the strength of the knowledge emerges.

The personal characteristics and actions of the 8 include administration, authority, large company, busy work, efficiency, carelessness, comprehension, focused effort, command, brutality, excentricious, intensive, energy-efficient, wasteful and executive strength, radical individualism, frustration.

Number 9 —Finishing The number 9 is known as the ennead or nonad. It's the first male cube. It is also known as incorruptible because it returns to itself, no matter how many times it is compounded. The nine can be known as a very religious number or a winning number because it is three three three. The 9 is similar to the 7 because it is very spiritual and seeks solitude and relaxation. In addition, it is the last numerological number as all other numbers can be reduced to 1, 2, 3, 4, 5, 6, 7, 8, or 9. The 9 represents the duration of human gestation that ends with one cycle and the start of the next. The fact that the actual activity of creation is not visible to the material world also resembles gestation. The nine can be related to Uranus, Neptune, or Pluto. It can be related to all colors of the spectrum, bright blue and surreal, because of its intrinsic qualities.

The nine points for imagination, faith, isolation, and completion in the numeroscope. A 9 in the numeroscope shows that the person will bring about the development of spiritual ideas, mysticism, and psychic phenomena, probably several times. The 9 is Neptune in esoteric psychology and the utopian elements and the desire for improved conditions.

Personality features and conducts associated with 9 include achieving, good-will, mercy, completion, creativity, devotion, disorder, emotion, intensity, intuition, unlimited power, meditation, mysticism, personal loss, philanthropy, psychic phenomena, regeneration, commitment to religion, service, and salt.

Number 10— Rebirth The decade is referred to like the number 10. It is completion, infinity, and rebirth. It's also our finger and toe numbers. The ten is said to include all the numbers since the numbers are repeated after 10. The number 10 is not generally used in numerology as the 10 in numerology is reduced to 1 (1 + 0=1). The 10 has both the 0 and the nine features. To occult psychology, the 10 means Pluto and fundamental elements of wellbeing and conservation to collaboration between people.

Number 0 — Everything and nothing Pythagorean numerology does not include 0. It stands for God without manifestation, that is to say, Spirit without Matter and without things. It is Allah, above all physical or material life, before creation. It's Godhead without knowledge. The 0 or ring is a divine ability that has not been acted upon. It is the universe before the stars, before the Big Bang, or anything else. It is also a sign of endlessness. The 0 reminds us also of the positive value of impotence. A circle with a dot in its middle, in spiritual symbolism, means that creation or physical manifestation has begun. It mainly symbolizes that the Spirit of God, so that he may know himself, is divided into individual parts. This is not a real division. It is the wrong perception of material objects. In astrology, the manifested God is represented by the Sun's symbol. The Sun is the personalized spirit that sustains us all. The 0 is not used in most numerological or numeroscope measurements. This is because 0 + any number= the total. The 0 has its own importance but adds nothing to numerological calculations.

Master Numbers The term master number refers to 2, 3, or 4 numbers considered above and beyond the average human range. Such numbers suggest brilliance and exceptional contributions from past lives. Master numbers may have higher potential or vibrations than others. These can be highly charged and hard to handle. You should make a significant effort to blend into your personality. The knowledge of master numbers will take time and maturity. Usually, the number is numerically reduced to a single digit after interpreting it as a master number, and the standard interpretation is used as well.

The 11, 22, 33, and 44 numbers are all called master numbers. Before they are reduced to single digits, master numbers are interpreted. Many numerologists have recognized 11 and 22 as master numbers, as described above. Many people use 33 as their master number and even less use 44 as their master number. Those numerologists use no master numbers.

Number 11— Inspiration and light Number 11 applies to idealism and remarkable accomplishments of an intellectual or psychological kind. It often shows creative or musical talent. The person with an 11 is said to be inspired and usually inspired by others. An 11 may also display 2's features. Naturally, not everyone with an 11 is able to show the talents and characteristics of an 11. In such cases, the 11 is an ordinary 2.

The attributes and behaviors associated with 11 include altruism, aviation, creativeness, uncertainty, ecstasy, elation, electricity, evangelism, religion, fanaticism, grandeur, idealism, morality, emancipation, debauchery, frustration, illusion, devastation, internal struggle, creativity, intangibility, inspiration, imagination, limelight, mysticism, nervousness.

Number 22— Master Builder The 22 is seen as a number of excellent material achievements, often with spiritual or magical abilities. It's the strongest of the numbers. A 22-year-old turns dreams into reality. It is regarded as a Master Builder. A 22 may also show the features of a 4. Not everyone with a 22 can, of course, show the skills and characteristics of a 22. In such instances, the 22 transforms into a typical 4.

The traits and conduct of 22 people included: achievement, ambition, broad vision, discipline, distribution, intensity, boundlessness, materialism, methodology, pressure, practicality, resourcefulness, self-confidence, strength, and success.

Number 33— Instructor Initiate / Master The number 33 symbolizes the guiding principle. It is the most significant of all numbers. The 33-year-old person has achieved great spiritual achievements in past lives. He or she integrated the 11 and the 22 successfully and increased to a higher level. He or she has become the Master Teacher, and its dharma or religious aim, through its transmission of the wisdom of the ages, is to improve humanity spiritually. He or she should give up all personal ambitions.

The Master Teacher shows a high commitment to the facts. Until preaching to others, he or she must seek understanding and wisdom. The Master Teacher needs to find original ways to promote spiritual development. Arts, medicine, or some alternative means of healing can be used by the Master Teacher to talk to the public. He or she needs to tell the things he or she learns. If not, the Teacher Master can stagnate. His chances for further development diminish until he or she does the tasks of the Master Teacher. A 33 may also display 6's features. Of course, not everyone with 33 will show the skills and characteristics of a 33. In these cases, the 33 transforms into a regular 6.

33 personality and the behavior of 33 are artists, blessings, bravery, Christian, compassionate, courageous, teachers, teachers, self-sacrifice, inspiration, love, martyrs, monks, doctors, protection, self-sacrifice, teachers and truth.

The 33 happens only when the day of birth, the month of birth and the year of birth (day/month/year) is 11, when the month and the days are 22 and year 11, when month and year are 22 and the day and year 11 and when day and year is 22 and the month 11 and the month is 11. The years 2009, 2018, 2027, 2037, 2045, 2054, 2063, 2072, 2081, and 2090 are 11 years in the 21st century. In the 20th century, just 1901 amounted to eleven. Years such as 1991 add up to a second. $1991 = 1 + 9 + 9 1 = 20$ ($1 + 9 = 10$, $10 + 9 = 20$, $2 + 0 = 2$), $19 + 1 = 20$.

The master numbers 11, 22, and 33 represent a triangle called the Enlightenment Triangle. The number 11 reflects hope with respect to the Triangle, 22 blends sight with practice, and 33 provides guidance for the universe.

Number 44— Master / Master Manager The Master Manager's number is 44. The Master Manager is unusual. He or she is a conscious link to higher planes/realms between the physical plane. The Master Manager is able to show anything he or she wants to focus on. He or she trains to be a model. A 44 may also show 8's features. Not everybody with a 44 is, of course, able to show the strengths and features of a 44. In these cases, the 44 is an average of 8.

Money and Number Mysticism

Numerology is the symbolism of numbers. Numbers appoint amount and can also, in relation to personal money, unbelievably represent qualities.

If you're unconvinced, we understand. In modern times the old science of numerology (i.e., spiritual numerology) was adulterated. We also don't believe in the numerology to which you were exposed. Nobody's a number-one who feels they're "a 3," for example, is incorrect.

Just as you have several physicals, mental and emotive parts of your body and facets, you are represented by a multitude of individual numerological factors (using the full date of birth, the place of birth, and the complete legal name of the birth), which form patterns. The different designs reflect your personal character and destiny.

The present numerology term "Life Path" is known to you, which is the sum of the month, day, and year of birth. All four of these numbers are symbolic and combine the other 500 + factors that represent the tapestry of your unique predetermination.

While it's like trying to explain the workings of numerology science to you in a foreign language in this section, you can still learn about the characteristics of the various numbers to start. Please note: the fadic addition in numerology allows the number to be added to give a single number. 578= 5 + 7 + 8=20, 2 + 0=2 for example. All numbers ultimately decrease to one of the root numbers, 1-9.

Below, together with others, we define the financial qualities of the root numbers 1-9.

1. While 1 is a sound money vibration, it's not so hot, for instance, for a period of 8, and worse for a period of 19/1. 19/1 usually talks in most timing roles in balancing negative karma. Yet ten can be incredibly fruitful after 3, for example. In terms of karma, 10 is usually a very satisfying number.

2. 2 isn't a sound financial vibration unless it is combined with money loss numbers like 7 and 9 after a more rewarding timeframe. 20, as with any of the master numbers (11, 29, 38, etc.), which are reduced to 2, particularly 38, maybe an exceptional financial number. 2 is a follower, not a leader, yet an incredible amount of funding is linked to 2, mainly if the collective energy of the topic includes healthy energy from 3 to 6 and 9.

3. Numbers like 1 and 4 before the 3 yield prosperity expansion under the 3. Fund dissipation takes place if the three is preceded by a banal number of vibrations such as more 3 and 5 and mainly if the collective timing is strict (13/4 and 19/1) after the 3. The collective difficulties can also be observed under other numbers, but robust 19/1 and 13/4 are common.

4. Stability is the organizational word for4-born economy, but substantial, except for 22, worldly, and enormous in reach. Starting with weighty financial matters in the long term would usually result in the retention of the funds, without

significant growth, unless the common birth trends suggest an upward correction. Great fun and carefree energy (e.g., three and five) before four will be a warning to avoid wasting resources later on.

5. One of the more adventurous and progressive numbers, 5, can produce dynamic gains and prosperity if the subject is on the ground and avoids over-risk. His versatility, his craze that he and friends in the high places are at the right place at the right time, helps him to make his fortune. Otherwise, five maybe the irresponsible speculator (14/5, for example, active 13/4), who makes the wrong bet, or the player who bets the family farm, which gives rise to a massive disappointment. Worse, the five (for example, with 9 and 2 stable) are the professional robber, also later to be characterized by 13/4 strong, but other numbers which form horrific patterns symbolizing him or her will be torn off (or make modifications, sometimes reluctantly and sometimes willingly) until the negative Karma is balanced. For example, 13/4 or 14/5 days of birth are not enough to symbolize the above-mentioned adverse circumstances. No "this (single indicator) in the forms of comprehensive numerology and astrology we use is equal to that (specific characteristic or elements of life). Multiple factors shape patterns that symbolize features and conditions of life, as always.

6. 6 is one of the most desirable vibrations for financial timing (and birth), mainly after 1, 3, or 5. Long-term multiple six allow for a wonderful life that takes care of all needs, and some of them. Continuous growth and stability are the keywords of 6. The problem with the 6 is that it can also be associated with a substantial karmic return, such as 13/4 or 16/7.

7. As such, a substantial spiritual, non-mundane, and other-dimensional number, seven are not known for prosperity. It often symbolizes the opposite difficulty and lack of wealth. Yet seven is also known for its fast turnaround (16/7). It is usual for subjects with lots of 7, particularly those engaged in

self-mastery (e.g., meditation, strict discipline, etc.) to become extremely rich with appropriate behavior when assisted by his / her birth patterns. The exact source of the richness of 7 is often a mystery. Most successful gangsters have an abundance of 7 (and 9 and 22) that symbolize intellectual abilities, anxiety, and no-one trust.

8. In combination with a ton of 9, 8 ends in great financial success. But after 9, 8 can spell catastrophe. Eight often is a talented investor, a mover, and a shaker, particularly in combination with 5 and 22. Full eight times early in life often lead to abuse of power or wasted resources, being too young to profit from favorable circumstances. High eight times later in life is tantamount to working late in years and maybe not withdrawing at all.

9. Big money in and a big payout, it amounts to the nine. Those with more births and times of 9 and 8 also make headlines as power brokers and influencers. For example, after 6 or 3 big nine times yields huge money gains, but for example, strong 19/1 or 16/7 precede heavy losses. Powerful collective 9 (with a 19/1 and 13/4 absence and other vibrations) makes for a beautiful retirement later in life.

As studying every language, it takes years of regular training to understand the mysticism of numbers. It is a fascinating way of understanding the notion of personal time and predetermination, particularly in financial matters.

Partner Up with Compatibility with Numerology

What are you saying, hoping for, but rarely finding? The perfect partner for the ideal relationship, of course! Why do you believe this is happening?

The first response to give is that many people don't like the dating scene, and don't want to find the right partner with extra energy. Others may not want to undergo the "rising and dining" routine, while others simply don't know who they are or what they're looking for in a partner. The bottom line is that you have to kiss a lot of toads and toadlets before you find your perfect mate. What a process and this could be entirely unwanted these days if you know.

Nothing about your compatibility sign needs to be known. We are going to show you a practical way to find your ideal partner and your love compatibility without a significant investment of time, emotion, or cash. If everything else fails, you will at least learn to communicate with each other better. Whether or not you stay together, it is always your choice.

What would you say if you knew that the spelling of your name and date of birth has a numerical value that sets the stage for your life? This is far beyond the accuracy of birthdates. Your birth name and date of birth show a map of your tasks to fulfill or evaluate your character carefully. We will decide if you were born as a construction worker, business manager, ambassador, entertainer, healer, humanitarian worker, leader, or educator.

Do you want to undersatnd the results of the model research you will be testing for and whether you and your potential partner are really suitable to each other before the dating game? Consumer reports prepare us for making the best decisions based on the detailed data on the advantages and functionality of the specific product. So why not try a similar strategy, in order for those who wisely choose their perfect soul mate or spouse to find happiness, success, and the joy of living.

What data is contained in a specific chart or character analysis There are two types of charts; the master chart of basic and basics numerology is used for two different purposes. There are two types of charts. These charts are individual and unique to each person.

The simple graph includes the nine tasks you have encountered in this period, which are broken up by the name and date of birth. The name reveals your soul desire, personality, intent, the aim of life, creation of soul value during the birth date, which reveals your destiny, birthday cycles, your personal years, and challenges (growth ranges by age) and Pinnacles. Our mission to learn is simply to understand better how we are "made" or "wired." We appreciate our relationships, compatibilities, attitudes, behaviors, strengths, or weaknesses better by understanding what our nature shows.

The Essence chart is a complete view of your entire life, from the age of 1 to the age of 5 years. The diagram offers perspective, clarification, comprehension, acceptance, and hope for the future, as we can see in advance what kind of experiences we are going to experience in five years ' time. Why does that matter? Understanding what type of vibrational patterns you can create will help prevent you from making wrong decisions for a given year. The diagram is then used as a roadmap or guide.

The secret to your life success is to know who you are, and how you are, and so everything starts with the term, "YOU!" If you understand your personal properties/features, development, strengths, and weaknesses intellectually and the work or failure of all your components (aggressive versus non-aggressive), then you can make better choices in life as we do.

Numerology charts and reading (consultations) are valuable tools to get a much deeper understanding of different aspects of your life, whether private or business-related. Numerology is like a mirror showing the story of your life in numbers.

Two examples that illustrate how the numerology charts proved to be useful as a compatibility test: Single Woman A customer wanted to make sure her husband was as successful as she was. A customer wanted to ensure the guy she was dating. A relationship compatibility analysis confirmed that this matched both of them because they are influential people who match their drive and ambition with outgoing personalities. He was undoubtedly a "keeper," ensuring that she had made the right decision. Six months later, they were engaged.

Man Wanting to date a certain woman, A customer has ordered compatibility charts for the woman he and his own chart dated. It was quite apparent from the study that she was an outgoing free spirit and liked her independence and that she was totally against her personality of being intelligent and substantial when we categorized such an individual. He was told that it wasn't a game, and she won't because she had specific figures in her graph that made her independence more critical than dedication. He decided to ignore the research data and proceeded to date it for another three months. At the end of the time, he called to say they're not dating, because she wanted her independence and couldn't trust herself. This man thought he could fight the wiring of his blueprint to produce a different result. In that case, he would not agree that they were never compatible first, as shown by the compatibility graphs because he understood deep within intuitively.

The Chaldean Numerology is the science of the ancient numbers that say that we have a set of unique numbers with meanings and that from those meanings, we can find out who we are, what our personality is, and more, compatible with our destiny. What an opportunity to make better social and life-time choices by using numerology diagrams. Consider this approach to your future investment.

Gift Number in Numerology Meanings

The date of birth is called the gift count. The Gift Number is an exceptional talent or skill that can help you fulfill the purpose of your life. This chapter will teach you how to receive your gift number in numerology and what this number means.

Some of the six digits in your full numerology table is the gift number. You can get from your name three numbers and from your name three numbers. The gift number is the actual date of birth. The gift number can, therefore, be any number between 1 and 31. For example, if you were born on 4 January (1/4), your Gift Number is 4 (4).

Keep in mind that no number alone controls control over your life. Each of us has many components. Numerology and all other sciences help us to understand ourselves better. Nevertheless, research must be discussed in a systematic way instead of preferring one field over the other. It talks about the donation figure, but the other numbers continue to influence how these donations are communicated.

The gift number is the actual date on which you were born. The gift numbers were 31 (1-31). If you have a binary number, you can add two digits to have one. You can also add the two digits. All numbers can be read without breaking to one digit, particularly master numbers in the gift number.

Example 1–11/18/2001–The donation amount is 18 and is also set to a total of 9(1+ 8), Example 2–5/15/1979–The gift number is 15 which also adds up to the number of 6(1+ 5), Example 3–6/22/2012 –The gift number is 22. When working with others, you are passionate and motivating. People follow what you say and do, of course.

You have the gift to congratulate most people. Of course, you like to play the backdrop, but if you see that it's a worthy cause, you support anyone or anything. You are intuitive and receptive, too.

Silly and social. Social. You inspire others to feel better with your gift. You seem to have encouraging words for people who are experiencing issues.

You enjoy knowledge, and you bring together ideas. Born with discernment, you have a gift to reveal the truth and tell others what you have found.

Doubled with an active mind and a determination to travel, you remind others that life should be purposeful and fun. You don't want to keep it moving somewhere too long mentally or physically.

The six gift number makes you a perfect custodian. You make people innately feel comfortable and tend to look after other needs and desires. You've got an eye for beauty too.

Intuitive and intuitive with many questions. You are an out-of-boxes thinker, and you see reality differently. You need a fair amount of time alone, physically and mentally.

You have no difficulty in exercising your strength. Money and business are essential points for your career. Once your power is controlled, you are talented to lead other men.

Motivator, diplomat, and aid worker. You were called to be an example of how to live and inspire others. You love to give back to others when you master those areas of life.

An example leader who is aware of the Spirit. You know intimately that you are guided by spiritual forces. You tend to do things based on well-being and positive thinking.

An enthusiastic leader was leading by example. You have a gift to inspire others when you are interested in something emotionally. When you trust what you are doing, you can't stop.

You have the ability to express great ideas and thoughts. You may identify areas in which to grow with a natural ability to make things full and whole.

Obviously, you are looking for information and suggestions in many respects. You enjoy learning as you read, hear, watch, and observe. Your style of teaching or sharing is unique and distinct from most.

A walker with love for many people, places, and things. You tend to attract a wide range of situations. You thrive on diversity and are developed in many respects.

Smart and imaginative in one way or another. You are searching for peace and willing to go far, physically and mentally, to put together things. You love serving others in different ways.

In art and life, you love to uncover the hidden meanings. In films, video, art, music, and poetry, you can see the more profound messages. You also want to express deeper problems with your friends.

A formidable ruler who can fight alone. You have the gift to encourage others to step and not tell them what to do. When you are driven and happy, people naturally follow your lead.

You have the ability to manifest and give back great things. Even after the years, someone who can help others emerges. You love helping others to be better.

You saw a great deal in your life, and that helped to make you a well-rounded person. You've got a rare talent to start and finish anything if you see the quality in anything you do.

Active compassion, you take up the emotions, feelings, and energy of others. You are blessed with the ability to gather more data than is available. Your lesson isn't overly emotional.

You have the ability to express the feelings in various ways, shapes, and forms. There is a certain degree of intuition when you share your ideas.

A prolific maker of ideas and things. You have the ability to put something together masterfully. These can be information to link points or anything else that seems random and unrelated.

You take steps to express yourself personally. You are talented at communicating with others profoundly and emotionally. You seem unpredictable, but in most situations, you follow your heart.

You want to be around beautiful physical things and people. When you see it, you know balance and harmony. It is usual for you to increase the attraction of hideous situations and people.

An innate capacity to be with or alone. You love your own business, but you also attract people who bring emotional balance and fun. Significant journeys and discussions are essential to you.

Doubtful with the power to get what you want, but with humility and concern to share with those you love and care for. You attract people you can support, of course.

Blessed with many experiences that contributed to your spiritual and emotional growth, you tend to help others less fortunate. You are interested in learning and discussing "taboo" subjects.

A natural leader who can collect whatever you are looking for. You see nothing wrong with creating a strong networking circle. The creative mind is a great gift.

A compassionate individual with a message. You know how important it is to offer less fortunate people. Most notably, you want to promote spirituality.

You tend to talk or say what others think or do, but don't say. Once you open yourself up to others, you have the ability to share things that help people see things differently. You have the gift of attracting people and knowledge to improve yourself. You are information thesaurus in many areas. You don't just like reading, but it's also important to share.

CHAPTER FOUR

Numerology with Meaning of Numbers

Have you ever wondered what significance a number might have, perhaps one that continues to reappear in your life? Since time immemorial, humanity has wondered how numbers are and how they contribute to growth. Numerologists assume nine distinct archetypes corresponding to 9 development cycles-numbers 1 to 9. Such amounts are also known as central or digital root numbers. Since compound numbers are just combinations of these nine core numbers, an in-depth study of these roots is necessary to understand the significance of a number. We will now look at the evolution of these root numbers.

We're starting with the Zero. This is the un manifesto where all is possible. The Zero does not contain or contain a number. It persists beyond any process. When the zero is applied to any name, it represents the perfection of the importance of that number. While 1 is the root of 10, 10 does not necessarily mean 1. This is because of the addition of zero means the perfection of the one effect, which actually moves from cycle 1 to cycle nine and into higher order-from 10 to 19. Once Zero is applied to a number, it tends to give its root number a universal obligation. It is from this formless beauty that there is something.

Moving away from the formless domain of the Zero is something that is complete, inclusive, and independent of the Zero. The one is a masculine power, which hits modern, original, and energy seething on pioneers and its own.

All other numbers are between the Zero and the One. The One appears to be put in conjunction with the unmanifest Zero. To order for the One to be One, it must be free of something, number two. The Two creates a relationship, and it has the power of the One but humility that represents its character. The icon itself, 2, shows a man bowing to a higher power during his prayer (1).

When we realize that something "higher" emerges from ourselves and our relationship, we sense the need to convey this feeling. The third number takes us into the social sphere. From the unmanifest Zero, 0, there arises an independent form, 1, which brings us into a core relationship, 2, which we must somehow express, 3. The Three's character, 3, represents this openness. It is open at its top, receives more prominent influences, and is open to others at its bottom.

If we want to have lasting value, we need to work to create a solid foundation–the Four. Once reaching this point, most projects fail to make it into three, but never bridge the gap between voicing a higher ideal, three, and integrating a higher ideal, 4. To preserve its balance, the four have to shut down or restrict their power. The Number Four takes the ideas expressed by the Three and introduces a self-imposed constraint to create a stable and lasting basis.

After the Four discipline, we consider the shift and operation of The Five, which tests the solidity of our base. The Four, 5, transforms and adds independence and adventure. The front and the back are open. It is a point where decisions need to be taken, and these decisions, correct to their shape, could radically change the results.

The freedom that the Four through the Five introduces leads to a new balance symbolized by the Six. At the same time, it expands the boundaries of the Four and puts the burden required on the five. The Twins, 6, are lovingly pregnant — the number of families and social responsibilities. The social roles of the Six establish the need to learn and gain insight and to find a way to turn perceptions into a cohesive whole.

The seven questions and quests for answers to the great riddle of creation. It is a mysterious and beautiful maturity. His character, 7, can be likened to that of an elderly man who holds a lantern or staff projecting its light into the darkness around him. It is the number of introspection, design, and internal research. By controlling, insight, and planning the 7, we realize that we harvest what we sow.

The number 8 is a carrier of dynamic power and the success of seeds planted with the One. His son, 8, shows a perfect balance between the concept world and the acting world. It is closed to show the power that will make ideas work.

After the Eight bonuses, we know that we reach the end, The Number Nine — the emphasis shifts from the material to the spiritual as we face this end. Simple concepts and self-service are paramount. The character of the 9 is very similar to the 6. While the Six bring their love into the material world of friends and family, the Nine completes the process with their love and compassion restored to higher ideals.

And we see the Zero again. We can start a new process, beginning with One again. It is possible that we can continue our endeavor to raise the One to the relative perfection of the

Ten. In either case, between nothing (0) and something (1), we consider everything.

Numerology and The New Millennium

It is said that Pythagoreans have founded schools to research this subject. As a numerologist, this discipline can be used to examine significant and evolving factors impacting us and our environment. It can also be used as an instrument to analyze the personalities and destinies of individuals.

Numerology is a positive discipline as it encourages free will and does not foresee fatalism. This focuses instead on the prevalent patterns in our lives and conveys the actions and attitudes needed to achieve success and happiness. We've always got a choice. We can choose to follow the spirit of that advice or decide to develop our own path. The latter decision could lead us to swim against the tide, but that's what it is. With this in mind, take this opportunity to address briefly the main power that believes influences all of our lives.

The new millennium, like its precursor, has a governing number, which would be a time to explain the difference. The last millennium was overwhelmingly masculine in nature, and its number was ONE. This was the first digit every year until 1999. Throughout his rule, it represented an entity, single and dominant drive, and men governed the world. However, the last part of the previous century led to a change, causing the influence of the ONE to surrender to the female head of the TWO as of 2000. At this time, Britain voted in its first female prime minister, and women began to play critical roles in a groundbreaking manner. Two examples of this trend with many more to follow are Margaret Thatcher and Princess Diana.

The TWO expresses itself as a pair by its very definition. This emphasizes duality in all its forms and covers all circumstances that give rise to two things or situations. Sadly, it reflects this symbolic attribute when we think of the Twin Towers, which were demolished at the beginning of the new millennium in New York. The most excellent value that can be applied to it involves partnerships on all levels and the commitment required to execute them successfully. This tells us that, if we want to lead a fuller and happier life, we need to build fellowship skills in all areas of life. Sanity and treatment should be relevant to our minds. That's because we are currently experiencing a time of increased sensitivity when we are all likely to feel insecure or sometimes lose emotional control. An example of this, in the recent past for Britain, has been the previously unknown outpouring of grief after the death of Princess Diana. There will be a growing need for courtesy and good manners to be handled. These are essential skills that have been lacking in recent years, contributing to dangerous circumstances like' road rage.' The saying goes that' no man is an island,' and what good are we, after all, if we are isolated by egoism or greed and disregard for anyone other than ourselves?

Because this is now a primarily feminine stage of our lives, the positive qualities underlined are maternal. We saw these recent examples as an over-protective mentality that has led to health and safety concerns reaching absurd levels. Political correctness is another example of the potential good of fixation.

This is a more intuitive time now when we should develop our spiritual values and increase our awareness of ourselves. Slow action is encouraged because the TWO takes many decisions, and we shouldn't emotionally react to them. This is a waiting period where thoughts and ideas will gradually rise to the surface and in their own time. In the past, daydreams were deemed punishable, but are regarded in the future as a useful instrument for progress.

The optimistic future will encourage us to co-exist and to be ready to work with others. There will be a spirit of cooperation, and we will strive towards the common good internationally. We must try peaceful solutions and use weapons instead of arbitration.

The last millennium called for an independent attitude, but the current one certainly does not. Now no one person or government can go alone. This is not a cycle that promotes independence and rewards only through harmonious partnerships with others. Diplomacy and tact will play an essential role in the agenda. Uniting opposites is also illustrated in this figure, and in our modern world, we face many challenges of this sort. Some of these examples include the widening gap between rich and poor or the shifting roles of men and women and political and religious tensions between East and West.

An adverse reaction means that we don't understand or accept each other's ways. Fear will make us see each other rather than prospective mates as potential threats. People and countries will use frustration to achieve imagined benefits. Excessive greed will drive the scales that will dramatically fluctuate our financial systems. They are mostly unaware of other needs and will not put resources into partnerships and personal relationships. We could see a fracturing or separation of the world population and a sudden and dramatic end to social and international relations. There will be rising aggression and materialism spiraling out of control before our present societies crumble. This will make us totally unprepared for the world crises that will occur over the next decade.

One of the toughest challenges the world's population has to face is that of shared life. The new century will judge us by our ability to live side by side. This is, of course, a challenging lesson to learn, as a change of attitude is expected from all of us. We will have to rewrite our own personal prejudices and stop living apart. It refers both to social and international partnerships. A detrimental example of the TWO demonstrations is now known as 9/11 when a terrorist attack was carried out on New York City, and the Two Towers were demolished.

One worrying aspect that will cause concern in the coming years is the increasing degree of control by the government. In the past, communism arose when the negative influence of the TWO was at its peak. The inevitable police state and a two-tier society were brought about. The people, in general, live in relative poverty behind the Iron Curtain under a strict regime, and their masters lead a totally different lifestyle. Western governments are now trying to enforce tighter control on their population for national security reasons, but the inherent risk should be clear. Sadly, Apathy is likely to be one of the negative things in this millennium, and this can cause us to sit back and accept anything that is given to us. Tao Buddhism suggests that "the price of liberty is a constant consciousness."

Marilyn Monroe Numerology of a Sex Symbol

• Which figures represented the individual of Monroe's sex symbol?
• Which percentage of tragic lives in Marilyn's chart?
• Which number trend shows father-abandonment issues in her early life?
• What IR (Influence / Reality) collection revealed her mother's problems?

There are three critical numbers that show the magnetic sexual image of Marilyn Monroe: master number 33-6 Master number 66-3 Number 5 Master number 33 One of the wonderfully fascinating components of the graph of Monroe is the inner stacking sum of master number 33. The material soul comprises a distortion of this intensely articulate sexual energy, an energy that can also lead to serious addiction because of its quality of pleasure. It is powerful to have one set of 33 fuel, but three are extremely rare. This internal tri stack of 33 energies can be written as 33-33-33, which, when combined, produces a 99, the number one of universal energy and law. Any master number in a simple matrix part is scarce. In the Material Soul position, the sexual power, pleasure, and image-saturated master number 33 are almost incomprehensible three times, and as the Soul Rules Material one's worldly wants, needs, and desires, Monroe reflected its motivations, which were to symbolize sex.

The master number 66 is the 66-3 master number in the design of Monroe's stuff. This is also a robust sexual master number. It's not as popular as the 33, but yet strong.

The number 5 The third number that generates the sexual identity of Monroe is the number 5. This controls the five senses, individuality, diversity, motivation, knowledge, independence, and discovery. The single numbers 5 and 6 are the most powerful sexual intercourse. The essence of Monroe was a third. She enjoyed the variety and adventure. Therefore, her lovers are many. One man just wasn't sufficient for her. In theory, Marilyn Monroe could be represented as being sexually embodied. Her delightful image manifested her inmost desires, personality, and life.

The number 7 is the number of spiritual tests and carries the most considerable possible degree of disturbance, tragedy, and suffering. The Life path of Marilyn Monroe was 7, the same as John F. Kennedy. Princess Diana also had a lifecycle of 7, and it was this number that caused Marilyn Monroe's life trouble right after the go, as it was for JRK and Diana.

The chart of Monroe contained a void of 7 (written in 7v). In other words, in her birth name, she had no Gs, Ps, or Ys. Her first called "Norma" is also a seventh. The active schedule was from birth to 25 years of age. Combined with its seven lifecycles, the resulting number is 5, switch power, loss, separation, discovery, experimentation, five senses. Thus this 7v/5 IR (influence/reality) intensified its seven life paths from birth to age 25, creating the condition of heartbreak and tragedy.

The numerology number 1 regulates father, male power, self, ego, autonomy, freedom, and practice. Father Abandonment Questions. Number 5 controls isolation, displacement, independence, fear, transition, and separation. Because Monroe was born on June 1st, her first Epoch IR set was a 1/5, resulting from her 1 filtering through her four speech to create a five outcome. It indicates issues with male energy loss or detachment (5) (1). Princess Diana, who also had the fourth term, and who was born on 1 July, also had the same 1/5 IR ruling on her first part of life. Another example of 1/5 and its loss/detachment problems is the famous aviator Charles Lindbergh. During this 1/5 IR set in Lindbergh's 2nd Challenge, his son was kidnapped and killed.

As the number 1 represents the energy of the male, the number 2 is the energy of the female. birth mother Marilyn was really known to get mental problems, and Monroe spent her beginning life in foster homes because of her condition. During Monroe's first peak, 7v/11-2, this chaos with her mother is seen. The seven voids represent mental instability, and the 11-2 shows that the woman, others, and relationships are very stressful. That would not only apply to the mother of Monroe, but also to Monroe herself. It would also play a general role in her relationships.

Marilyn Monroe is undoubtedly a legend of legends. Her life was hard but influential, powerful enough to keep her image alive after her death half a century. The enormous 33 and 66 master energy in her chart, together with five powers, created the image of her sex symbol. The combination of 1/5 and 7v/11-2 in the fundamental part of its graph clearly showed some problems with both mother and father. Wrapping all these together in a Life path of 7 was a massive with an incredibly tragic but declared career.

Divining The Life Path Number

The way of life is decided by the number you get after your birth date has been decreased by adding digits together. This number represents the characteristics and talents with which you are born and the likely journey during your life. In some ways, it indicates which direction you can take, regardless of your heart, which is expressed by the soul number calculation. When you measure your soul count, you will compare these two figures to see your life's unique challenges.

Convert the month to a single number or master number first. Remember that double-digit months, such as September, November, and December, do not decrease to one digit when measuring months. For example, November, the eleventh month, is number 2 after adding 1 + 1 together.

The birthday of Angelina Jolie does not decrease to a single digit. Her sixth month of birth is the year. Her month is six.

Your next step is to turn your birthday into a single digit. If you were born on the 17th, for example, you can add 1 and 7, reducing the number to 8. If you were born on the 29th, you would be reduced to the 11th master. In that case, the number is further reduced to 1.

The birthday of Angelina Jolie must not be diminished since she was born on the 4th, and her number is 4.

Next, add the total number of the year of birth and reduce it to one single number. Joe was born in 1975, and you said 1 + 9 + 7 + 5 to a total of the number of the year. In the case of Jolie, the year is Master 22. This would easily be reduced to 2.

Reduce your own birthday to a single number and then consider the following description explaining your journey. Settings that also lead to a master's number such as 11, 22, or

33 should also read the life path forecast for that number. For example, if your birthday falls to 22 and then to 4, you can read both 4 and 22 interoperations.

Life Path Number 1 If you are 1, you are motivated by the need for soul freedom and personal achievement. Your primary instruction is to learn how to be autonomous in all ways, emotionally and financially, in particular.

Number 1 often has the potential to be great leaders, but when it comes to teamwork and cooperation, they often fail abysmally. They make great business people, administrators, leaders, freelancers, CEOs, and manufacturers for this purpose.

Number one generally spends at least two-thirds of their lives trying to shake off others ' emotional and financial gags. We are usually self-made people who have to face high odds of succeeding like salmon swimming upstream. We change typically the world in some way, creative and imaginative personalities.

A person with a life path number 1 typically has motivation, passion, imagination, and inspiration. We seem to be better physically and mentally smarter than most. Excellent looks of youth and a passion for life cause us respect, who often admire the perseverance and the ability to act together.

Nevertheless, a person who travels the number 1 path can sometimes be self-sustaining, pushy, and intimidating. They often interpret their aggression and ambition as hostility and egoism. Most of the first people learn hard lessons about the value of good time and patience on their journey through life.

Most people who try to have connections with numbers one cannot afford the driving ambition and social climb, which is reflective of their desire for success (particularly material) at all costs. We tend to regard people as objects, and they are jealous, greedy, and possessive. We are also not without infidelity that advances their careers.

Number 1 people who go away often end up in a coded relationship with mentally ill or addicted partners. If you are number one and have this kind of situation, it is a clear message that you fail to achieve the intention of your life to become autonomous in life.

Life Path No. 2 Those who follow the 2nd Life Path tend to be polite, sensitive people. Because they have an innate sense of morality and equality, they appear to be cautious because they can see both sides clearly. We also nominate excellent judges, mediators, prosecutors, psychologists, or social workers because they have an unbelievable talent for dispute resolution.

Such caring, optimistic people only want to see the best in others. We are almost honest to the point of failure. We have high emotional quotients and perform best in a teamwork setting. Number 2 is always valued because of its politeness, patience, and ability to inspire people to conduct voluntary and philanthropic actions. Number 2 is never "stop winning" and finds itself above fighting with others.

Number 2s works best in 9 to 5 careers, where the routine is the same each day. They are upset by erratic behavior, drama queens, and open displays of physical affection.

Such natural collectors are also packed rats and are the kind they have owned since birth in the shelter or in the basement. Many of them collect antiques and photos of lovers, as they are also very emotional and nostalgic.

Since the life goal of a number 2 is to add peace to group situations, it is imperative that we get out and socialize with them. Number 2 has isolated itself from its path of life. This is usually identified by pessimism, lethargy, and depression. The best way to get back on track for number 2 is to find a job that involves working with the general public or finding a way to practice charity or philanthropy. Nothing more efficiently corrects number 2 karma than acts of random kindness or voluntary work in a hospital, school, or shelter. Indeed, this is how many of them meet their fellow souls.

Life Path Number 3 Followers of Life Path Number 3 are sparkling figures whose path always leads to creative appreciation or social success. Number three is world entertainers, and most of them are very talented dancers, musicians, actors, poets, speakers, and politicians.

A number 3 is not satisfied until there is public recognition of its unique talent. The 3rd life path is characterized by elegance, anticipation, creativity, and social success. Often these unusual, charismatic personalities gain fame and glory quickly.

This number also has a warm, charismatic personality and an incredible sense of personal faith and optimism. Their distinctive physical appearance also often catches many people's imaginations and makes excellent muscles and models.

Often a number 3 is also a humorous or poetic individual who is a conversationalist. At the same time, they are known for their understanding and the ability to listen to others and truly understand their emotional needs.

Number 3 is also great chefs and hosts and has an exquisite taste in fashion and home design. They are often socially sought, as others physically and spiritually find them beautiful.

A number 3 is typically very stubborn and won regardless of how high the cost of success is. Their extraordinary strength and vigor help their recovery from life's losses than most men. Such failures are often economic or emotional, as they are sometimes driven by their idealism and spontaneity to make bad decisions.

Nonetheless, a number three is generally very patient and willing, to be frank about their mistakes.

Number 3 is quitting their course of life by giving up their hopes and talents. Many seek alcohol or drug abuse to avoid their constant inspiration from hearing the stinging voice. If you are three and are not in the spotlight because of personal problems, then this is a wake-up call that meets the urge of your heart. Your exuberant nature will take you beyond most people, particularly if you are permitted to focus your energies and talents.

Life Path No. 4 Those who follow the 4th Life Path often end up becoming the foundation of the community. Such people work hard, are realistic and trustworthy. You have the practical ability to make others ' dreams come true.

Self-sacrificing number 4, however, also demands too much of itself and others. Many of them thus establish a personal reputation as martyrs or tyrants. The persistence and stubbornness of number 4 can also be translated as arrogance and egoism. This disturbs the confused number 4 whose goals are generally to help everybody.

Such sensitive people can also be extremely motivated and traumatized by changes to their routines. A number 4 can hardly ever be convinced that he or she might be incorrect as they don't address criticism well. The tenacity and the obsessive disposition of figure 4 also give him the nickname workaholic. Much still profit from the dedication of number four to unfortunate tasks and a rigid sense of organization.

Such loyal people make great relationships and business partners. At first, a number 4 can be hard to know because you usually play your cards very close to your chest. They don't believe life is a popularity competition and so tend to make a few close friends instead of shining in a crowd on the festival circuit.

Dependable and predictable number 4s are connected to the Earth element so that they can influence others very fundamentally. Yet their fear of talking will make them look very cheerful. They can also focus so much on the tasks at hand that they lack great opportunities.

People who follow the 4th way of life often learn lessons about emotional insecurity. Signs that a number 4 is walking away from others are jealousy, hostility, possessiveness, and the presence of a lack of humor.

Sometimes a number 4 dedication to the schedule is pathologically repetitive. When you assume that altering your routine in one way or another will ruin your company or happiness, you could become a 4, crippled by fear. The way back on the road would be to let go and cultivate versatility and empathy for others.

Life Path Number 5 Those who follow the 5th Life Path are adventurous and extremely inquisitive people who consider managing knowledge as the best teacher of life. Many of them are profoundly philosophical, intelligent, and spiritual. We like to theorize about the nature of life. Despite their sometimes spatial attitude, many seek real solutions to the problems of mankind.

The routine and everyday duties of Number 5 abhor. They are often good at initiating many projects, but they rarely do. Number 5 is terrible at homework and self-care but likes to follow its whims and desires. For this reason, in office environments, they don't perform well.

Nonetheless, number 5 can be great communicators and excellent in the abstraction of any subject. This is why they are creating great cultural anthropologists, archeologists, and historians. Some of the five teachers are also excellent.

Usually, at a point in their lives, a number of 5 experiences some kind of spiritual or emotional catharsis that lead to an artist, investigator, or journalist in a standard career for a self-made profession. Most of the five are talented but do not have the discipline or desire to follow a path. For this reason, numbers five eventually lead to unstable and even catastrophic financial lives.

Number 5 is also hateful to plan and prefer to live today. Happy-Go-Lucky attitudes are proof of incredible confidence in the world. The opposite sex also finds its approaches to the devil's treatment thrilling and romantic, before they finally embrace a number 5 that lacks a way of life.

The lack of commitment of number 5 also covers personal relations. We tend to be self-absorbed and unaware of the effects on other people of their acts. There is also a propensity to put what others might see as the last and the least essential thing in life. Since different people frequently feel deceived or deluded by numbers 5, they have a number of relationships that are broken.

A sign that a number 5 has wholly strayed from its life path would be an emphasis on the decline or demoralization of everybody. If you are 5, who are continuously faced with criticism, mockery, dissonance, and lack of stability in life, you probably have turned away from the intent of your life, which is to create a more compassionate and hopeful future for others.

Life Path Number 6 Those pursuing the Life Path Number 6 are often people who love to feel important to others. For this reason, numbers six also devote their lives to providing care of physicians, nurses, therapists, firefighters, and law enforcement officers.

Such selfless people feel that they should share the struggles of others as they go on their journey through life. These are usually patient people who don't care about taking responsibility or taking responsibility for difficult situations.

Number 6 usually feels a moral obligation to assist others by showing kindness, tenderness, and compassion for all they meet. As children, these born leaders typically have wisdom, bravery, and self-control far beyond their generation.

Number 6 is also domestic beings whose actions are often driven by the love of kids and the family. It is unusual that a number 6 has money problems, other than helping a less unfortunate person. You are also more likely than others to adopt a child or work to be a mentor for young people (such as a baseball team). We usually earn a confident trust of family and friends because they are willing to bear more than a fair share of the responsibility while engaging with the public.

Number 6 has very few negative qualities, apart from a codetermination tendency. Six who are enslaved to a dedicated or mentally ill partner may not follow their correct path, as this is a sign that they are becoming facilitators rather than healers of illnesses. Their purpose in life is to love and nurture everyone they meet, not just an individual, exclusive person.

Life Path Number 7 Those who pursue Life Paths Number 7 are fond, peace-loving people who prefer reason rather than motivation. Top mathematicians, engineers, inventors, scientists, and doctors are these reserved and logical deep-thinkers.

Often these intellectual and scholarly leaders have advanced academic careers. As you like to read and absorb information, it usually takes you a lot of private time to cultivate your knowledge. There are often seven children at school, and, for their age, they tend to be "old souls."

Number 7 s are perfectionists who prefer music, noise, and crowds to remain silent. They are methodical and thorough analysts who believe,' if you can't do the job correctly, don't do it at all.' They disregard the stupidities and manipulations of popular culture and reject all those who do not meet their strict moral standards. Seven often appear very reserved and distant to others, and many find that it takes time to get up to them. Once a 7 becomes a mate, it is typically a lifetime.

While critical and logical, seven rely more on their gut instincts than on numbers, public opinion polls, or other advice. As they don't like bullying, TV or the press are very gross.

These hermits enjoy being alone and far from the excitement of modern life. This is why many of them prefer to living in a country where the hectic pace of urban life does not irritate their nerves.

The shadow of a 7 appears to be gloomy, excessively rational, divisive, and harmful. Many of the seven are smart and (maybe right) feel the world owes them a living. When you're seven who don't seem to deal with people at all, it's possible the abrasive, formally thought of as excentricious traits have been demoted to repulsive. A warning that Number 7 is ultimately out of its way of life is a complete withdrawal from society. In this case, the troubled seven should seek to acknowledge their original ambitions to improve the world by applying wisdom.

Life Path Number 8 Followers of life path number 8 are, of course, lucky people whose soul strives to accumulate material wealth. Those on this road have relatively little time for dreams and visions when they apply themselves to the real world.

Number 8s are usually trustworthy, charismatic people who can spot trends and opportunities. Their purpose in life is typically to learn to exploit money and power without becoming corrupt.

These social climbers will go to the right person at the right time. Although an 8 has an unfavorable history, it will be challenging to see him or her at the right parties, wearing the right clothes and lobbying with the actual players in the space. People who praise the past of "from rags to riches" are often 8.

Eight who make good use of their natural ability have tremendous potential to improve the lives of thousands, maybe millions of people. Eight are realistic and relentless in achieving key objectives, and their tenacity and determination allow them always to beat their competition. Courageous 8s also have a remarkable ability to "not sweat the little stuff," and often simply beat their rivals by stamina or strength.

Some 8 take a dark turn away from their correct path by voicing greed, desire, and unchecked ambition. They may be tyrants at work, and at home, they look cold and heartless. You should avoid discounting others ' views, especially in emotional relations.

The pursuit of wealth sometimes becomes more important than personal relations. Eight is considered as on the wrong path to take the desire to share the material and spiritual wealth with the rest of the world by binding themselves to material objects.

Life path number 9 Those on the 9th Life path are destined for a humanitarian journey. We are excellent negotiators, ecologists, veterinarians, educators, magistrates, social workers, clergy, priests, and healers.

This sophisticated person is very selfless and often cautious, trustworthy, and honest from the start to the end of his life.

We are often characterized by their moral correctness, empathy, and kindness.

In the name of justice or fighting for the oppressed, Noble Number 9 is willing to assume significant responsibilities. Very few of them are interested in gaining content. Most believe that they will earn their rewards in heaven for good deeds performed on earth. Nor is it unusual for a number 9 to abandon all their material possessions for the common good.

Often 9 express their in-depth knowledge of life by means of drawing, poetry, music, or other forms of art. Many are also mystics, channelers, light students, practitioners of Reiki, witches, and holistic healers.

The number 9 personality is best suited for the profession of healing and caring. They seem to be absolutely trampled under their vulnerability in conventional, competitive business environments.

Number 9 has winning smiles and very quickly makes mates. They're fantastic listeners, and many of them just have a fast punch on their hands to make us feel better. Although they are phenomenal with strangers, in one relationship, they are not so smart. One partnership also seems poisonous to sophisticated nine who are put off by the tension, possessiveness, and fatal singularity, which are synonymous with a soul mate's ideal. Nine does not really like gender unless it is linked to tantra or is done for procreation purposes. Many of them deliberately remain alone to treat everyone like their soul mate.

Nine who are diverted from their false directions, frequently feel angry or hostile to those they support. You can think that your generosity was misused or abused. Your way of life is to have faith in God or a higher power instead of other people. The 9th person who receives a bonus has to rethink his or her own inner core and values.

The negative side of 9's occurs when others are out of the loop. Others are viewed as village idiots because of their eccentricity. Often nine high ideals are seen as ridiculous, spacious, or funny to others. Part of the 9th way of life to communicate religious values through acts and not by preaching or proselytizing.

Life Path Number 11 The Life Path Number 11 is about spiritual enlightenment. Often a number 11 shows an understanding and knowledge of metaphysics far beyond the reach of others.

11 tends to lead an unhealthy life. We also follow the most diverse religions and cultures in their quest for a balance between the rational and the irrational. These forward-looking and forward-looking people are great learners, musicians, psychics, teachers, writers, healers, mystics, and artists.

Number 11 also sacrifices everything in search of spiritual or supernatural knowledge. Their ability to know persuades many of them to join the cult or movements of the New Age. Luckily, they also show great courage when they get in trouble.

Eleven can also be camelons in the career. Many try jobs the same way others work clothes. The strange thing is that these "fast studies" seem to excel in everything they do. Many of them often have two careers at once, often anti-theoretical. There are 11 of you who work as managers of a bank every day, and then lighting the moon in the night as a tarot reader.

Nevertheless, 11 use their life's ambition effectively by seeking to be educators or counselors. Most 11 of them are highly qualified subconscious healers, and others are often healed by their insightful and touching words.

On the negative side, 11 also expect a lot of itself and others. Many of them are "wounded healers" who undergo a traumatic experience at some point in their life, which forces them to pursue spirituality. But in these cases, a lot of negative emotional baggage and a harsh internal criticism usually come. It takes many eleven years to get rid of the chip on their shoulder.

Eleven are also very nervous people who are vulnerable to double-like conditions, such as manic depression and schizophrenia. Sometimes a propensity towards dreaminess delays it in seeking its real purpose in life. In fact, 11 are often late bloomers who don't make money until the age of 40.

An 11 has strayed from his course when he or she still dreams of big projects but never takes practical steps to execute such proposals. This means that the 11 is not moving forward and trapped in the "visionary" cycle of illumination.

Life Path No. 22 Master teachers are those who follow 22's life path. These are the most potent and powerful of the Life Path numbers. We have a remarkable ability to bring theories into the realm of reality.

Anything a 22 thinks of will be almost guaranteed, and so it is imperative that they carefully select their thoughts. You can achieve enormous success, prestige, and fame if you are willing to work for what you want. Twenty-two people often find it convenient to describe things that they often describe as "born with a silver spoon."

Contrary 22's are very rare, but they display insensitivity occasionally. This is part of a divine instruction that is isolated from events and performance. Many of them work for material gain with a view to increasing their wealth among the people.

Life Path Number 33 A date of birth, which decreases to 33, is scarce. If it happens, you look at a high spiritual figure along the lines of the Dalai Lama or Gandhi.

These people have no characteristic of their lives, but generally, they acquire renown by acts of kindness, tenderness, and empathy that change the consciousness of the world.

The Prosperity of Magic Numbers and Psychic Numerology

Numerology is the number science in our world. The ancients used numbers in which physical structures and behavior of living entities were aligned and linked. Numerology is used in our present age to predict future events and emotional readings. Numbers or numerical codes dictate our existence. Numbers are considered to be the universal language of this universe and, if you cannot understand another person's speech, you will appreciate the number of fingers and toes he counts.

Numerology is also used for a deeper understanding of the nature of human behavior. Our DNA and consciousness are programmed like the way a machine operates. In the following paragraph, we will go over the numbers 0-9 and their meanings.

The first number zero is related to high power and brings about a very drastic transformation. The number zero is associated with so much intensity that wherever there is this number, there is a huge need for care and attention to ensure that extreme polarities are not manifested. The cosmic egg, the number zero, is depicted. It is a circle with nothing within it that reveals space and death and the completeness of existence. Both sides of the ring go up and down, evolution and devolution. This is the ultimate infinity, the incomprehensible mystery.

One, when used as an adjective, represents a human being or entity always referred to as unity or unit. This is regarded as the start and is the sum of all possibilities. One can be considered as the center or essence of creation that leads to duality. One as the number of the way of life is independence and individuality. It is used as a term and conveyed in self-help and self-confidence. The first number counted is considered as having high power, and since it represents the beginning, it is very self-centered in nature and prefers to be in the center of the whole attention. The upsides of number one impact are a caring, healthy, compassionate, energetic, and creative individual. The downside to the nature of number one is egotism and selfishness.

The second is duality, plurality, and conflict. Three are called a stable state that can be known as equilibrium, reflection, and stability. Two give rise to the polarity game, which has two opposite poles, representing human beings ' dual nature. Two is the duration as one is a point. Two as the amount of the way of life signify love and peace. One's accomplishments are not as realistic as the teams ' work and co-operation, for that is how best achievements are accomplished. Two are feminine numbers that correspond with intuitive and protective actions if a positive nature if a negative influence is possible.

Everything happens in three, mainly because we live in the third dimension. Nothing could manifest in our realm other than in threes. The cornerstone is the understanding of multiplicity, creative power, and development. Three is a dramatic force of energy that overcomes duality, thought, manifestation, and synthesis. Three is also the first number to which everything's significance has been issued. The triad is three because it has a start, center, and end. The energy and strength of three are universal as it is represented by heaven, waters, and earth in our galaxy.

Within humans, it is reflected by our diverse mind, body, and spirit. Three are reflected in terms of our existence through the past, the present, and the future. The number three is celestial, and it's best illustrated physically as a triangle. In regard to three as the amount of the way of life, it implies communication and imagination. When properly expressed, it is manifested through art and speech. Three are also considered an auspicious number. The influence and nature of three depend on knowledge, knowledge, and understanding. The negative side is shown to be cynical, naive, and cautious.

The fourth dimension is symbolic of the fourth, which creates an impression of time. Four is referred to by its spatial schemes as the first solid figure. Four are most deeply portrayed on our earth plane through the four-season period, four cardinal points, the four earth signs, the four elements. Four is related to endurance, practicality, and tenacity as the number of a life path. Four are expressed in hard work and strong ethics of practice. The fourth leads to very independent thinking.

Five is the human microcosm, the amount of the human being. Bracelet, hand, leg, chest, face, and our five senses. This forms a pentagon as our body is stretched, and the pentagon is infinite, synonymous with the strength and power of the process and perfection. The number of men is three, plus the number of women is two, making five. Five reflect meditation and spirituality, as well. Five means the love of freedom and adventure as a number of life directions.

Five are expressed through change and various experiences as development. Five are members of the highly analytical and critical system to other orientations. One disadvantage of the influence of critical thinking for Number Five is that it tends to overthink a subject or problem so that its relevance is eliminated altogether. The upside of the five is that it drives life to the frontier and encourages good physical and mental health.

The sixth is stable and harmonious and is the most productive of all numbers. The sixth number is also symbolic of the polarity group. Six is called the symbol of love, luck, beauty, opportunity, health, and prosperity. Six are linked to responsibility and attention for others as a life path number. When adequately articulated, six are known as a support structure for the most vulnerable or needing help. Six of the materials we are most attracted to and enjoy. The number six offers beauty, elegance, and the ability to conjure up idle talk at a finger's snap. The sixth is also incredibly nutritious. Number six is jealous, angry, unfaithful, and vengeful in a negative sense.

As the sixth number is symbolic of mankind, then the seventh must signify the relationship between humanity and the creator, god, or the grace of Christ, it is the number of the Universe. It is not essential to have affiliations and links to the number 7 in our world because the representation of seven, which most can be seen, is the seven days of the week. Seven are linked to intellect and the analytical mind as the number of ways of life. The strength of its speech suggests abstract thought and a desire to be alone. Seven contain veils to be sought before enlightenment can be attained, so they are considered to be a religious number. The number seven's negative qualities are doubtfulness, deceit, and insincerity. Positive, robust gains are cognitive insight and a deeper understanding of spirituality.

Eight if the infinity number is remembered, heaven. This number is the intention of the initiator on the path to enlightenment, which has spiritually completed the first seven phases. In its form of life, eight is related to materialistic accomplishments, resilience, and discipline of the dynamic mind, body, and spirit. The number 8 is the karmic cleaner, and we have to pay the karmic debt for our current and preceding lives. The number eight reflects hard lessons learned from life's experience and is restrictive in nature so that it can be considered as a complicated number. The number eight is a desire for money and material prosperity, although the difficulties faced by its wealth and resources are severe.

Nine is the final phase before completion and renaissance. Nine is the earthly paradise number, the angelic, and the heavenly number. Nine means deep love and compassion as a life path number. Nine as an expression suggest idealism by recognizing the value of supporting others. Nine is the change and growth that is inspired.

As stated in our mission statement, we strive to provide our viewers with the necessary knowledge to activate the energy spark required to start the desire to seek reality. We are trained in this exact approach. The only precondition for success is that you read the information we offer with an open heart and an educated mind.

CONCLUSION

Nowadays, our world recovers all its ancient knowledge and uses it to help in our lives, and numerology is one of Pythagorean's oldest sciences.

Physics and chemistry are focused on mathematics as well as biology, and physics and chemistry are based on psychology, which makes numerology the basis of all sciences.

Numbers are used in our everyday lives. Every number of an alphabet has a number assigned to It. Governs the astrology as the Moon, the Sun, and other planets.

There are three primary numbers that will affect your life, the date of birth, the number on the way of life (by adding all the day/month/year of birth), and the numbers which will make your name. That explains all the hula hoo behind changing names or adding a new alphabet to improve the' luck factor.' It can all seem like hokey pokey switches names and does extraordinary things on certain occasions, etc., but it is a very profound science. It's not only in our vet's but also the tarot, the root of Egypt, based on numbers. It has been lost somewhere over time and now is understood in great depth by those who have studied it.

The common assumption that numerological calculations are very advanced and require a high intellect for mathematics is for individuals who have not undergone numerological research. Nothing could go beyond the truth. Numerology calculations are actually quite easy to perform, but unraveling numerological calculations can become a little more complicated. Like any specialized craft, numerology requires expertise and skills to develop.

The calculations of numerology are divided into two common categories: the date of birth in numerology and the number name. Every letter of the name has a number associated with a particular vibration, which, together with the numbers at the birth date, provides information about the underlying abilities, the character of an individual and enables him or her to make informed decisions on life.

Life Path Number: The number of life paths is the simplest of all calculations, but usually, it is considered the essential numerological number. It is an external impact number and can help to reveal deep-rooted talents, attributes of your personality, and possibilities and show you your journey into life.

Your destiny number, which describes all your talents and potential in this lifetime, is based on letters that make up your full birth name. This is not your married name, but the full name written on your birth certificate. If your birth certificate name is misprinted, use it to customize your destination number.

The definitions of your destiny number below suggest what you have to do or do in this lifetime. This calculation gives you a glimpse of which opportunities you should have during the journey through life, unlike the Life Path Number, which is more about your limitations because of your ancestry or physicality. The beauty of your destiny is that it teaches you what you really can or should look for when you know your most significant potential.

Tarot for Beginners

The Complete Guide to Understanding Tarots, Learning to Read Magic Cards Meanings and Secrets, Simple Spreads to Get You Started

By Jade K. Star

Introduction

Tarot is a fantastic, mind-blowing leisure activity, and this book will certainly assist you to get going on your journey of self-discovery and also expedition.

The following sections will cover the intriguing history of the tarot deck and the detailed, extensive meanings for every one of the 78 memory cards of the minor as well as major arcana. It will also discuss just how you may use the importance of the tarot pictures to recognize what is going on in your life. The book will also introduce you to the methods on how to utilize your tarot deck in everyday life, such as tarot for daily consideration, meditation, help to avoid problems, in addition to manifesting your dreams and also objectives.

The tarot is a lot more than a mysterious artifact traditionally enjoyed by occultists. It is a real and useful tool that can be taken advantage of to improve one's lifestyle. These may include the individual's development, relationships, wealth, occupation, loved ones, and also lasting objectives and aspirations.

The imagery of the tarot is based on old knowledge and phenomenon of archetypes, which are global tasks and symbolic representations that all of us attach to on some point. These teach us beneficial things about ourselves, ensuring that our team quit making the same mistakes and stop choosing that mistake for our team. Also, start appreciating the lifestyle that we got today, and even taking actions for a brighter, healthier tomorrow.

Chapter 1: History of the Tarot

What is Tarot?

It's helpful to consider the Tarot as a symbolic map of mindset. This map has our life's journey in all aspects, including spiritual or practical means. Checking out Tarot memory cards is a technique of divining support and also wisdom with how our experts placed or even dispersed them out. Their positioning, and also the way they connect to the various other cards around them are how readers decipher the meanings they have.

Tarot memory cards are indicated to provide understanding into our lifestyles and disclose what our experts may already recognize a subconsciousness amount. This suggests that you don't have to possess clairvoyant skills to read through Tarot cards. The amount of foreknowledge of the audience is going to govern the reading that one will certainly obtain. A single person generally reads through for another, yet it is feasible to read through for our selves.

It's important to remember that cards on their own are not oracles. They do not reveal a future that is waiting for us along the way, but instead, they can be used to make the future that we want. It is that revelation that the cards may hold that attracts us to the Tarot. The lore and the mystery bordering the cards always keep some folks away, for worry of negative consequence, yet others seek to comprehend all of them on a much deeper level.

A lot of Fortuneteller understand that training books on the subject function as tips as well as provide us simple interpretations. However, it's the individual strategy that builds a style, technique, and much more in-depth expertise. It is necessary to remember that cards themselves do not certainly consist of any truth. They only function as our mirrors as well as also windows where people can easily view a higher certainty. When they deliver intuition and level of sensitivity to their approach, every person can access this info.

History of the Tarot

Where did Tarot originate from, and also what was its initial purpose? The majority of versions about the origin of the Tarot state that they started as hand-painted cards made use of by Italian nobles in saloons during the Rennaissance. This card mirrors the activity we called Bridge. The Tarot has changed over the years right up to the modern art and decks that we currently possess. There is still a lot of the Tarot story that continues to be unknown. It is because many perspectives, including those of wise women that review cards in their residences, were undoubtedly never passed along in books and resources for the general public. A lot of knowledge has been passed down orally overtimes. Some past histories suggest the Tarot is much older than the Awakening. It's much easier to watch the history of the Tarot as a progressing timeline. Most historical publications suggest the early 1400's as the era when the first decks showed up, but it had not been till the mid to late 1600's that The Marseille Tarot spread over Europe. Between this moment and early 1900s, occultists examined and changed the Tarot to be used for divination. In the 1960s and 70s, Tarot became famous all around the globe. This was also when dozens of brand-new decks were generated. The Rider Waite Smith contains some of the most universally acknowledged pictures in the Tarot. This deck was posted in the early '70s by USA Video Games

Solutions. In the '90s, much of the Pagan, as well as Wiccan icons, were traded for standard Christian significance.

In Europe, etched stencils created by expert paper producers were passed on over many ages producing fundamental iconography of the Tarot. In the 18th and also 19th centuries, Tarot dispersed all around Europe as a card game. Before the publishing empires occurred, a lot of the general public played Tarot utilizing thin paper, meant to be thrown away, printed along with woodblock seals.

The French Marseille Tarot is probably the one that succeeded the most and, in time, became the reference for future manufacturers and card dealers. Still considered a top deck for amateurs, the Marseille Tarot seems to be to have details that will pop out at you even after you're familiar with the deck. In a minimalistic way, the memory cards keep a regular structure throughout. The small pips or cards (1-10) are merely only a sign repeated as many times as the card stands for. The 5 of Cups would undoubtedly have five real cups and nothing else. In the Minor Arcana section of the manual, we will look into the Marseille Tarot representations. It will be beneficial in your learning quest as it will assist you in focusing on the Major Arcana representations and also its relevance to the minor arcana.

In the mid-19th century, the Tarot was even considered to be connected with alchemical symbology, the Kabbala, zodiac signs, elements, and also the planets. Eliphas Levi and the reports of others during this period generated the connection between the Tarot and antiquity, divinatory powers, and Egypt. Cartomancy, the use of cards for divination, grew in level of mystery and popularity during this moment. Many are still pulled to the Marseille deck, particularly beginners to Tarot, given that it's the oldest set of the deck. The graphics it utilizes are prototypes from our earliest history documented. Those illustrations consist of noble or major primitive characters. The 22 symbolical images are associated with the individual's journey.

It's pretty feasible in current times to find a deck with illustrations that interprets almost everything that we wanted. These are practically based on a mix between the

Marseille deck as well as the more recent Rider Waite Johnson Tarot deck. The Rider Waite Smith decks were made for telling the fortune. And for the first time, the Minor Arcana are represented with images. Pamela Coleman Smith's pictures within this deck became the inspirations of many other manufacturers. There are revisionist decks including the Morgan-Greer and post-modern decks like Starchild Tarot that are all deserving of checking.

Tarot in the Modern Time

You might have seen an increase in passion encompassing the Tarot. It seems to be as if we are currently experiencing a form of Tarot revival where you can see videos online performing Tarot readings. Tarot Clubs are meeting up in public areas to perform readings and also interact with likeminded people. What began as a more mystical practice that aided the masterpieces of the previous theorists and artists is now used even more for giving an insight into our everyday lives. Interpretations of the card can be offered without being mystical and present other intentions. By taking away the mirrors and smoke that concealed the true essence of the Tarot for a very long time, it is now more open to modern audiences that treat it as an art rather than a mystical activity. This ability to artistically go through a story that the cards found and also administer it to specific facets in our lives is relatively appealing. This pull is, to some extent, due to the reason that it's all about us. No one can understand absolutely the card's interpretations on a more personal level besides us.

If you've never had your Tarot cards reviewed, be sure to start there. You can do this quickly if you are acquainted with someone who knows how to use and read Tarot cards. You may pull one card, or even determine your Birth Cards, or also pose a question that you need understanding. There is still a particular preconception that comes with the Tarot. Numerous followers of religious beliefs are still against the notion of managing our fate and not letting or believing the plans that God has for our lives. Some forerunners in faith are even creating anxiety around the Tarot by saying its usage will undoubtedly draw in demons and bogeys. Despite the negative thoughts that still borders the Tarot, many youths are drawn to take advantage of the mystic. As more mature generations sought alleviation and order to their lives with religious beliefs, lots of people right now are locating a sense of control through the Tarot.

For a lot of people, the meditative method of reading through Tarot cards remains the main reason to proceed to do it. Surrendering major lifestyle problems and also decisions to the historical illustrations located in the Tarot could be both enlightening and calming during times where assistance is required.

Chapter 2: Getting Start with Tarot

You're now ready to obtain a Tarot deck as well as begin the learning method. The primary thing you should do is to discover your personal Tarot deck and make it yours. You can then start to build an individual link with those cards as well as build the groundwork that will provide you with guidance and also understanding for the next years.

How to Properly Pick the Right Deck

It may be actually challenging when to begin with choosing which deck to use because there are a lot of Tarot card decks now offered. Don't worry about picking the inappropriate deck, since just about anything that calls to you will likely be the ideal match. You aren't confined to only having one deck, either. You may and also probably are going to wind up with numerous decks that you use for different reasons. Some will always keep one deck private, and also only utilize it when they read cards for themselves. Others will undoubtedly use one deck for every little thing. Many educators of Tarot card advise that you find a deck that you resonate with as well as utilize it to discover and perform along. Once you are confident about reading Tarot for other people, you will certainly know if you require a brand-new deck for that objective or if the one you already have is enough.

Regardless of which deck you end up choosing, possessing a sense of link using it is actually critical. Take your time and scan all the alternatives accessible to you. Look for a brand new deck if you find a deck and decide that the illustrations don't really relate to you. You hold no commitment to any deck of cards until you feel that it resonates with you. When you found a deck that you like, you'll need to clear the powers that could exist around it and also purify the deck. If that appears a little bit very metaphysical for you, think about it as introducing your own to the deck and also starting fresh.

How to Properly Sort your Tarot Deck

To begin, you will undoubtedly wish to sort out your cards and take note of any energies that you may get coming from them. On a neat table or even surface, sort your cards out in front of you in order. Begin with the Major Arcana cards and afterward arrange the suits of the Minor Arcana. Have a swift peek at every card while doing this. This is a technique of making sure that you possess all the cards in your deck. Aside from that, it is to familiarize yourself with the illustrations of the cards. When managing the Minor Arcana cards, sort the Suits through type and afterward through number. You begin by arranging in order from Ace through Ten. Next comes the Page, the Knight, the Queen, and finally, the King card.

For the grounds of learning, you might desire to sort your cards into the Major Arcana and also the Minor Arcana. After that, placed one or even the other away in the place you assign for storage. When we concentrate on either one of these, especially, we enable space for additional knowledge and growth in that specific area. For example, it's rather usual to start with the Minor Arcana as well as to develop a good understanding of what each Court, Number, or Suit card is telling us. It allows us to concentrate solely on a restricted amount of cards to ensure that we can easily make use of the reoccurrence to build on our initial notions and perceptions.

How to Cleanse the Tarot Deck's Energies

When you have examined each card and also have it arranged, you may use a smudging stick like sweetgrass or sage to get rid of any stored energies in the cards. This is particularly helpful if you possess cards that have been used before, but it is also an excellent base for new decks. Now, you might wish to contemplate the cards and then imagine the energy arising from you and moving in the direction of and into the cards. If you have knowledge about visualization techniques or guided meditations, you can use them to make a protecting white light that covers you and your cards. This may be a highly effective cleansing, as well as a bonding exercise between you and the cards.

There are different techniques used for cleansing the energy such as water clearing, moon bathing, and salt burials. Get the opportunity to execute a purifying routine with all of them if you experience your cards have any bad energies linked or even clinging to them. For newbies, though, easy sorting and also simple meditation is good enough. It's encouraged that you do some energy clearing, however little, prior to performing readings to focus on the concerns and client.

How to Make Your Card your Own

When the energy of the cards is cleansed, pick them up and then shuffle them to bring your energy into the cards. Continue to reshuffle however way you like until you're satisfied. You may prefer to shuffle them by your lucky number or choose to put cards at the bottom or top of the deck. Your first deck will be ready to be used whatever method you choose to use. Your deck also needs a proper storage area where you can store them when they are not used. For some, the box that comes with the deck is perfect. However, others prefer to have a dedicated space to store their cards. Since it is related to magical properties, silk is considered to be the preferred fabric to wrap the deck before storing it away in a box. While it's fine to choose whatever you prefer, always keep in mind that the Tarot is an artform from the ancient times that deserves our reverence and respect.

Develop a Personal Connection

You are now ready to start using your cards and create a personal bond with them. This link should be with every single card in the Tarot deck. You might decide to start with the Major Arcana to establish a connection on the representations of the illustrations found within. You might opt to start with the Minor Arcana to build a sense of what each Suit interprets. No matter which way you go, you still need to determine what each of them means. You will definitely begin to create a partnership with your cards. This is the reason why it is essential to work with a deck that you prefer and resonates with you. When utilizing it, you are primarily connecting with the deck and noting just how you feel.

You do not have to remember the significance of each card. You just need to cultivate a pure feeling of what the card works with at first. You are going to get a sense of what they mean as you keep on working with them. You are going to, at one point, share what they mean to other individuals. So, try to familiarize yourself with making associations that can be deciphered, repeated, and recognized quickly. This should be enjoyable for you. If you start to feel overwhelmed with too much information, you can step back for a while and return when you are ready. You are not required to learn and know the whole deck right away. You may take one card and ponder over it until you are ready to get on with the next one. Some individuals even choose a single card and meditate on it, discovering all the little things that emanate from it, for a whole month. This may seem very long, but if you are truly serious in learning Tarot, then this is a highly recommended approach to familiarize yourself with it entirely. Remember that you can do this when you practice daily.

Meanwhile, any type of importance and also the representation that you locate in each card is entirely fine. Spread your cards out and take note of all the details and patterns that emerge from a birds-eye-view. Record in a notebook all the feelings and themes that the cards express to you. You can always refer back to your journal as you build your relationship with the cards. You can only see their interpretations when you always interact with them. When you need their interpretations, you can easily find and use them. You can create your own opinions of them as you use this time to connect with the cards. The deck you picked basically becomes an expansion of your voice. Be straightforward along with anybody that may approach you for a reading beforehand. Let them know that you may do it for fun, but that they shouldn't take them seriously because you're still learning them. Always remember, these meanings are actually theoretical and not essentially pythonic. You and the individuals you might perform readings for are free from harm.

Shuffling

Learn to shuffle your Tarot deck. It can be difficult to shuffle a deck of cards unless it's on the smaller size. The reason why is that the cards are larger and thicker than the usual deck of playing cards. Shuffling a deck of cards can be done in different ways. Remember, though, that you should only spread them out and circulate them in a clean and even surface to avoid damaging them. You may attempt to shuffle them like a usual deck of cards, or by separating them in half, and more. You may shuffle or cut them a number of times or you may let your client shuffle or cut them personally. The goal is to randomized their shuffling as you contemplate the questions asked by your clients. This is actually the distinction between obtaining a meaningful reading and not just plainly interpreting random cards.

If you're reading for someone else, think about letting your client shuffle the deck so that they can be in tune with their energies. If that's one thing you're not comfortable with, that's alright! You can just let them separate the deck several times without really giving them your cards. Discover where your limits are regarding your cards and emphasize that they should always be respected.

You can also just choose a spread, reshuffle them, and then spread them out again. If you find it hard to relate to the questions being asked by your client or that you are not in the zone to interpret the cards, you will find them hard to do. Remove all the energies around both of you and your cards and then start again. It is not really wise to pull out interpretations forcefully out of the cards. This must take exertion on your part as the cards are going to deliver the understanding you are searching for only through your sight. You can easily build intuitive readings quickly by always practicing!

Chapter 3: Obtaining your First Tarot Deck

Let's carry on and talk about the most important piece of this whole process: the deck itself. As with any skill, obtaining the right tools is key to advancement. Choosing your tarot deck is as essential a step of discovering the meanings of the cards. What many don't understand at first is simply the number of decks that exist. When you're a novice, there are a lot of different types of decks available, and it can get mind-boggling.

First of all, where does one obtain a deck? Crystal shops are the first place a beginner should look at, which is a kind of metaphysical shop. These shops offer items tailored towards Wicca specialists and contemporary witches and deal prophecy decks, angel medallions, besoms, candles, incense, stones, and of course, crystals.

You don't have to worry about not finding any since Tarot is already widely available commercially. It's not limited to metaphysical stores anymore. The decks, along with books about the subject, can also be found and bought in popular stores like Barnes & Noble, which has a dedicated spiritual section on their store. Although they don't have a lot to offer compared to actual metaphysical stores do, it is still an excellent place to start if there are no crystal shops around your area.

Naturally, there is always the web. Amazon has a variety in their catalog, and there are online stores that specialize in prophecy decks that can be found with a fast search. It's also possible to get them straight from the publishers. Llewellyn Worldwide and U.S. Games are the two primary companies that manufacture decks in the U.S. They have all their decks offered for order right on their website.

The great thing about the internet, however, is stumbling upon something that isn't commonly readily available. Also, tarot decks have seen such an increase in popularity that lots of artists have self-published their decks. It takes some digging to find these indie decks, but the variety of designs and the charm of a few of them makes it beneficial. Signing up with a tarot forum can point you in the right instructions, as there are lots of passionate deck collectors who spend a lot of time looking for simply these kinds of tarot art.

The general guideline of purchasing a tarot deck is to choose the one you feel drawn to. Much of reading depends upon interpreting the images on the cards, so if you dislike the art, it's most likely you're going to dislike reading the deck. There's likewise the more mystical component of feeling the energy of the deck. It's a common phenomenon for readers to describe their decks as if they have unique personalities. Some deal with you and some do not, just like people. There's absolutely nothing more discouraging than purchasing a deck just to recognize it's challenging to work with. When selecting a deck to discover the Tarot, it's crucial to get the one that feels right for you. Do not over-analyze; just opt for your intuition.

That stated, it is recommended that you think about the Rider Waite-Smith Tarot as your very first deck. Made by A.E. Waite and Pamela Coleman Smith, in charge of the illustrations, the Rider Waite-Smith Tarot Cards works as the basis for the style of many decks available now. It's hard to understate just how prominent this deck is. It turned the pip cards into clean, clear, detailed styles that reflect the cartomantic significance for ease of reading. Aside from that, it was instrumental in making the Tarot approachable, bringing it out of the hands of magical mystics and into the general public sphere. It is the most commonly offered deck worldwide. You can guarantee that this deck can be found in any stores that offer Tarots. You'll have a much easier time analyzing the other cards that followed suit when you know how to read the Rider Waite-Smith deck properly. If you're having difficulty choosing on a deck, it's an excellent bet to go with this one.

Aleister Crowley, a fellow occultist of A.E> Waite, also produced a deck, which is also worth checking out. Along with Lady Frieda Harris, an artist, he developed the Thoth Tarot. This is a lot more ambitious deck, soaked in the deeply mystical folklore and astrology of the Order of the Golden Dawn. Typically, it's only suggested you get this deck if you're an innovative reader thinking about exploring the more profound mysticism of the Tarot. This is because it is notoriously difficult to read for prophecy. It's only raised here due to the fact that some contemporary decks are affected by its focus on Kabbalic hermeticism, and anyone entering the Tarot should be aware of it. Once again, go with your gut, but usually speaking, any deck created after the Rider Waite-Smith will be a more approachable than one following in the steps of the Thoth deck.

There are a total of seventy-eight cards in each tarot pack, what deck it is. It contains 56 Minor Arcana and 22 Major Arcana. There are similar archetypes in every Major Arcana, which begins with the Fool and ends with the World. Every Minor Arcana is separated into four suits that contain 14 cards in each. Tarot is an extremely stiff system with this extremely specific structure to the deck style. It can get confusing when looking at decks for the first time, but remember that any deck that does not have this structure is not Tarot. There are other divination card systems; however, they all have their own different symbolism and read really differently. Like for example, you cannot consider Tarot the Oracle cards. The same goes for the Kipper as well as the Lenormand. They are extremely interesting systems, and you are encouraged to explore them as well, but this book will not help you to comprehend them.

What's the distinction in between all the tarot decks offered? Basically, it remains in the method the artist chose to interpret the significances of each card.

Typically, through theme is how you can see the difference in every kind of decks. An extremely popular deck is the Wildwood Tarot, which utilizes Celtic influence and nature as its imagery. Although it is based on the Rider Waite-Smith Tarot, the image on the card in this deck is usually not the same as the card that it corresponds to in the Rider Waite-Smith deck. Often, the cards are even relabeled to suit the theme. In the Wildwood Tarot, you call the Seer the High Priestess card in the Rider-Waite Tarot. As well as you call Ancestor, what you commonly refer to as Hierophant in Rider-Waite.

More modifications can be seen from deck to deck. In some cases, you call the Wands suit as Rod and the Pentacles as Disks or Coins. A Page in one deck is called Princess in another, or Daughter in yet another. Some decks get rid of the images totally from European tradition and positions it instead in the context of another culture with all the legendary connections consisted of. Even with these changes, the significance of the cards stays the same, and the underlying structure of the Tarot remains intact. It is still four suits, still a Significant and Minor Arcana, and still seventy-eight cards. What's different is how the message through the cards stumbles upon.

Typically, however, tarot decks adhere to custom and keep the old names, instead of utilizing imagery alone to offer new viewpoints. This is the reason why picking a deck you connect with is very important as far as the artwork is worried. The art assists you in unlocking the significances of each card and how they link together to provide you a photo of what's going on in your reading.

There is likewise the alternative of making your own deck. There are blank sets you can purchase where you can draw on and use immediately. If you are really into arts and crafts, though, all you require is a corner cutter, a paper slicer, and card stock. Then you can produce them to be any size you desire. If you draw your own analyses of the cards, it will resonate that far more, considering that you'll understand exactly what the illustration implies and why you picked it. It's an incredibly wonderful process worth checking out for anyone with a flair for creative expression. It helps to be knowledgeable about the cards first, to understand their meanings, and how they work together, but Tarot does not need to be sophisticated, comprehensive art.

Whatever deck you decide on, take it out while we go through the principles of the card's significances. Let the cards speak with you while you find out.

Chapter 4: Introduction to Minor Arcana: The Pips Cards

'Arcana' is the plural form of the term 'arcanum,' which refers to the mystical, specialized understanding. It is often related to alchemy, which sought to transmutate the disparate components of nature into something cleansed and never-ceasing, most commonly, gold. The Minor and Major Arcana are two sets of secret knowledge that we get from within the tarot. As alchemists of the soul, we can use them to connect the pieces of ourselves and turn them into spiritual gold, which is an elixir of life. It is the Fountain of Life that comes from within and is not actually a drink.

Their significance might pertain to more ordinary things, but because of that, they also tend to be far more relatable and specific. In this chapter, we will be checking out the pip cards, which are the varieties of the suits Ace through Ten.

The Minor Arcana is composed of four suits, which include the Pentacles, Swords, Cups, and Wands. Following the approach of alchemy, these are the four components that combine to produce the world we live in. They are the standard onto themselves, but it is in the synthesis of these that we are produced as spiritual beings.

The component of fire is the Wands. They are a masculine, active property that associates with the spirit. They are the creative will, effort, and enthusiasm. The cards in this suit typically mention pursuing objectives.

The Cups represent the passive and feminine aspects of water. This suits displays the depths of our feelings. They are our fantasies and dreams, relationships of all kinds, and love.

Swords associate with air. The dourest of the suits, it has a manly, active personality and relates to pain of the mind. It is the mind, communication, conflict, and strife, especially as it deals with reasoning and reality.

Pentacles, often called Coins, is the earth element. It is feminine and passive and often shows money. More symbolically, it is the body. It is our material sensations. Endurance, persistence, and practicality are the theme of this suit, and among a slow, stable technique.

To explore the pips, rather than going through each match separately from Ace to Ten, we're going to use the framework of numerology, the study of the mystical relationships of numbers. In regards to our subject, numerology has ancient connections to the Kabbalah and alchemy, and so was used along with those to determine the significances of the cards.

In this chapter, the four suits will be broken down into the numbers, talking about each set of 4 cards as the numerology applies to the match's characteristics. The Kabbalic placement of each set of numbers on the Tree of Life will be noted at the top of the page. Each card has a title that is a couple of word summation of what the card comes down to. Astrological significance will be noted with the card's significance and shadow element.

As with the Major Arcana, the astrological and Kabbalic info is more for a future recommendation if you pick to delve deeper into hermetic associations. While doing so can help you open much deeper meanings into the cards, in the meantime, while you're learning, it will not impact your capability to read the cards.

While the Major Arcana checks out the archetypes of universal influence, these cards deal with the elements of our daily lives. We will be focusing, in this chapter, the pip cards, which are the numbers of the suits Ace through Ten.

The cards in this suit frequently speak of pursuing objectives. In this chapter, the four suits will be broken down into the numbers, going over each set of four cards as the numerology applies to the fit's attributes. Each card has a title that is a one or two-word summation of what the card boils down to.

Aces: Kether, the Source

Aces are the quintessence for each of their matches. They are each element in their purest spiritual sense, symbolized by the fact that even in decks with detailed pip cards, the Aces normally do not have a figure on the card. They are energy unmanifested, endless in their possibilities, but without shape or form themselves. When they appear in a reading, they are an offering of what could be, if you take what they need to offer and understand something concrete with it. All Aces can indicate pregnancy or birth.

Ace of Pentacles: The Root of Earth. Virgo, Taurus, and Capricorn. This is pure abundance. While it can suggest wealth is coming, more frequently, it means the materialization of tangible things that will assist you. It is your desires turning real. In the shadow element, this reveals the evil of wealth. You might be getting what you desire, but it is not what you need, and it will stop working to improve you truly.

Ace of Swords: The Root of Air. Libra, Aquarius, and Gemini. This is the Sword of Truth. With it comes total clarity of idea. It is a powerful card, showing victory in understanding. It is likewise the energy of learning something new. In the shadow element, this indicates misdirected judgment. You have actually made a call without the complete fact, resulting in disaster.

Ace of Cups: The Root of Water. Pisces, Scorpio, and Cancer. This is an open heart that is overflowing with love. Your subconscious is a vessel for spiritual happiness, and now you can't help but reveal it. Let your imagination unfurl and pursue something innovative. It is the expression of self-love that penetrates into everything around you. In the shadow aspect, this is false love that damages. This can indicate either yourself or someone taking advantage of you.

Ace of Wands: The Root of Fire. Sagittarius, Leo, and Aries. This is the motivation of inspiration. This is the card that tells you to follow your visions. This is your hint to go for it if you have a brand-new idea. In the shadow aspect, a burst of energy with no instructions.

Twos: Chokmah, the Wisdom

In numerology, 2 is the number of dualities. With this, likewise, the sense of balance required to keep the dual elements steady. So within the tarot, twos frequently show up to point out options that need to be made, or collaborations.

Two of Pentacles: Balance, Change. Jupiter in Capricorn. In practical Pentacles, the earth energy in the number two produces a juggling act. It is the balance of all the important things you must handle in day-to-day life. It is work and play, pain and enjoyment, and responsibility and rest. All these elements remain in balance, and you are in control of them, despite any trouble that may try to interrupt your concentration. In the shadow aspect, the balls have dropped. You're trying to keep an excellent face, but beneath, there is a sense of panic you may not be able to maintain, and the tension is setting in.

Two of Swords: Peace Restored, Inner Balance. Moon in Libra. This is the anxious harmony of a stalemate. In spite of the favorable connotations of words like 'peace' and 'balance,' in Sword energy, this becomes tense conformity. It is declining to decide so as not to rock the boat. In the shadow element, this ends up being straight-out duplicity, of using falsehood to take a simple way rather than do the work facing a decision would bring.

Two of Cups: Love. Venus in Cancer. In water, the energy of 2 becomes one of loving connection. The card is the most favorable symbol when reading on love. It can likewise show relationships of friendship and family. This is synergy and sympathy at its highest level. In the shadow aspect, this translates to clinginess or co-dependence.

Two of Wands: Dominion. Mars in Aries. This is discovery, risks, and establishing a strategy. In the energy of fire, the duality of this card recommends weighing the dangers of remaining where you are or gambling. In the shadow element, it is fear of surprise. It can also mean wishful thinking.

Within the tarot, twos typically reveal themselves to point out options that require to be made, or partnerships.

In water, the energy of 2 ends up being one of caring connection. Two of Swords: Peace Restored, Inner Balance. Two of Pentacles: Change, Balance. In practical Pentacles, the earth energy in the number 2 produces a juggling act.

Threes: Binah, the Understanding

Threes are the presentation of development. They are groups congregating for a function. They sustain imaginative endeavors, therefore, represent energy progressing. If ace was the self, and two were people coming together, then three is their unity developing something more. This is similar to how couples come together to make a family.

Three of Pentacles: Works. Mars in Capricorn. This is team effort at its finest. Strategies have come together, everybody has been assigned their tasks, and the partnership of craft and ability is at its creative peak. You are on the right track. In the shadow element, this card is mediocrity. Either the work took into a job isn't at its finest, or the project itself does not permit the very best the shine through. It may also show that the work is not taken seriously by those included.

Three of Swords: Sorrow. Saturn in Libra. Another name for this is the heartbreak card. This is deep hurt and sorrow, and in this sense, it is psychological release as your mind processes the discomfort. In the shadow element, instead of processing unhappiness, you dwell on it, and the psychological alienation creates unfavorable self-talk and confusion.

Three of Cups: Abundance, Pleasure. Mercury in Cancer. It is joy in society and having a good time. You are surrounded by people who wish to celebrate with you, to assist you, to raise you as you lift them up. In the shadow aspect, it is an overindulgence in your social life, perhaps spending too much time with friends or drinking too much rather than on your daily obligations. There is likewise a component of gossip.

Three of Wands: Virtue, Established Strength. Sun in Aries. This card is development, of taking established strategies and building them into a working system. Dare to dream larger. It can likewise symbolize organization, undertakings, or travel. In the shadow aspect, it is avoiding obstacles and remaining within existing restrictions. It can also be dissatisfaction with the method things are going.

Fours: Chesed, the Empathy

Like the four corners of a square, four represents form and stability. Things have materialized and developed structure. No longer is the energy merely an idea in advancement, instead, now a solid truth.

Four of Pentacles: Power. Sun in Capricorn. This is securing accumulated resources. Thriftiness is needed, and keeping a close eye on what is coming in or being spent. In the shadow element, this deteriorates to opposing and hoarding anything that may change the status quo.

Four of Cups: High-end, Blended Pleasure. Moon in Cancer. This card has to do with having a lot that you can't, or won't, accept anything else. There is a sense of discontent here, of being spoiled for choice. The stability of four in watery energy develops into discontentment and monotony. In the shadow aspect, there is a lot of disillusionment, so you may not notice when something really incredible enters your life.

Four of Swords: Truce, Rest. Jupiter in Libra. When this card shows up, a retreat is presented. This is the time for healing. Seclusion is needed. Recovery is needed before marching out to battle again. Some readers see this as a card of illness and death. In the shadow aspect, this is deliberate avoidance of hunching down when it's time for action.

Four of Wands: Completion, Abundance. Venus in Aries. This is the card of the home. With the intense energy of the Wands settled, it demonstrates how far you've come and all the important things you have actually achieved. It is a time for commemoration and acknowledging all you have. It has no shadow element since this card is so positive. It just serves to stress just how much charm and success there is in your life.

Fives: Gevurah, the Judgment

Five is the number that interrupts the stability of the previous fours. The look of this interruption brings stress over the changes it instigates because balance feels ideal and safe. Nevertheless, it is a natural progression and must not always be considered a bad thing.

Five of Pentacles: Trouble, Worry. Mercury in Taurus. This is a material challenge, typically a precursor of financial problems. It is the poverty feared by the hoarder from the 4 of Pentacles. How well you can make it through this time depends upon your ability to bring all that you have left and piece it back together. In the shadow element, this loss comes down into mayhem that will squander what resources you have.

Five of Swords: Defeat. Venus in Aquarius. Rather than a fair battle like in the Five of Wands, there is damage for the sake of destruction here. This is the card of bad blood. If it appears in questions of litigation, it's to state that some fights are unworthy having. This card is so negative; there is extremely little positive to state about it. Therefore it becomes its own shadow aspect. Its only advice is to pick your battles.

Five of Cups: Pleasure Lost, Disappointment. Mars in Scorpio. The strife of five becomes the shock of loss because of the emotional quality of the Cups. Things didn't meet your expectations, and so you grieve what could have been. In the shadow aspect, this advances into a dwelling in regret and remorse.

Five of Wands: Strife. Saturn in Leo. This represents competitors. In a sense, it resembles entry into a competition where you should display your skills to come out on top. Everybody wishes to win, but there is no genuine vitriol between the players. In the shadow element, this competition develops into a battle and ends up being a personal war. With everyone battling so tough to be heard, it only causes interruption with no resolution in sight.

Sixes: Tiferet, the Beauty

Sixes are the energy of harmony. While possibly not as stable as Four, all aspects are nonetheless stabilized after the schism of the Fives. Sixes guideline cooperation and interaction and have the energy in them to adjust to possible difficulties in the future.

Six of Pentacles: Success. Moon in Taurus. To some readers, it is the card of loans and financial obligations. Inherent in this message, however, is the intricate interaction of offering and getting. On the surface, this card speaks of the security and implies to provide to others and the gratification that originates from a charity.

Meanwhile, it also raises the act of receiving. One can not provide to one who does not wish to get. In numerous circumstances, favors are given up the expectation that something will be returned later on, and so getting is not as passive as drawing from the open hand. This relationship is not a simple hierarchy but an exchange. In the shadow aspect, it reveals the greediness in this relationship at its worst. The giver might hesitate to share although they have sufficient. The receiver may beg for more without any objective of repaying or with any mind towards the giver's resources. Thus, the exchange crumbles.

Six of Swords: Earned Success, Science. Mercury in Aquarius. In the Thoth deck, this card is called 'Science' since it represents intelligence not divided, however, united to achieve its goals. In most other decks, this idea is illustrated as the focus of the mind to bring itself out of distressed waters. It's generally provided as a card of shift, however, it does not always carry that meaning at all times. In the shadow element, it is merely these intellectual aspects not being harmonized.

Six of Cups: Friendship, Pleasure. Sun in Scorpio. This reveals harmony in all your relationships. There are fun and liberty in this card and typically illustrated with children.

This is generally called the card of fond memories and is frequently read as the past coming back into play, or enjoyment in memories. Either way, it is an extremely favorable card in a reading. In the shadow element, instead of exposing some negative quality, this card turns its positivity towards the future and might suggest a renewal of some sort.

Six of Wands: Victory. Jupiter in Leo. This is excellent news coming in and triumph over misfortune. This is a crucial milestone that shows your perseverance has been rewarded. You are recognized for your ability to overcome difficulties. In the shadow element, there is fear of somebody else's victory and the betrayal of conceit.

Sevens: Netzah, the Stamina

Consistency has been unbalanced, therefore once again, each match should go through a duration of pain. The Sevens bring with them a sense of assessment the Fives did not. Through knowledge attained, each fit has more capability to reflect on their battles and deal with them appropriately.

Seven of Pentacles: Unsatisfied Success, Failure. Saturn in Taurus. On the one hand, this card's titles offer it the significance of a job that is draining you. You have actually committed a lot of effort to something, and now there are no results of your work. On another, however, this card mentions the persistence required for the long-lasting view. Since the harvest is not here now doesn't imply it will not be enjoyed later. The difference lays in the connotation of the reading, and whether or not you're putting your efforts into the best things. In the shadow aspect, this shows you do not have the persistence to see a task through to the end. You have actually thrown down the stake and have quit. Once again, the connotation will expose if that is called for or just the result of frustration.

Seven of Swords: Reduced Force, Futility. Moon in Aquarius. This card is among the biggest red flags in the deck. This is deception, trickery, and theft in all aspects. Strategies will fail when this card is around. Nevertheless, unlike the Five of Swords, this is a passive card that can be overturned easily. In a more positive undertone, it reveals that some workaround may be sussed out if you look at a problem from a different point of view. In the shadow aspect, it reveals secrets, bad advice, and slander.

Seven of Cups: Illusory Success, Debauch. Venus in Scorpio. The impression of dream sidetracks you on this card. You imagine a lot of ideas that it's impractical to harp on all of them, and yet stay you do, indulging the dream rather than working to make it real. This is one card in which the shadow element is actually an improvement, suggesting the focus of your will on one option and revealing the decision to make it concern fruition.

Seven of Wands: Courage, Valour. Mars in Leo. This is a card of struggle, but of one where you have the vantage position. You are a rising star, reaching the top of your field, and others are shouting to take you down or take on you for what you have. This typically shows a scenario where you must work out and compromise to be successful. In shadow aspects, this pressure is triggering stress and anxiety, which only makes you susceptible. You have the advantage, and you are on the back foot.

Eights: Hod, the Submission

Eights reveal the proficiency of each suit and the ability to turn its energy into directed action. The Eights came through the imbalance of the Sevens and now work to respond versus it. It is through them that we can head towards real accomplishment.

Eight of Pentacles: Vigilance. Sun in Virgo. Discipline motivates this card's energy. This is the card of the apprentice, one who toils at their work with the pure intent of acquiring artistry. This is a skill at work and business. In the shadow element, it is the vanity of your craft. May likewise be excessive attention to information to your detriment.

Eight of Swords: Chains, Interference. Jupiter in Gemini. This is a card of entrapment. Intentional sabotage might be indicated. You were put in this scenario, possibly by circumstance outside your impact, but this is only short-lived chains. You're the only one keeping you here. The impact of the eights in airy Swords indicates you can take your power back. In the shadow aspect, this is an unanticipated catastrophe with no apparent way through.

Eight of Cups: Abandoned Success, Indolence. Saturn in Pisces. This is another card of loss, but unlike the Five of Cups, this reveals a loss you select. In the Eight of Cups, you ignore something. In its titles, it is recommended this is due to laziness. There might be a tendency to drift from one thing to the next and always leaving things unfinished. In some cases, though, this can indicate something in which you put a lot of emotion into only to find it wasn't nearly as crucial as you believed. A loss, yes, but an acknowledged one, and something that requires to be left, although it's a hard thing to do. Another card with a favorable shadow aspect, it exposes finding happiness in carrying on and voluntarily dropping the weight you've carried.

Eight of Wands: Swiftness. Mercury in Sagittarius. This is an extremely dynamic card. It is pure movement, a fantastic burst of speed towards the end of an endeavor. You are focusing straight at your goal, like an arrow flying. In the shadow element, this energy can turn on itself and create disagreement and in-fighting. There is no room for doubt at this speed.

Unlike the Five of Swords, this is a passive card that can be reversed easily. On the one hand, this card's titles provide it the significance of a task that is draining you. On another, however, this card speaks of the perseverance required for the long-term view. Another card with a positive shadow element, it exposes discovering pleasure in moving on and willingly dropping the weight you've brought. Discipline motivates this card's energy.

Nines: Yesod, the Connection

Nines are complete fulfillment. In some schools of thought, nine is the top of excellence. However, in the tarot, this has actually been obtained in each suit. All accomplishments and struggles are now given their maximum capacity.

Nine of Pentacles: Wealth, Gain. Venus in Virgo. This is the outcome of the discipline displayed in the Eight of Pentacles.

You have actually been rewarded, and now reside in luxury and comfort, able to take pleasure in the riches of life. This is the pinnacle of self-worth. In the shadow aspect, this is bad faith in something that won't work out.

Nine of Swords: Anguish, Cruelty. Mars in Gemini. Since the Swords are so negative, in their culmination, they only bring desolation. This is pure stress and anxiety, the dark ideas that keep you up at night, and utter failure. In the shadow aspect, it is still doubt and pity.

Nine of Cups: Joy. Jupiter in Pisces. Referred to as the Wish card or the Yes card, this is complete satisfaction. Everything is going your way, and there's nothing to be unhappy about when this shows up. In the shadow aspect, something seems like it's missing from what needs to be an excellent fortune, as the emptiness in wealth.

Nine of Wands: Strength. Moon in Sagittarius. This is the energy of having come through misfortune and being all the stronger for it. You have developed your ground and can base on it. It's a great deal of responsibility to protect it, but you understand you can take on the obstacles. In the shadow aspect, it suggests weariness and fear.

Tens: Malkuth, the Kingdom

Ten is the end of the cycle and the promise of something new. In that sense, they could be considered as the period between one sentence and the next. They are completion after fulfillment and renewal.

Ten of Pentacles: Wealth. Mercury in Virgo. Legacy is the center of this card. While the Ten of Cups shows the emotional home, the Ten of Pentacles shows family inheritance. Your goals have provided for you, and now you can provide for everyone else. In the shadow aspect, rather than showing a secure fortune, there is a sense of chance here and the possibility of loss. This is like putting all your money into the lottery.

Ten of Swords: Ruin. Sun in Gemini. This is the card of ultimate pain. All things seem to be going wrong, and you are defeated. Many tears will be had in this card's energy. Being ten energy, there is a sense that it is not permanent. In the shadow aspect, this energy turns positive and promises new dawn.

Ten of Cups: Perfected Success, Satiety. Mars in Pisces. This the heart's desires wholly fulfilled. This is family, friendship, and romance perfected in love. In the shadow aspect, disruption of this state.

Ten of Wands: Oppression. Saturn in Sagittarius. This card shows the weight of the many responsibilities garnered by attaining the goals you set. Any success comes with its own problems. A choice is implied here: you can either carry on or drop the load. In the shadow aspect, the responsibilities actually inhibit success. There is a warning here against using force for all things at all times.

Chapter 5: The Court Cards of the Minor Arcana

The Court cards, which are composed of figures of royalties, rule every suit in the deck. There is the King, the Queen, the Knight, and the Page. These can be a few of the most perplexing cards to figure out as their significances range extensively and need to be contextualized within each individual reading.

They can indicate people, wherein every single card in the suit may represent a certain type of personality. In some cases, they mean particularly a man or woman; however, it can also mean somebody of any gender who shows that type of feminine or masculine energy. They also personify elements of ourselves, the different attitudes we can utilize to fix issues. Once you have an understanding of every single one, it will be easier to obtain their meanings within readings.

Pages

This is the youngest among the Court cards. They are students and messengers, an expression of vibrant vitality without any sense of being aware of themselves. They are hungry for learning and bring with them the possibilities of new projects or ideas. In the Rider Waite-Smith, they are represented by young boys, but their energy corresponds more towards the feminine side. That is why in many other decks, they are girls and will be described as such here. They often suggest teens or kids, but they can likewise appear to highlight a situation you do not know much about or parts of yourself that are inexperienced. They are associated with the component of Earth because of their potential for development.

Page of Pentacles: Earth of Earth. Slow and consistent is this Page's work principles. She's a coordinator, somebody who sets objectives in mind and applies themselves thoroughly in order to achieve it. While she is enthusiastic, she's practical, more interested in getting it right than in bowling everybody over. Among all of the Pages, she is the one probably to suggest a literal student. In the shadow element, she is irregular and susceptible to wasting her time and resources if she has no set goal to deal with.

Page of Swords: Earth of Air. She is a firm character, in some cases, even called aggressive, but shows critical practicality. She is related to spying in the sense that she accumulates info with terrific enthusiasm for future usage. At her finest, she can fix conflicts with ease of logic. In the shadow element, she becomes vengeful and utilizes her presents to pull underhanded strategies that win her no pals.

Page of Cups: Earth of Water. She is a gentle and sweet romantic and poetic mind who likes to study literature and art. She is known to have a delicate, pleasant soul. She typically brings messages of a new romance, pregnancy, or marital relationships. She also gives new opportunities, usually in a vein of creativity. In the shadow aspect, she can quickly become lazy.

Page of Wands: Earth of Fire. She has many things to improve and is quite ambitious. She is an active catalyst, someone teeming with ideas; however, maybe not the patience to see a project through to the end. There is a light-heartedness to her that can be motivating. At her worst, though, in shadow element, she is all theatrics without compound and shows undeserved self-confidence.

Knights

Knights are action-oriented. They represent masculine energies and young adult years. More mature than the Pages, they nonetheless tend towards extreme habits, not having the experience to temper their ideologies. They are always on the go and represent change and motion, and for that reason, are gotten in touch with the element of Air.

Knight of Pentacles: Air of Earth. This is the systematic, useful Knight. Though he may be slower than the others, he is incredibly capable because of his competence. His cautious nature permits him to prepare ahead and think through a job before moving forward. In his shadow element, he can end up being persistent and decline to take in any concepts which do not align with his own. His practical, grounded method to things may make him insensitive to the psychological needs of others.

Knight of Swords: Air of Air. The most war-like of the Knights, he's the sort to charge ahead with no regard to risk. He is intellectual and supports the highest standards of logical thought, focused just on his ambitions. In the shadow aspect, his degree of rationality can leave him without a moral compass to develop his concepts. He might readily turn an indifferent eye to the consequences of his actions, resulting in a wrathful disregard for others.

Knight of Cups: Air of Water. A captivating dreamer, this is the romantic Knight ruled by his heart, who utilizes his passions as his guide. He is an idealist, which provides him the appealing quality of having a grand vision he's working towards. He often brings tidings of a relationship or an invite. In the shadow aspect, he is selfish and secretive, believing his creative creed is more critical than goodwill towards others. His ideas might be too high to reach; therefore, he winds up distracting himself going after dreams instead of focusing on the here and now. There's likewise an aspect of seduction.

Knight of Wands: Air of Fire. He is the courageous harbinger of change. He's reckless and impulsive; however, he does not seek conflict for the sake of dispute. He merely wants to throw his strength into that which he believes in. He enjoys taking action and can be generous in considering that energy to others who need it. If he's not careful, however, in his shadow aspect, he can turn prideful and vicious. He also refuses to listen if he's on the wrong side of ethical concern.

Queens

Queens is the card that shows the feminine maturity and perceived to be the middle age amongst the other cards. Each rule through the experiences of starting to understand herself and others. They all care to some degree and generally show the various ways imagination can reveal itself. While not prideful, they nonetheless significantly affect those around them and garner regard for the insight they supply. They are associated with the element of Water due to their psychological strength.

Queen of Pentacles: Water of Earth. She shows the strength of peacefulness, hard work, and achievement of heart. She is frequently extremely domestic. Through practical means, she keeps a secure budget plan and shows a lot of sound judgment. She does what she can with what she has and still finds the resources to be kind to others. In her shadow element, she ends up being mechanical, living daily without any drive to change her lot. She can be vulnerable to drug abuse, choosing an escape instead of action to deal with drudgery.

Queen of Swords: Water of Air. Highly observant, this Queen does not handle insincerity from anybody. She is a smart and keen observer, and swift to bring her foot down if she senses unethical action. Ruled by her head, she stays, at all times, independent in an idea and is characterized by efficient bluntness. She never allows her feelings to determine her will. In the shadow element, her bluntness can be harsh if her intent turns malicious. If she uses her quick observational abilities versus others, her intellectual talents can be sly.

Queen of Cups: Water of Water. She is the relaxing mom who is deeply sensitive to the psychological wellness of those she loves. Empathy and dreaminess are her most distinct qualities. She lives by her imagination and is usually highly talented in the arts. She has a keen intuition that makes her a psychic or a healer. In the shadow element, she can be susceptible to sinking so deep into her mind that she becomes confused by illusions. She might have a tough time differentiating her feelings from those of others.

Queen of Wands: Water of Fire. This dominant Queen wields authority with strong independence. Her imagination springs from her perseverance and adaptability. She is magnetic, frequently controlling the conversation in a room by the force of her character. She is the best buddy anybody could ever hope for, efficient in deep love and generosity. However, in her shadow element, she is the worst enemy you ever got. She has a tendency to brood, exhibit a quick temper, vain, and can be envious.

Kings

Here, in the Kings, we see the complete conclusion of each suit's potential in older, manly energy. He is the most fully grown, the most knowledgeable, the most steady, the one with complete control of himself and that which he rules over. He is a giver who creates stability for those around him. Because of their drive to bring things to completion, they are related to the aspect of Fire.

King of Pentacles: Fire of Earth. To use a legend to him, he is King Midas, metaphorically turning to gold all that he touches. He achieves success in service with an excellent instinct for the worth of his resources and labor. He cultivates the richness of life, whether it is monetarily or otherwise. In the shadow aspect, he lacks insight or effort, preoccupied with just what is in front of him. At his worst, he has a deformity over petty matters and can be oppressive.

King of Swords: Fire of Air. He is a militant king, a stern authority who wields a hefty sword of judgment. He commands harshly; however, with fairness, supporting the law to the very best of his capabilities. In the shadow aspect, he acts on choice without reflection and implements his rule with futile violence.

King of Cups: Fire of Water. Like all Cup Court cards, he embodies creativity; however, his is the mind that can apply emotional intelligence to his developments. In personality, he is delicate and passive, with a peaceful authority. In the shadow aspect, he is superficial and easily influenced, and vulnerable to come down with his own sensual tastes.

King of Wands: Fire of Fire. A natural leader who rules with absolute honesty and nobility. He is quick to act and understands how to push individuals to produce what he visualizes. In the shadow aspect, he can be vicious and fierce, even ruthless, in driving towards his goals.

Chapter 6: Major Arcana –
The Fool's Journey

The Major Arcana agrees to grand, overarching principles. Each card represents an archetype of the human condition and deep space. They express deep occultist meaning, and by themselves, can be totally studied for their magical weight. For the functions of divination, though, their primary significance is highlighting a point in a reading. If a Major Arcana card appears, it's usually informing the reader, "This is significant. Take note."

We will go over the significances of Major Arcana using the Journey of the Fool. This is a design of checking out the cards by visualizing the series of cards as a story, one in which we all begin as ignorant fools but, we become one with the world by taking this Journey. It is the tale of the soul becoming whole.

Each card will be described initially by it's more substantial, more spiritual implications, followed by the divinatory meanings for a fast recommendation in your readings. The matching Kabbalic qualities and astrological associations will likewise be listed with each card. This is in case you decide to fall down the tarot rabbit-hole of hermetic approach; you'll already have a concept of each card's undertone in your research studies.

Each card of the Major Arcana has a favorable and unfavorable context. We will discuss the shadow aspect of the negative card in this book. Some call this ill-dignified, or how some readers reversals. It is important that we read the shadow element as part of the card's general messages and significances.

Also, it should be noted that all tarot decks have the same number of cards and utilize the very same significances for each card. Some decks have the card Justice as XI and Strength as VIII, while others changed them around. Rider Waite-Smith deck has to do with this. Generally, due to the fact that tarot had so much relation to the mysteries of the Kabbala, the cards were numbered according to their order on the Tree of Life. This puts Justice as VIII and Strength as XI. A.E. Waite chose to switch them for his deck to line up more with their astrological significance. For the basic reader, this has little consequence. It is only discussed here due to the fact that this book follows the Rider Waite-Smith model of Justice as XI and Strength as VIII because that deck is basic for most. If your deck has them the other way, it is not a misprint; it was a choice of the deck designer.

The first half of the Major Arcana will be talked about in this chapter. This is the Journey of the Fool through the Mundane Realm. All the figures we will fulfill here are the archetypes of humanity. Here exist the elements of the Divine Masculine and the Divine Feminine. We will explore and challenge in here the relationship between us and the external world surrounding us and the way these influences show how we associate with ourselves. By checking out the Mundane Realm, we develop the spiritual knowledge and perseverance we need to turn within. We should understand and learn the elements of our nature if we are to transmutate them into something higher.

Order Number: 0 - The Fool

Association to Alchemy: Elemental Air
Path to Kabbala: Aleph, the Ox
This is the beginning of the Journey, as well as paradoxically, its end also. As the number zero suggests, it is a limitless possibility, the nothingness which all things come and all things look for to balance back to.

Frequently, the images in this card show a young man about to step off a cliff with his stare up to skies, willfully ignorant or heedless of the gorge before him. Despite all preparation and foresight, life will take us where it takes us. As often, there is absolutely nothing we can do but embrace and follow the mystery, knowing we may never ever understand its true nature.

Yet this card is not one of hopelessness by the hands of destiny. It is the commemoration of taking the very first steps to self-discovery, no matter the failures or successes, pleasures, or uncertainties. It does not matter what the ending is, for you can not know it anyway. Beginning the Journey in any way-- that is what holds effect.

Interpretations: This is a positive card of affirmation. It is typically an indication that something will come and that it is time to go into a new cycle in your life. This is the radical chance that comes along that makes you wonder if you're crazy for even thinking of it. Even more than the Aces, the Fool says go for it, regardless of what anybody else states or what questions you may have over you. Take the opportunity and jump over that high cliff. You never ever know where you may wind up, or moreover, just how you will change as a result of it.

Negative Meanings: In some cases, this card suggests authentic foolhardiness. Taking action is essential, yet if misused, it can result in a brash mindset that will throw you around without any more knowledge than you had before. All of it boils down to timing. If this card shows up on the negative side, take a U-turn, assess your activities, and hold your horses. A true opportunity will certainly come when it's ready.

Order Number: I - The Magician

Association to Alchemy: Mercury
Path to Kabbala: Beth, the House
As above, so below; as below, so above. This expression, divined centuries ago by the hermetic thinkers of the old past, envelops the power of the Magician. It expresses the hermetic

concept of communication, which specifies that one reality is a reflection of all truths, as well as any action taken in one, is also revealed with the others. There is a mirroring between the microcosm of the Self and the macrocosm of the Universe. Hence, if you can comprehend one, you can understand the other.

The initial aspect of the Divine Masculine, this card shows the will of the Self over the external. He acts creatively, one who exerts influence not by bending the world to his will but by mirroring the world. He materializes that which is within himself right into the truth around him, and also, in return, the Universe manifests something above himself within him.

The Magician helps you in aligning yourself with the world as well as to find liberation in that unity. It is the shock of power that will undoubtedly set the Journey rolling onward with whatever might come.

Interpretations: Whatever big ideas or plans you may have developed in the past, the Universe has lined up to aid you in bringing them to fruition. All the little actions and setbacks that may develop are insignificant when faced with your will to manifest your desires into reality. Now is the time, so take action.

Negative Meanings: The kind of unconscious creation exhibited by the Magician does not come with an innate conscience. Make sure your purposes come from the aligned Self and also not from individual gain before you take further action.

Often, it signifies that something is coming in and that it is time to enter a brand-new cycle in your life. If this card comes up in darkness element, take a step back, review your actions, and also be patient.

Order Number: II - The High Priestess

Association to Astrology: The Moon
Path to Kabbala: Gimel, the Camel

One of Major Arcana's most mysterious cards, the High Priestess brings a subtlety that only exhibits her deeper definition. A. E. Waite defined her as, in some respects, "the Great Arcana's holiest and highest figure."

The very first facet of the Divine Feminine, she remains, in many ways, the personification of mystery. She sits in equilibrium between the mind and the subconscious, the tangible and the astral, and functions as the conduit between them. She is frequently illustrated in front of a cloak, but her significances place her as the cloak between us and the enigma behind it. She holds the reality; however, she is the fact. She reflects the light; therefore, she is the light. What is concealed can be disclosed, and also what is revealed can be concealed, similar to the phases of the moon with which she is so very closely associated.

The High Priestess needs your intuition for real understanding due to the fact that her riddles can not be gleaned through reasonable thought. By silence, she informs you to use the knowledge you have without understanding just how you have it and advises you to listen closely. Half of the Journey happens within.

Interpretations: When the High Priestess displays in a reading, there is an indication that not all facets can be defined for you. Instinct, as well as wisdom, is the secret to opening additional expertise. Rather than searching through outside sources, hideaway within. Feel out the situation without effort, and also let your gut guide you. Occasionally, you currently have the answers you require. Have faith in that.

Negative Meanings: Sometimes, this card reveals the presence of tricks or concealed schemes. In this case, there's a requirement for open and also sincere communication to disclose what is being kept from you, or what you may be keeping from others. As always, though, when it involves the High Priestess, do so with compassion and also guided instinct. It is through quiet contemplation that we can hear the tiniest whispers.

Order Number: III - The Empress

Association to Astrology: Venus
Path to Kabbala: Daleth, the Door

The second element of the Divine Feminine, the Empress personifies abundance. She is the representation of Mother Earth, this Garden of Paradise we have actually been offered. She is life itself streaming in the sheer desert.

Bounty, as well as satisfaction, is a substantial interpretation of this card. She is the imaginative power of the greater love in all things revealed through the material plane. When the world is experienced by complete awareness of the present moment, that is the Empress manifesting. The greater realm and the physical world are not separated but an expression of it that should be understood as a piece of spiritual development. It is through our physical detects, by recognizing our bodies and our world, that we can attain greater understanding beyond what we can see. It is the platform from which we can spring off right into higher consciousness, as well as our guard when we swim out deeper and need rest. It is very important to care for our physical selves.

As your Journey takes you to the Earth, the Empress will certainly be there to hold your hand when situations appear overwhelming. She is also there to advise you to stop, pause if you need to, and quit to scent the flowers.

Interpretations: The Empress comes when nurturing is needed. Open your eyes. Walk and also appreciate nature. Express yourself artistically. Make something lovely. She is love objectified, so allow it stream from you and right into you via self-care as well as supporting others. Through her, there is more than enough to walk around. The Empress can likewise represent parenthood itself, or somebody who exhibits these high qualities.

Negative Meanings: Occasionally, overindulgence can do even more injury than good. Taking some time to appreciate the pleasures in life is critical, but without self-control, it's easy to slip into inertia and laziness. In a negative context, this card may be showing precisely what's taking place, whether it be you or a person in your life who is using your love for their advantage. Focus your creative power. It might be time to leave the garden and go handle difficulty.

Order Number: IV - The Emperor

Association to Astrology: Aries
Path to Kabbala: Heh, the Home window

If the Empress was the Holy Mother, right here, we have her counterpart, the Holy Father. He is the second aspect of the Divine Masculine. He is the hand that pushes us out of the nest.

Self-control composes the central feature of this card's message. Unlike the Magician that creates by showing a higher function, or the creative power inherent in the Empress, the Emperor is creating through the force of will. He gives policies to live by and after that, applies them for our very own gain. He is a representation of government and manifests just how it creates a structure so we might effectively live our lives as opposed to running through widespread turmoil. He shields by offering a method to prosper. Sometimes, it may appear severe, but this rigorous strategy enables us to discover how to base on our very own feet.

In your Journey, he's there to encourage you to go out there and make something on your own. It is a type of love that does not cater to due to the fact that he knows you can do more. When you also get comfy, he will undoubtedly hold you to a higher criterion as well as push you along. Through his leadership, you can be ensured that you will certainly complete your Journey.

Interpretations: Firstly, this card brings signs of authority. Recognition, framework, and also the order is exposed with the Emperor. His message is justness via a firm hand, as well as the regard that type of power can bring if used sensibly. It can likewise present more essentially a trustworthy leader or father figure.

Negative Interpretations: This card additionally provides the threat of burning out. It takes a great deal of energy to wield this much power. If not managed or permitted to relax, it can very quickly turn dangerous as well as damage what was created. This is the leader that does not know how to lead anymore. Perhaps all the focus, as well as intent you're putting into a task, is doing more damage than good. Ease up. Release control and also accept that while your power was required to create, it does not need your stringent interest anymore to maintain.

Order Number: V - The Hierophant

Association to Astrology: Taurus
Path to Kabbala: Vav, the Nail

Unlike the Emperor, who proclaims the virtue of stringent discipline, or the High Priestess, who speaks of the spirit hiding within each of us, the Hierophant uses dogma to preach redemption. He is not our guiding intuition or government. He is the whisper of culture in our ear and the exoteric pledge of faith.

The Hierophant enforces the orthodox customs of society. He is the keeper of where we have actually come from, and through the collective knowledge of the ages, he supplies essential insight. He is the instructor who guards the sacred. In return, those who yearn to discover should follow the teaching of the sacred and willing to acknowledge ignorance to seek knowledge.

The Hierophant provides the basic concepts that will guide you further on your Journey than you thought possible. He can explain the pitfalls in your path and show you shortcuts you would never have discovered. Through his mentors and your humility, there is an opportunity to find out greater spiritual knowledge than you might ever find out by yourself. You just need to be ready to follow his word.

Interpretations: This card's most immediate meaning brings to mind faith and spiritual beliefs. It can also indicate other institutions that require obedience to tradition, such as school or a court. The Hierophant is what's tried-and-true, not innovation. Discover a coach or a facility that can assist you in getting to study more. Take the opportunity to grow under guidance. Then, you can reach more learning when you lay down the groundwork that has already been found.

Negative Interpretations: The hierarchical leadership depicted in the Hierophant can take on a sadistic aspect if abused. A good teacher must help their students in going further than they themselves have reached. Customs are the ground upon which we can develop progress, not the end-all-be-all. Holding understanding back only hinders that procedure and can harm the trainee. Do not follow blindly-- if your teacher can not teach you, restore individual freedom, and seek your own course.

Order Number: VI - The Lovers

Association to Astrology: Gemini
Path to Kabbala: Zain, the Sword

As the name suggests, the Lovers represent pure human love. Romantic love is the first thing that comes to mind; however, it likewise represents the deep love we can feel in all relationships. It is our human connection with each other. It is the card of wholeness.

The Lovers is among the most challenging cards to interpret. Its instant significance is obvious, but there are many layers to this card that require much more in-depth scrutiny. While the imagery of the Lovers depicts the joy in coming together, it's fundamental implication is that there was a separation in the first place. By being two instead of one, they produce duality. Their unity provides and keeps a balance between their opposite aspects. Why is it these two instead of another set? The response and the Lovers' much more profound significance is about choice. Each choice is a duality, and tossing the balance towards one answer or another creates the life we lead. All these meanings come together to bring a message of picking with love, not with fear or embarrassment. The options based on the respect of the higher Self will combine the most harmonious components and join that which appears in conflict.

With the Hierophant's teachings, you have now pertained to the part of your Journey where the road diverges. With all the knowledge and assistance you have received so far, you are now prepared to choose your own method. You select who you like and what you believe. The choice may not always be simple; however, your honest love will be your guide from now on. Keep in mind the knowledge that was imparted to you before, and you will remain real to your higher course.

Interpretations: In its purest sense, unity, and options. It implies a relationship that has a deep soul connection if this card is drawn to show love. In other contexts, it suggests that separate parts are coming together or that a choice needs to be made. It can likewise suggest oaths, pledges, and commitment.

Negative Interpretations: The Lovers can imply the agony of separation. The aspects at work fight each other and see-saw in confusion and discomfort. The balance is wildly skewed.

Deal with bringing things together rather than letting them swing around each other. Evaluate your options more carefully.

Order Number: VII - The Chariot

Association to Astrology: Cancer
Path to Kabbala: Cheth, the Fence

The Chariot reveals accomplishment in its most exuberant form. He is the conquest of the external world.

The Chariot applies his will over in all his journeys. By focusing his mind, he drives forward to satisfy the obstacles waiting outside himself. He hurries forward and seeks to control in the name of more understanding. He wishes to know all the answers to his questions and to achieve the objectives he has in his heart. With all this focus on the external, the High Priestess speaking from within can not be heard. He has actually considered enough. He knows where he has originated from and where he desires to go. He has eyes only for the roadway ahead. He is the time for action.

Having picked your path, the Chariot comes along and sweeps you off your feet. Now that you know where you want to go on your Journey, handle the challenges ahead with your head held high.

Significances: With a goal in mind or a project at hand, the Chariot gets here to motivate you to move forward with all speed. The road to success might not be easy; however, with determination, there is no reason that you cannot accomplish what you're fated to do. Have confidence and do something about it. It can also suggest travel.

Negative Interpretations: Without the inner guidance of instinct, it is easy for the Chariot to divert off course rapidly. The Chariot's power depends on his confidence, of understanding where he stands and what he's defending. In the shadow aspect, this ends up with will with no instructions, energy with no focus. You must show an understanding of why you are moving forward. You need to read the signs, so you need to slow down. You may think you're headed on the right path, but maybe you're not.

Order Number: VIII - Strength

Association to Astrology: Leo
Path to Kabbala: Teth, the Serpent

The Chariot reveals the strength in the rule of getting rid of the external world. Strength in and of itself is the fortitude of the human spirit.

Strength turns herself inward, focusing on the exertion of will over the self instead of the world outside. She shows not just the discussion of strength, but the pleasure of that strength. She acknowledges the enthusiasm within and controls them, both to release and subdue as she allows. She is personal power, the will of the Self happy in its own authority as it aligns with its more significant purpose. For this reason, it is one of the most powerful cards in the tarot and brings the force to negate all negativity around it.

On your journey, there will be times when you will question if you can sustain any further. Strength will occur within you to bring you back to your feet and require you to continue. No matter how many kingdoms you dominate or trophies you hold on your wall, real Strength resides within. Will over the Self is the greatest prize of all.

Interpretations: Stamina and self-confidence in purpose. No matter how burnt-out you feel, know there is still heart within you to stand firm. Acknowledge that will within and savor it. You're the only one to give it to your self, and you are the only one that could take it away. This is the essential element of personal power.

Negative Interpretations: Individual power only means anything if it has self-discipline. It takes Strength to pick your fights and not let raw emotion overcome you. Permit them to stream when the time is right and keep them under wraps when they would just bring damage. Tame what is wild, and you will have an understanding of the fortitude and patience that lies within you.

Order Number: IX - The Hermit

Association to Astrology: Virgo
Path to Kabbala: Yod, the Open Hand

The Hermit lights up the course on which he strolls. He is the wise man who does not desire to conquer, but instead, holds the light of Truth, understanding that even in the darkest times, this light will direct him more than sheer self-discipline ever could.

While the Hermit is a design of knowledge and experience, his true significance relates more to attainment. He is the fertility of understanding Truth. He is, in some cases, connected with seclusion. However, it should be explained that he is not withdrawn because of abhorrence to humanity or to keep Truth from others. Rather, because attaining this knowledge frequently leads down a solitary path. The Divine Mysteries, by their very nature, position themselves where it is challenging to reach them. The extremely existence of the Hermit shows that. He sought them out, and so too can anyone.

The Journey leads you down a winding road. You might find yourself alone at times; however, in the distance, the Hermit holds up the light of Truth to guide your method. It is your inner assistance alone, which obliges you to reach it. The Hermit will not bring it to you. When obtained, it will expose the fertile ground of an entirely new level of spiritual ascension, and your Journey will continue.

Interpretation: The Hermit talks about the introspection of self-discovery. This can indicate actually withdrawing from social life, but it can likewise describe merely not permitting the outside world to sidetrack you. Instead, finding out to observe your own inner light. The Hermit is a pivotal point where your current path may not indicate much to you anymore. Nobody but yourself can direct you to the next action. Contemplate, and seek your Truth.

Negative Interpretations: The Hermit, at his worst, represents unmerited seclusion. Spiritual growth does not require cutting off the world completely. You do that, and you reject others the opportunity to find Truth on their own because you have actually hidden your light from them. Everyone has the ability to redeem themselves and seek a greater purpose. Though we might stroll the path to Truth alone, we expand the light of it by helping others to explore it too.

Order Number: X - The Wheel of Fortune

Association to Astrology: Jupiter
Path to Kabbala: Kaph, the Palm

The Wheel of Fortune is a state of constant modification. What goes up should come down, and what walks around comes around.

The Wheel flows the fortunes of everybody, often bestowing good, sometimes bad, but always with the understanding that all will alter in time. When things appear dreadful, and you're stuck in a rut, this can be excellent news. If fortune seems to be preferring you now, however, keep in mind that the good times can't last permanently. The Wheel exemplifies the hermetic concept of rhythm. A pendulum swings both methods. Things can't stay the same, and that's alright. That is the universe at work. Just know that, in time, the Wheel will swing right back around, and around, and around. In all this change, though, there is a stability to the Wheel's turning, a providence around which all fortunes take place. The center o-f the Wheel is Divine Intent and the understanding that all things happen for a reason. The Wheel will take you where you need to be when you require to be there. It is within this framework that our free will lies.

Your journey takes you past the realms of the ordinary. Now, you enter where the fantastic cosmic forces rule, and for the very first time, with the light of Truth, you can finally begin to see them at work. The Wheel of Fortune eternally cycles overhead, revolving with the sun and the moon, the change of the seasons, and the rotation of the stars through the year. From here on, you walk your Journey with the clarity of that rhythm.

Interpretations: As the Wheel swings, you require to grab hold and choose its flow. Adjust to the modification it declares, for worse or for much better, and benefit from where it leads. Courses open and close throughout your life, sometimes without warning, but always as a chance to enter a new direction.

Negative Interpretations: The Wheel is a force greater than yourself. It moves beyond your impact, and absolutely nothing you can do will stop it. If you try, it will grind you down and require you into its rhythm anyhow. Stop battling it. Instead, learn the wisdom to work within its system.

Chapter 7: Major Arcana – The Justice in the World

We enter the Cosmic World as we discuss the second half of the Major Arcana. Here, our Journey brings us face to face with the concepts that rule over our lives, so big of a force that we do not even see them from our restricted viewpoint.

By learning control over the Self through the Mundane World, now when we peel back the curtain and see the greater powers, we are more able to assess our location within them. We can not alter how deep space works. We are only able to change our actions within it. But we belong to the Universe, a reflection of it, a spiritual being eternally connected to the greater picture. These figures in the Cosmic Realm exist within us also. By acknowledging how they rule our lives, we can, in turn, control them within ourselves, and pertain to a higher understanding of our Selves as a whole being. Through this part of the Journey, we should put aside the ego and dive more profound still.

Order Number: XI - Justice

Association to Astrology: Libra
Path to Kabbala: Lamed, the Ox Goad

Justice, in spite of her name, does not personify what is simply in the typical sense of the term. There are no ethical disputes to confuse the concern before her. Justice of the tarot is Karmic Law, and she does not care for moral debate.

In some circles, Justice is believed to be the female counterpart of the Fool. Zero is the number of the Fool, emphasizing the nothingness where a thing came from. On the other hand, Justice is the system that rigorously stabilizes everything to this potential, like a mathematical formula. Ramifications are administered to maintain stability, in which equilibrium is not controlled by reasons. Every action has a response. That is the Law. Her estimations cause constant modification and satisfy all possibilities. Unlike the Wheel of Fortune, which turns, whether we want it or not, and will always cycle back around, Justice deals in absolutes. When she brings her sword down, there is no going back. There is no argument to make, for her word is entirely grounded by what is fair, whether you like it or not.

Your Journey brings you to the feet of Justice. She will hold you responsible for your actions thus far. Karmic Law needs to be supported before you can continue, and while she will not judge you to be wrong or great, she will bring you to deal with the consequences of your choices. Observe her well and understand her absolute hand. This will enable you to make wiser, more well-considered choices as you move on.

Interpretations: Justice calls you for judgment. Typically, this is not a pleasant experience. It is hard to deal with consequences. Nevertheless, this can bring a sense of relief. As soon as Justice has been served, you can carry on without the weight of your past. Face the music so you can move on. She can likewise suggest an actual lawsuit, often with a favorable outcome.

Negative Interpretations: If you attempt to blame your mistakes on others or decline to own up to the fact that where you are is because of what you have actually done, you just frustrate yourself. Justice has cast judgment on you already. It depends on you to accept the judgment and get a wider perspective. Otherwise, you will stay stuck with karmic weight.

Order Number: XII - The Hanged Man

Association to Alchemy: Elemental Water
Path to Kabbala: Mem, the Water

The Hanged Man is an extremely complicated card and of specific significance to mystical mystics. He reveals the spiritual function of the act of baptism and sacrifice. The 'Drowned Guy' is what it is called in the old days, which emphasized this significance and his connection to water more plainly.

The Hanged Man is the acceptance of the divine will. The old mythologies about the journeys to the underworld are closely related to the Hanged Man, most specifically Odin of the Norse mythology and Orpheus from the Greek. In fact, the illustrations on this card are influenced by the story of Odin, who, for nine days, dangled upside-down in a tree so that he can go to the underworld. The Hanged Man dangles upside down by one ankle, putting himself at the mercy of suffering so that he might be initiated to secret knowledge. Like baptism, it is a symbolic death of the old Self, so a more authentic viewpoint might be discovered. The Hanged Man is linked to water as a symbol of the underworld. He suspends himself near death so that he can find what he sensed to be missing. By crossing that barrier, he gets insight into the relation of the divine to the universe and reanimates to bring that knowledge back to the world, just as Odin restored the runes when he returned.

Who you were on your Journey needs to be compromised to what you will end up being. The Hanged Man sets the example for you. However, it is not he who can hand you the rope. You need to submit by your own hand so you might enter into the worlds of the unknown. Your will for the divine is the exchange for greater understanding.

Interpretations: In the standard significances derived for prophecy, this card generally indicates surrender. The Hanged Man tells you to launch the previous outlook, for they no longer serve you. Submit to the process voluntarily. This time out in your life is required.

Negative Interpretations: The Hanged Man likewise displays the discomfort of suspension. You may not desire this brand-new perspective; however, you are now feeling strung up. In some cases, stagnating at all is the very best strategy. Aggravation won't fix the scenario, and more force will not assist you.

Order Number: XIII - Death

Association to Astrology: Scorpio
Path to Kabbala: Nun, the Fish

This is the card of supreme improvement. It does not describe what came before or what will come after. It just embodies the process of one becoming the other.

In the previous card of the Hanged Man, death was utilized symbolically as a means to insight. The Hanged Man baptizes himself in the waters of death, hangs from the tree in a gesture of death, but all with the intent of returning to himself with more understanding acquired. In the Death card, there is no returning. It is the door from one phase to the next, and whoever crosses it will not come back. What is scary about Death is the finality that it brings. This card does not normally prophesize doom and gloom. It is very rare for it to show a literal death. Rather, it is the harbinger of change. Whatever that was will be taken down to the ground to make room for what will be. There would be no space for anything brand-new if whatever stayed the very same. Death brings with it a message of painful passage into a new phase of life.

On Journey's course, a dark figure stands in the way. There is no going around-- with Death, you either turn back or you send yourself to his scythe. There is no going back to what you were as soon as you are on this Journey. Despite your worry, with the knowledge gained from the sacrifice of the Hanged Man, you know the value in enabling change to occur. You can not continue forward without it. And so you kneel before Death, and he cuts you down.

Interpretations: The most significant promise of Death is Renewal. Like a forest after a fire, there is now the opportunity for new development to rise from the ashes of the old that would have smothered it. There is filtration in the process of purging what no longer serves you.

Negative Interpretations: Life has become an overload of decay. Things have actually stagnated and begun to decompose. There is a clinging to the old methods, and without any flush of water to clean things out, life itself has actually become sick.

Order Number: XIV - Temperance

Association to Astrology: Sagittarius
Path to Kabbala: Samekh, the Personnel

Temperance evokes balance, but the card is not just about balance the same as with Justice. Temperance is the art of creating that balance.

This card is also known in some decks as Art or Alchemy. This brings to light that the balance here is sought through the synthesis of things. It can be straight connected back to the idea started in the Lovers, which talked about separate parts stabilizing to produce a steady working relationship. In Temperance, these different parts are somewhat unified, and balance is created not by weighing something against another; however, by enabling them to chemically combine and react into something which is stabilized in and of itself. That act is a form of production; however, instead of springing from the ground, it is the creativity of taking what currently exists and reforming it. These elements can become disorderly when separated. When fused together, they form a cohesive whole.

On your Journey, you wake from Death and find yourself altered. All the pieces of you from your Journey already lay spread on the ground. The love of the Empress. The enthusiasm of the Chariot. The knowledge of the Hermit. All of them are a part of you but have not come together to form who you are. Temperance comes and gathers them and mixes them before your eyes. All you have gone through has tempered to a whole. You know where you have originated from; now, pieced back together, you understand where you must go from here.

Interpretations: By accommodating the different parts of yourself and of your life, you strike a balance. You have actually ended up being very particular in who you are; therefore, you are able to deal with what comes your way with patience and clarity. You produce order out of chaos. On a more ordinary level, it can suggest small amounts.

Negative Interpretations: There is a sense of excess in this card. If the balance is required to be developed, then something was off in the first place. There is also the possibility that some things simply can't be harmonized.

Order Number: XV - The Devil

Association to Astrology: Capricorn
Path to Kabbala: Ayin, the Eye

The Devil shows a carelessness of results. In a manner, he presents the bliss of material things, but likewise how far they can drag us down.

There is a basic pleasure in indulging the desires, of letting go and letting wild. On its surface, there is nothing incorrect with that. The issue with the Devil is that he is unsystematic in what he enjoys. He revels in everything, be it healthy or harmful, and does not suffer from ethical dilemmas. He does not care what is wrong or best, just what makes him feel excellent. The Devil tempts with his easy joy, and when you're not looking, binds you to worldly satisfaction he offers. He reveals the short-sighted view of pursuing what you desire without concerning the repercussions. He likewise shows the desertion of the spiritual. One does not require to be austere to satisfy their spirit. However, the Devil's trap is an easy one to fall under, and if not cautious, the worldly can replace the spiritual exceptionally quickly.

The Devil comes and offers you a drink. "It's a long journey. You should take a break and have a good time for a while," he says. You join him, and one drink turns into another, then another, then another, for many days. It feels so good and simple at the time. One night you pass out, and when you wake up, you find a chained shackle around your ankle — the Devil towers above you, chain in hand. "You have actually done so much already. Do you require to keep having a hard time? You must just stay here," he states and gives you another beverage.

Interpretations: The Devil's mantra is known to be instant gratification. This is you giving over to your shadow side and enabling bad choices to rule your life. You are stuck in the rut of the patterns of your habits. At his worst, he typically reveals addiction or abuse, even violence. His look in a reading shows the chains that bind you from living as your finest self. Nevertheless, in seeing the chains, you are that much closer to releasing yourself of them.

Negative Interpretations: The Devil has completely blinded you. Under his impact, you have actually grown weak and allowed your petty desires to own you totally. As a result, you suffer the effects.

Order Number: XVI - The Tower

Association to Astrology: Mars
Path to Kabbala: Peh, the Mouth

More than the Death card, this is the sign that makes a tarot reader sweat. The Tower is a speedy catastrophe. Everything is annihilated whenever this card is drawn.

The Tower is that which shakes your essential understanding of deep space. All the rules you have lived by thus far are revealed to be lies, and you are left without a leg to base on. You are left disoriented most of the time. How can you ensure what to count on when everything can come crashing down at a moment's notification? As agonizing as it might be, this is the quintessential core of spiritual awakening. It resembles the principles from the philosophy of the Eastern culture. Therefore, all symptoms of this world, for great or wicked, are rot upon Nothingness. The Tower, then, ends up being the automobile of emancipation from the existence that traps us. Its destruction shows you how absurd it was to cling to it in the first place. Life is all impression. Not even your ego suggests anything. The Tower strips you of everything so that you might see nothing within everything.

The Devil has you locked up in a Tower. He binds you there by soothing you with an easy life and informs you how sensible you are. So you stay. You think about your Journey, every once in a while, and see the course of it from your window. However, you constantly turn back to the convenience of the Tower. The Journey was hard, and you discovered enough. Life here is great. Lightning strikes. In a rain of fire, it comes crumbling down, and the only method to conserve yourself is to leap from the window. You land on your Journey's course and watch as whatever in which you found solace is damaged. Right that moment, you realize that all that matters is being present in the moment.

Interpretations: This card declares an imminent disaster. Utter devastation is foreseen, and the suffering of having to pick up the pieces. The confusion will destabilize everything you have actually ever known.

Negative Interpretations: This card is one in which the shadow element actually draws out the good in it. In this case, this means spiritual knowledge. You have actually seen the chaos around you and utilized it as a means of personal development. You now know the facade and become aware of the true worth crazes.

Order Number: XVII - The Star

Astrological Association: Aquarius
Path to Kabbala: Tzaddi, the Fish Hook

After the tragedy of the Tower, we can now see the truth being revealed in the full light of the Star. She is the free-flowing presents given by the Spirit.

The immortality is brought about by the Star because there is no separation between the Divine Spirit and the core of the Self. She embodies the individual growth that happens after the Tower. This is the soul who held up against the worst and came out its best. This is because of the idea that with the Star, all things are valued and fully comprehended for what they are, be they bad or good. All things have a purpose in this world. In her light, true blessings stream forth, and the outermost Star is within reach.

Through the taking down of the Tower, your Journey has cleaned out all of the things that have kept you away from what you truly are inside of you. The ego has been gotten rid of, and your purest sense now exists within you. The Star shines down on you and puts the Divine down onto you like water. Faith is your power.

Interpretations: Its most fundamental analysis is hope in the sense that the Star presents the brightest possibilities. That's just a surface reading. The Star represents a lot more. The Divine is all over, and you are connected to it. One does not require hope when joined fully and absolutely to Spirit. Stay open to the gifts pouring down on you.

Negative Interpretations: There's an arrogance here, a mindset of being higher than you. This is not a real spiritual motivation. If your faith is checked, you may find it to be easily shaken until the Star can really shine.

Order Number: XVIII - The Moon

Association to Astrology: Pisces
Path to Kabbala: Koph, the Mind

This is considered the Soul's dark knight. After the knowledge found in the Star, after that euphoric, ideal satisfaction, the soul swings back into doubt and worry. This is the power of the Moon.

This is a time when it will seem like you're feeling your method through the dark. The Moon is the unknown. This type of pressure raises the animalistic instinct in all of us as well as our tendency to feel fear. This is all subconscious activity of the deep processes that drive us. In defense of the intensity of the previous two cards, the subconscious draws up veils again and makes us see bogeymen where there are just shadows. Now, more than ever, our intuition is our only guide.

The brightness of the Star fades, and you are just left with the light of the Moon on your Journey. You stumble and fall, and freeze in worry. Everywhere around you, threat lurks, and wolves growl. You don't know how you will ever make it through. Deep within you, something pushes you along, makes you look twice at the shadows. You begin to see they are just branches moving in the wind, and that the wolves are only dogs alert to your presence. Uneasily, you move through your fear and push forward through the night.

Interpretations: This card serves to show you that there may be numerous things hidden deep within your psyche that are rearing their heads. You might not know what they are precisely, but they are affecting you, and you feel their existence. This card embodies uncertainty and worry. Things are never what they seem under the light of the Moon.

Negative Interpretations: This is the silence when you know that the sound should be there. There is still the component of fear, but this silence just brings out what is unidentified. You know innate signs are coming your way, but you can't hear them. And yet, you're still scared, due to the fact that you understand there's something out there you need to be aware of. Be still and listen more.

Order Number: XIX - The Sun

Association to Astrology: The Sun
Path to Kabbalah: Resh, the Head

The Sun exposes all visions for what they are and detangles all secrets. It is the most positive card in the deck and shines its light on whatever around it.

Instead of the subconscious rising, this is total awareness. This is the soul in complete realization of itself. There is a particular simpleness in this card, of just being what it is, the heat and joy and energy of all happiness made to manifest. The consciousness and subconsciousness are combined as one. The soul is considered a whole.

The dawn comes after the night. You can now see on the horizon as the Sun rises, repelling all shadows and leaving the Journey clear for you ahead. You indulge in its light, enable the heat to charge you, and with a deep breath, you continue on your course in its light.

Interpretations: This is a time when you can share the absolute best of yourself. This card has a lot of energy in it and might indicate a period where you will be so complete that you will not know what to do with yourself. Life is good with this card. If you're looking for a 'yes' in your reading, this is a 'yes' yelled from the mountaintops.

Negative Interpretations: The light of the Sun exposes everything. Some things might emerge that may not be pleasant to look at. The Sun is a uniformly favorable card, even in negative contexts, so this exposure is continuously a great thing, like hanging something out in the sun to air out. Absolutely nothing can destroy this beautiful day.

Order Number: XX - Judgment

Association to Alchemy: Fire
Path to Kabbala: Shin, the Tooth

The last transition is now happening. This is the stage beyond modification and death. This is the waiting of eternal life if there will be a response to the call.

'The Last Judgment' is what they call this card originally, referring to the Book of Revelations of the Christianity wherein the world's end is on the horizon, and the dead rise from their graves to deal with the completion of times. In the tarot, it represents the soul lining up with its greatest goal. The enlightened will rise and leave behind their worldliness once they have received the call, as the spirit leaves the body in death. It might sound a bit morbid; however, in actuality, this is the greatest aspiration the spirit can have. In Eastern terms, this is the receiving of Nirvana.

The Journey leads to you a gravesite, empty, and open. It is your size, and you know it is yours. You can hear the trumpet from up above. The clouds part and the angel of Judgment comes down to you and offers you a hand. "Your Journey has been completed," the angel states. "Come and carry out your real function in this life." You rise in the sky as you take hold of the hand of the angel.

Interpretations: This card shows entering into a substantial phase of your life. You might have encountered significant crossroads where you have two unique options: go the safe way and remain where you are, or go and follow the call in the hidden desires of your heart. Your function in this life may take lots of twists and turns to get to. However, with every weave that brings you closer to it, Judgment will exist to remind you that you are on the method.

Negative Interpretations: The flesh is still weak, no matter how willing the soul is. You hear the call, but you do not listen whether out of a sense of comfort or fear. Instead of growing, you stay where you are. In some readings, this card also appears to refer to legal concerns, usually suggesting a sentence will be passed.

Order Number: XXI - The World

Association to Alchemy: Earth
Path to Kabbala: Tav, the Mark

The World is a card of commemoration. It is the Cosmic Joke, of the pure and utter belly-laugh bliss that comes when you attain knowledge and understand that you are what you are looking for.

Here, as in the Fool, the paradox of the beginning and the end is the World. The Fool and the World are the same; however, also opposites. The Fool goes out from nothing, and the World goes back to nothing. They form a complete cycle. Manifestation has culminated to the highest degree, and with that process done, attempts to go back to zero and begin once again. For that is the cycle of the universe and all things within it, which has actually been shown several times throughout the Major Arcana. Endings develop beginnings, and beginnings create endings. The ending displayed in the World is the most perfect and intense. The great work of the soul has actually come to an end with the soul accompanying the universe. Because of this, it once again ends up in nothingness; therefore, you start from the beginning.

Having passed through Judgment, you come to the end of your Journey. You now acknowledge that all the difficulties you went through en route were there to prime you for this. You are the universe, and you always were. It just now, though, that you see this for what it is. You blend into the nothingness, whole and complete within yourself and whole and so fulfilled with the World. You understand you will manifest again as the Fool, ready to begin once again, but for now, you go into happiness.

Interpretations: This is a sign that change is coming. You already completed one phase of your life, so prepare to start another. A sense of closure accompanies this and the joy of having achieved a lot as well as excitement to what will come. Take the lessons learned from this phase of your life and utilize it to help you with the next. In a more grounded sense, the World can likewise show the literal globe, perhaps take a trip abroad.

Negative Interpretations: You can't move on. There is an unpleasant sense of being insufficient; therefore, you remain immobile in life, allowing inertia to dictate your life. Do not let the fear of challenges to hold you back-- they exist to assist you in growing.

Chapter 8: Methods in Reading the Tarot Cards

When you are ready to begin practicing spreads, look for a couple of cards that you feel comfortable working with. You just require simple spreads that utilize a few cards when you're just beginning to learn. Even the most experienced Fortuneteller still takes advantage of a three-card spread.

Start by making sure that you're cards are free of energy then begin to shuffle them properly. You will want to meditate on the questions asked while shuffling no matter what spreads you have. Continue to shuffle the cards as you repeat your concern till you feel ready to lay them down.

Feel free to cut the deck a lot of times as you want or have the person you read for shuffle and cut them. Find a routine that gets you in the best head area to analyze and interpret the images you are about to see. You might feel the need to use a "clarifying card." When you pull an extra card to provide more context to a spread, this is. You do not wish to use this as a crutch; however, it can be utilized when more info is required.

If you have a friend that has the ability to help you, try doing this workout to improve your ability to compare and contrast. You can utilize this method of practicing for concentrating on the whole deck, the Major Arcana by itself, or the Minor Arcana independently. In any case, you'll start by shuffling the deck. As soon as mixed, take the card on the top and put it to the right in front of you. This is the card for your friend. Get the succeeding card and put it quite a bit to the left of the former card, as the card will represent the event that will happen to you. Perform a mini-reading. Do this once again with the next two cards and work your method through the entire deck. This will increase your familiarity with the cards and get you used to look at all the cards equally.

It should be noted that the cards are all equivalent, and we should have any reservations with drawing particular cards. Try to come up with different impressions and significances instead of one stiff definition of each card. Don't spend too much time on any card or set of cards. You can ask a simple question before each draw, or you can merely perform this exercise to create your own stories for the cards simply.

To look even further into the card's relationship in a spread, focus on if they are dealing with one another or if they are facing away from each other. What type of indicators turns up when we take note of the way the figures in the cards are facing? Check out your cards and discover characters in each card that are looking away or towards each other.

Ask yourself the questions listed below:

- Are they neglecting each other?
- What are these cards communicating?
- Why might they be dealing with away from each other, or facing each other regarding this situation or question?
- Is the subject unfavorable or favorable?
- What's the function of this interaction?

Spreads

One Card

As discussed in the past, you can just pull one card a day. Set your intent before you pull the card by asking what energy you require to concentrate on, or what you might experience in your day. Make a note about what card you drew and what stood out to you about it. At the end of the day, journal any correlations you discovered.

Three Card Spreads

1.   Scenario- Action- Result

In unclear circumstances, this three-card spread can be especially practical. The left card, the Circumstance, is the thing you've inquired about. This may look unlike what you expected, but it will give insight into what's going on. The middle card, the Action card, is a suggestion of the action needed to get to the Result Card, which can be found on the right.

2.   Blessings- Obstacles- Action

Another Three Card Spread is the Blessings, Obstacles, Action spread. This spread can be advantageous if you are seeking clearness regarding the next step. Laid the same way as the Past, Present, and Future spread, this reveals where you will find help in this aid in the Blessings position. For Obstacles, you see what problem you require to fix, or what you're up against. With the Action position, it represents what you need to or ought to refrain from doing to resolve the difficulty.

3.   Past-Present-Future

Lots of Three Card spreads connect to the Past, Present, and Future. Lay down the cards starting from the left to the right, and they will represent the past, present, and future positions. You can find the things that formed who you are and what's taking place in your life now as well as get an indication of where the energy in your life is leading. Your present actions have the power to alter all.

Five Card Spread

1.   The card on the top is the probable result if the course of action has complied.
2.   The fourth card shows our future results.
3.   The card positioned in the center is the representation of our present circumstances.
4.   The left of center position exposes those things in our past that still affect us currently.
5.   The bottom or the far-left position represents the causes that resulted in the situation at hand.

Celtic Cross Spread

Among the most popular spreads, the Celtic Cross uses ten cards in a circle/line design. There are numerous variations regarding how the cards are laid, but they will usually include five cards (one in the middle and four cards surrounding it-- one on each side of the middle card and one card laid sideways on the center card.). Then a line to the right of those 5 for cards 7 through 10.

1.   Center card on the bottom. The first card you lay. It represents the present condition.
2.   Center card laid on top of Card # 1. It represents your Current Barriers and Difficulties.
3.   Above the center card, expressing the very best result possible.
4.   To the Right of the center card, representing the cause for the current scenario.
5.   Listed below the center card, representing your near past.
6.   To the left of the center card, representing your future.

7.   On the Bottom of the Line to the right of the circle. This card represents, in general, who you are right now and your relationship to the theme of the concern.

8.   Directly above the other card, this position represents your existing environments as it connects to your question. (environment, family, buddies).

9.   Directly above the preceding card, representing worries and hopes concerning the scenario or your life in general if there is no specific question.

10.   The top and last card of the line, this card represents the result, or how this phase is ending up.

Horseshoe Spread

A seven-card spread where there is one main card placed in the center and has actually 3 cards laid on either side of it, forming a staggered version of a horseshoe. This spread is checked out from left to right.

1.   The Past (The first card on the bottom left working towards the Center and down the right side).

2.   Today.

3.   Surprise Influences.

4.   You, or the Querent.

5.   Attitudes of others.

6.   What you must do.

7.   The Outcome.

There are so many spreads for you to learn and multiple variations on each one that you must have plenty to experiment with. Find which spreads you are comfortable with. You can use certain spreads for certain types of questions or for a deeper understanding of the cards' relationships.

You may choose to include reverse cards in your readings, or not. Don't feel pressured to do anything you're not prepared to dedicate to!

The Fool's Journey

When establishing a greater connection with the Tarot, you may wish to begin with "The Fool's Journey." Imagine yourself as the Fool, and we will travel through each of the cards of the Major Arcana. This can assist you in developing those associations you will trust when carrying out readings. This exercise is a fantastic method to view the cards objectively. Using The Fool's Journey to practice learning the Tarot will also help you comprehend the personality and energies of each archetype.

On this journey, the Fool gets more informed as they travel.

1.   The Fool - The hero of our story into the Major Arcana. There is so much excitement for the approaching Divine journey that we don't always enjoy our step, and we have no awareness of the risks coming our way.

2.   The Magician - He teaches the Fool and ignites his inquisitiveness. All possibilities are set out in the form of tools from each Suit, and the Fool sees all the directions they can take. The Fool wonders if the Magician had these tools already or if they were developed just then.

3.   The High Priestess - Another instructor who pleads the Fool to utilize their instinct prior to entering into scenarios. She's the reverse of the Magician, being quiet and still. She hands the Fool ancient scrolls, and they discover that through introspection, they have actually chosen which action or path they will pursue.

4.   The Empress - A mom figure and developer. She advises the Fool that this path will need patience and that they will need to establish a way to manage this new production. She impresses the need for time to develop and loving attention.

5.   The Emperor - A father figure that reveals the Fool the importance of discipline and authority. The Fool is impressed at how the Emperor is complied with and discovers that

strong will and braveness will help them handle their quest. The Fool is now prepared to lead and heads away from the Emperor with a new purpose.

6. The Hierophant - Reveals the value of Custom to the Fool. The Fool realizes the fear they have regarding what they have constructed. The Hierophant begs the Fool to consider all choices and understand the legacy of what has been gotten. The Fool is at ease as he heads away on his journey.

7. The Lovers- The Fool comes across the Lovers in between the present path they are on and new love. They decide between continuing down the road they were currently on and deciding to take this new Love they have discovered along with them. The Fool makes the option to pick Love and heads down a whole brand-new road.

8. The Chariot - Teaches the Fool to make and keep the course up on their mind so that success is inescapable. The Fool eventually loses faith in the journey and enables enemies and situations, even their own confusion to delay and derail them. The Charioteer encourages the Fool to put on their armor, decide about their willpower, and to run over anything standing in the way. The Fool comprehends that triumph is just the beginning.

9. Strength - This is the figure that shows the Fool calm confidence and power. The Fool leaves the Charioteer feeling proud and effective. They stumble upon Strength closing the mouth of a lion, and they want to link to the greater energy that was used. Strength advises the Fool to direct their passions to get more out of them.

10. The Hermit - Encourages the Fool to believe introspectively of all the lessons learned so far. After the experiences gained from Strength, the Fool requires time to pull away. Meeting the Hermit, the Fool begins to see those hidden areas of their minds. The Fool understands they have the power to brighten the darkness.

11.   The Wheel of Fortune - The Fool sees that nothing is ever complete and that life is repeated cycles. The Fool comes out of hiding with the Hermit and discovers that they need an alteration. The Fool learns how things change by the hour, in a never-ending way. The Fool begins to feel that everything is coming back to them three-fold.

12.   Justice - The Fool discovers to be just and sensible. The Fool learns Justice is making a reasonable choice that benefits both parties even though they do not necessarily see it that way. Justice shows the Fool to straighten their inner scales and preserve balance.

13.   The Hanged Man - The Fool is changed by the experience of being turned upside down and inspecting life from a brand-new point of view. The Fool leaves Justice and hangs around under a tree in deep introspection. They awaken and begin to hang upside down from the tree and surrenders everything and receives an amazing minute of awareness. With their heads filled with these visions, the Fool continues.

14.   Death - The Fool finds out the value of death and cleaning out the old to bring in the brand-new. The Fool starts to feel sorrowful at the awareness the former methods are gone. Death took them due to the fact that the old ways and old self were compromised. The Fool is ravaged at a loss, however, understands it's natural to mourn so that new things have space. As Death leaves, the Fool seems as if everything has actually been stripped away. He starts to move again.

15.   Temperance - The Fool Learns to put two opposites together in the formation of a third, balanced force. The Fool encounters Temperance blending the contents of their cups together and is amazed to discover that all contrast can create a unified third.

16.   The Devil - The Fool sees the dependencies they have subjected themselves to. As the Fool passes by the mountain, they begin to feel desires come back, and they rail against them, thinking it's a test of spirituality. The Devil recommends the Fool that it's merely the critical things that already exist within them that are being realized which they can be used on the mission. The Fool learns that some utilize the impulses to reach the greatest heights and refuse to find contentment in the fixations. The Fool leaves understanding this key.

17.   The Tower - The Fool sees the collapse of whatever they formerly believed but discovers a method to start anew. When the Fool passes the Tower, they remember constructing it when they had to make a mark on the world and prove themselves. In a flash, the Fool understands that he is no different from the conceited individuals sitting inside the Tower. The Fool comprehends that he is not singular and superior. The Fool shouts out this realization, and the Tower is struck by lightning, bringing it down to debris. The Fool feels extensive worry; however, he feels their insight has actually opened. The lies on the Fool's life are damaged, and he is forced to restore the structure of reality.

18.   The Star - The Fool finds a period of quiet recovery. When they come across the woman reflecting starlight holding two urns, the Fool feels lost and is in anguish. She invites the Fool to be invigorated and assists in healing their injured heart. The Fool admires the stars, and the female explains that by concentrating on one possible future or start, that they will be directed to their destination.

19.   The Moon - The Fool finds out that the majority of their troubles are just impressions of the mind. With restored Hope, the Fool continues down the course that is now brightened by the Moon. The Fool realizes they are in a strange land that he thought to be beyond the veil. The Fool sees the boat in the distance and understands that while he can stay in this primal land of secret, he can also trust himself

to the river as the Moon is in control either way. In the boat, the Fool surrenders to the magic of the Moon and sleeps.

20.   The Sun - The Fool discovers a clean slate. When the Fool awakens to the dawn, a kid's laughter is heard, and the Fool enjoys the kid take joy in all the important things being discovered. The Fool finds himself smiling and feels light and brightened. The Fool sees the world in a new light and observes as the kid faces the sunlight realizing that he is actually the child. The Fool recognizes that they have actually satisfied their own inner light. Feeling that they are close to completion of their journey, the Fool continues to take the last steps.

21.   Judgment - The Fool learns how to carry on and how to forgive themselves. The Fool sees Judgement and discovers that there is only one last action to handle this journey; however, that it can not be taken up until the past is put to rest. Judgment discusses that the only way to eliminate the past that we stroll with under our feet is to call it up and comes to terms with it. The Fool is handed a small trumpet and understanding that Judgement is right; he needs to pertain to terms with whatever that has happened. When the Fool blows the trumpet, the Earth is split, and all the Fools past selves rise up to be faced. The Fool forgives all these past-selves and reaches an understanding with them. The Fool ends up being reborn and returned to reside in the present. He takes that final step.

22.   The World - The Fool comprehends the world is theirs and that the cycle begins again. When they initially began, the Fool is bemused to discover that same cliff they started from. Seeing this position in a different way, the Fool comprehends that everything is intertwined, and everything is One. The Fool makes his way to the edge of the cliff and is drawn upward to a place where he can view the entire world. He becomes one with the universe, and the journey begins as it concerns an end.

Guided Reading 1

In this example Reading, we will do a Three Card Spread suggesting Past, Present, and Future.

The question we are asking is, "How can I improve in my profession today?".

The cards laid from left to right are the Five of Cups, the Three of Cups, and the Queen of Cups.

Understanding that Cups represent Emotion, we currently know that Emotions are profoundly affecting how we (or the querent) conduct service.

Let's break down every card and the location they are in:

1.   Initial Position - Five of Cups.
We understand that the Five's represent Forfeiture and Remorse, along with Exploration. This tells us that the Five of Cups represent crying over spilled milk. It shows us not having a great mindset and what we have been delighting in the past.

2.   Second Position - Three of Cups.
We found out that the Three's show a Commitment and Togetherness in addition to Creativity. This informs us that we need to join forces with others. It can likewise suggest that we need to make time for a break for reflection.

3.   Third Position - Queen of Cups.
The Queen of Cups awakens the Spirituality in others and holds a space for herself. Once we get our Feelings under control, this can advise us that things are being brought back to success. This shows that the more adjusted you remain in your Psychological life, the much better your profession will be.

Bonus Carded Readings

Two Card Share

For this next example, we will use the two-card quick pull that we utilized to introduce ourselves to the cards. Presuming that you have a pal with you, start by shuffling and then each of you cutting the deck. Place the first card in front of yourself, and the 2nd card in front of your good friend. In this sample, we won't be asking a question of the deck; however, utilizing the cards to ask concerns of ourselves based upon the interpretation of the cards.

1. Your Card - The Chariot. This card brings us to ask what encourages us. What is driving us? What in your life are you fiercely determined to accomplish?
2. Friends Card - The Hanged Man. This card has us ask Where we require to include Compromise? It also has us ask what in our life is presently "on hold or stalled?"

Assess the cards you pull for a minute, bear in mind of any questions or insights that resonate with you and draw again!

Movie Scene Spread

Pull a card and describe the card as a scene in a movie. Don't bother with your instinct in the meantime. Just call what you see in the card as if it's a scene in a movie. For example, we'll pull The Tower. Ask yourself the following concerns relating to The Tower.

-       What kind of scene is this? Is it a beginning scene or an action scene? The Tower would profoundly resonate with an action scene.

-       What is taking place in this scene? People are falling out of the Tower, things are on fire, and it seems frightening.

Pull another card. We'll choose The Queen of Wands:

-       What type of scene is this? When you come across a Face card, they are normally just sitting there. Pull the 2nd card to place over it a little. Now, image the figure from your Court card in the scenario presented in the second card. We pull the Eight of Swords as our 2nd card.

-       How does the Queen function as the figure put into the Eight of Swords? The fertility and joy in the Queen card now look like she is in trouble with the connotation of the Eight of Swords.

-       Produce a summary of this "movie scene: You may describe this as somebody falling from grace or somebody that got themselves into problems.

When starting, keep in mind to keep things easy. At first, the smaller, the better. There is so much that you can check out and do without things becoming too overwhelming for you in the beginning. Keep your readings practical and keep them short-term. Keep your concerns easy. Ask the cards what you should focus on today and pull one card for yourself. Pull a Card of Gratitude. Find something in the card you pull that shows you how you can gather thankfulness from it and into your life. Pull a card asking What or Who can you embody today? Ask what you need to let go and release.

You will start to learn the capabilities of the Tarot, and what
the   cards   point   to.

Chapter 9: Exercises & Practice

The most important thing that can be done to improve at checking out tarot is to practice every day. You can check out on your own, obviously, however, you'll get to a point where you run out of questions, or you begin repeating. And as every knowledgeable fortuneteller knows, if you duplicate questions over and over, the cards tend to get a bit huffy and stop responding to. They provided you their response, now quit asking.

If you read for family or pals, you run into the exact same issue. Everybody's got problems, but once you do a reading on that issue, you'll begin striking obstructions if you try to over-extrapolate. You likewise wouldn't wish to wish ill on your liked ones just to have something to do a reading about.

In place of having particular questions to ask or anybody to practice on, here are some strategies you can use to keep going and work out that card-reading intuitive muscle.

Daily Draw

So, if there's no one around to read, how can you continue to practice? Probably the very best method is to do what's called a daily draw. You ask the tarot, "What is my message for today?" Draw one card. This is actually good to do at the end of the day when you've currently had all your routes and adversities. Then the card allows you to study the occasions of the day and reflect.

It's a great idea to keep a journal for this, specifically when you're discovering. At the start, document the meanings of the card as a bullet-point list to assist you in maintaining the details. Then contemplate the card, look at its message, and keep your mind open to any words, thoughts, and images that flow in. Write down what the message you're receiving through the tarot implies to you. Not only does this permit you to utilize your rational brain to memorize and use a specified definition to the occasions of your day. However, it likewise opens your intuitive mind to get more details.

If you're having a hard time opening up to your intuition, visualization helps. Take a look at the image of the tarot card you drew for the day. Research study it, and take a better take a look at the details on the card. What's the first thing you observe? What does the mood of the figures appear to be? What's going on in the background? And most notably, what is your gut reaction? Write all that down, too, and get as into the nitty-gritty as you seem like.

With the card now securely in your mind, close your eyes. In your mind, keep the image of the tarot card, most importantly. Typically, your mind will attempt to bring in various images to supersede it, but that's regular. It takes practice to hold the card there. Then, allow the tarot card to relocate your mind. Stimulate it, enable it to break free of the confines of the card dimensions, and see what it does without directing it. More often than not, the actions the figures in the cards take as you imagine them will give you a hint as to why this card showed up for you, and how it applies to your day. Document what you see, and then analyze.

You can also practice the one-card visualization method with a more specific question. If you're doing a reading on your own, it's a good concept to do this before setting a spread. It assists lead you into the spread out by already giving you an idea of how to piece together what you will read. With sufficient practice, you'll be able to do this without a tarot card as an aid, and simply open your mind to what your intuition can attune to.

Journaling your reads, in general, is so important, particularly as you're starting out. You 'd be fantastic just how much leave your head when the reading ends. If you document your predictions and impressions, and when you are even more along in your research studies, you can go back over your entries and see how far you've come. This is an indispensable present to offer your future self. Because it's just for you, there's no right or wrong. This is just a reflection. You get out of it only what you need to. Ultimately, you won't require to make a note of every little thing. You'll have the cards memorized, and your intuition will be sharpened to where impressions will come fluidly to you. Then you can blog about your daily draw easily and easily.

Utilizing the News

However, simply reviewing your day or practicing meditation doesn't sound incredibly amazing, you say. This is a prophecy. If you can predict the future, you want to know.

If you wish to check your predictive abilities, there's no better way than to do readings on the news and present events. This is info that can be verified easily, and if it's a huge story, it'll be tough to miss it as it unfolds. If there's a breaking news story, after you read up on the details, take the time to do a reading on it. You can ask particular questions about it, mainly if you've got that intuitive sensation about it. However, often, the news can take a while to conclude, so another method to approach it if you're impatient is just to ask how the situation will unfold within the next two weeks. Then you have a short time frame in which to wait.

The very best aspect of this method is how objective you can be about it. Often, if you're reading on your own or somebody you're close to, it can be tough to preserve sufficient emotional distance to offer a sincere reading. You desire the best, and your desires can cloud what is as you're interpreting the cards. When it comes to public events, you're not mentally near the center of the reading, so it's simpler to see the cards as they are.

It will also offer you a great concept of how varied some of the cards can be when it concerns applying them to a reading.

Typically what goes on in the news spans beyond the usual individual questions of love or careers. What a card like the Knight of Wands can indicate will be a lot various for a bigger, possibly more political question than you 'd ever get out of your own inquiries.

If you do readings on the news, make certain to document your predictions with the date. That way, you can refer back to what you read in the cards. Another excellent concept is to draw out the spread from that reading. That way, if you got a prediction incorrect, you can go back to the reading and go over what cards existed, and get a sense of which ones you may have misinterpreted.

Celebration Trick

The most obvious method to practice is to go check out for a wide variety of individuals. If you're not in service already, which we can presume, not if you're just beginning, then how would you find complete strangers to practice on? When you go to a party or barbecue and offer to read for anyone who's interested, one easy way is to take your deck.

Obviously, doing this requires some self-confidence, so you're not prepared right out eviction to do this, that's all right. Take whatever time you need to develop your skills to where you're comfortable with this. There may also be an element of shame about it as if being interested in the tarot is unusual, and individuals might think it odd. It's indisputable that some might, however, you 'd be amazed simply how many people are keen to get a reading, especially if it's complimentary. If you're honest about it and say right out the gate, it's for practice; most are more than happy to be your guinea pigs. It might likewise assist you in connecting with others and maybe even make a few pals, as tarot has a tendency to get people to open up and be more honest with themselves and with you as the reader.

Card Clubs

Discovering other individuals who have an interest in tarot and may have more experience is important for the development of your reading skill. While books such as this one can offer a great base knowledge, there's nothing to change actual human conversation and insight.

With the revival of appeal in the tarot, there are lots of tarot clubs forming. Specifically, in more industrialized areas, there are generally metaphysical shops that not just function as a store; however, they likewise provide space for workshops and weekly groups. If there is an esoteric shop in your location, it's worth going in and talking with the personnel to see if they offer anything like that, or at least if they understand of any group concentrated on the tarot in the location.

Create one yourself if there is no club already formed in your area! It can be pretty simple to discover other interested parties to develop a group. Probably, the best appropriate way to relate with your community is through Facebook, but if you'd rather tackle it more anonymously, Craigslist has a board for occasions where you can post the information and see who shows up. Easy paper posts at metaphysical stores or on a community board may appear old-fashioned, but these boards still get a lot of marketing traffic, and you 'd be surprised at the number of individuals who respond to these.

A word of care, though: there are individuals out there who like to take the mickey out of psychics and fortuneteller. If you market too widely, you might end up drawing in individuals who only want to come to tease everyone else there. It's an unpleasant fact of life, but something you should be aware of if you're going to develop an open community for spiritualists.

A simple method to dissuade these habits is to have a charge for every conference, something very little like $5. Usually, people who aren't that major about it will leave it at that, preferring to waste their time somewhere else instead of spending the cash. When it comes to authentic people, this cash can be returned to them later, or it can be pooled together as a resource for the group to buy supplies, or prepare an event, or lease a much better area to have meetings. Whatever works well for the group you have.

Online Resources

Another method to find more spreads, more exercises and more advice on how to continue getting better with your tarot practice is to look online.

As mentioned, there are a lot of tarot online forums available online. It was raised there as a method to find indie decks not commonly offered. However, an online community is a ripe source of discussion and concepts that can set your creativity on fire and make you itch to try something brand-new. Facebook hosts dozens of group online forums based around tarot. However, there are independent websites out there where tarot is the whole focus.

YouTube is likewise filled with channels committed to tarot. Some are specifically suggested to work as mentor guides, so searching for videos to check out the ideas set out in this book may assist you in understanding further what was introduced here.

Other channels are merely recorded readings, one popular format being the pick-a-card reading. This is when the readers will set out pre-drawn stacks of cards to respond to the question posed in the video. Those who watch the videos pick the pile they feel drawn to and get a reading. Certainly, because these are pre-filmed and indicated for a general audience, they're really broad and may not constantly resonate. Nevertheless, they can be tools to assist you in understanding how various readers find significances in their cards, what different kinds of spreads can be utilized, and how to bring a reading together. You might even get an unexpected handy message along the way.

It is likewise preferred among tarot readers online to use the news as a means to get traffic on their channel, much like we went over previously this chapter. This can be handy to you if you choose to practice your cards that way, given that their videos can be used to compare and contrast what you're getting when you check out the exact same concern.

It's not just the meaning of the cards; it's also the figures in the cards. The card's meaning, according to the book, absolutely informs the reading, but if you feel drawn to a card specifically because the figure in the card is doing something that attracts your interest, that's your intuition telling you that card is important.

You can reshuffle the cards and ask about those specific cards, and you'll likely find the answers in the next spread. To look at the cards and instead of thinking, "This is what this should mean," you read the cards and just let the intuition opened by meditation and the present moment guide your thoughts.

Very often, the actions the figures in the cards take as you're visualizing them will give you a clue as to why this card came up for you, and how it applies to your day.

Chapter 10: What Does Your Intuition Tell You?

Memorizing card meanings is something. Grasping how to read them is another. While having the ability to context them rationally is a big part of the skill of tarot reading. The art of tarot is the use of your intuition.

We have actually discussed intuition numerous times currently during the course of this book. It penetrates everything about tarot. The point of the images and using allegorical figures to describe our universe is tapped into our capacity for metaphor, which is at the heart of our cultures, our stories, and our dreams. By connecting themselves to our subconscious language, the tarot opens us as much as our instincts, and through that, offers the answers to our most important concerns.

Everyone has intuition. For some, it is far more established. Some individuals were born with it already strong while others need to work on it, much like how some individuals were born gifted at math, and others require tutoring to pass algebra. Just about everybody believes at least one point in their lives where they had a sensation about something that turned out to be proper despite there being no rational factor they should understand. This is a phenomenon often experienced by moms and dads, who have such strong intuitive bonds to their children that they just know something is wrong even when their kid is out of sight.

Usually, these kinds of stories are preceded with, "I do not know why I think of doing that," or, "I don't understand how I knew," or, "I simply got a feeling."

That 'sensation' is what the tarot trains you to tap into. For all the reasoning and memorization that goes into learning the cards and reading them in context, the genuine reading originates from that instinctive voice.

A lot of this can be done by finding out to take a look at the images on your tarot cards. It's common for beginners to set out their cards and look up the significances of the cards, and string them together from there. It's what we carried out in the preceding chapter when talking about context, and this is a legitimate way to do a reading, particularly when you're discovering. It's how pip cards were initially checked out prior to Rider-Waite making it popular to illustrate them.

In text, however, it's impossible to get throughout the value of the art on the tarot decks. This is why getting a deck you respond to aesthetically is so crucial to reading well. The meanings of the cards stay the same across all decks. You may get a different instinctive reading from one deck than you would from another, just because the images for the very same cards would be various.

Frequently, the tarot communicates a lot in the images drawn for a reading. It's not just the meaning of the cards, but it's also the figures in the cards. What are they doing? What are they wearing? Do you see patterns in the cards in the overall reading? With tarot, the big picture can often inform you a lot more than getting lost in the minutiae of what a card is supposed to indicate. The card's significance, according to the book, definitely informs the reading. Still, if you feel drawn to a card, particularly since the figure in the card is doing something that attracts your interest, that's your intuition informing you that card is necessary.

Intuition will also help you expand your readings. You might get an intuitive push during a reading that informs you that there's more to the question than fulfills the eye. Maybe, the querent does not fully trust you and is keeping the information, or maybe the best questions weren't asked in the first place. However, throughout your reading, there are a couple of cards that genuinely stand out to you, and don't seem to be fixed within the spread. You can reshuffle the cards and inquire about those particular cards, and you'll likely find the responses in the next spread. But it takes intuition to understand that.

Sadly, a book can't precisely teach you how to utilize your intuition. It's something you need to understand on your own. When you notice your intuition, you'll understand it. However, the procedure can just be felt. We can offer workouts to assist you in tuning in and nurturing it.

The first thing you can do for your intuition is to meditate, meditate, meditate. Both science and spirituality have proclaimed to the high paradises how healthy this is for the mind, so what are you waiting for? Even merely five to ten minutes a day will help you feel more unwinded and focused. In regards to your intuition, meditation takes advantage of the part of the brain where intuition speaks most plainly. It can direct you through your tarot readings more successfully if your intuition can speak clearly.

Meditate during a time of the day when you're most awake, not right before bed, and not right after getting up. Sit anywhere that's comfortable but also enables you to sit up directly. You need your spinal column aligned, so your physical energy is streaming even while the rest of you is relaxed. Close your eyes, and breathe deeply. It will help to count your breaths, generally in a pattern of breathing in for three counts, holding it for 3, then blurting in three counts. Breathe in using your nose, and then breath out by your mouth. You can do this for the whole five minutes, but in order to go into the meditative frame of mind, you only require to count for a handful of breaths.

The trick with meditation is to try and not think about anything in particular. Thoughts will go and come, but it's best to picture them as clouds floating by. Our mind typically wishes to get onto thoughts and follow them regularly, but in meditation, you let them go. The idea appears, then it drifts off. Ultimately, as you get more skilled with this, meditation will become a space of silence. You'll have the ability to induce a frame of mind where there are no thoughts, only a peaceful calm where your mind can totally unwind.

You do not even recognize just how tough you work your mind all the time up until you unwind it, like when you get a hand massage, and you feel the muscles in your palms and fingers lost their stress. By allowing the mind to unwind, not just will it work its logical processes more effectively, but it will also increase the more psychic capabilities like intuition.

This leads to the next method you can tune into your intuition. As you meditate regularly, you'll find you're more attentive and more aware of the space around you. Concentrate on that awareness, and let the minute really sink in. Know all the noises in the area. Observe the colors around you, in the rug, on your chair, out the window. Take a look at the quality of the light, and take the time to value shadows produced by the light. Notice your physical type, how it feels sitting where it is.

This is called existing at the moment. Let thoughts come and go, but do not hold onto them. The past isn't today. The future can't be completely known beyond the present. The most essential minute is the now, and the now is where the intuition resides. In the now, there is no depression about the past. In the now, there are no stress and anxieties about the future. All that matters is the now, and all the running thoughts you have about what you're doing and what you're refraining from doing and what you should be doing drop in the gratitude of where you are exactly this moment. Who you are as a complete, whole human being at this moment.

Comparable to meditation, taking the time to be present in the minute ought to be done every day. When you enable your awareness to leave the constant chatter of your mind and spread out into the world like that, even if only for a few moments at a time, you're opening the door to enabling your intuition to stream forth. That constant chatter typically overrides the intuition because it's so loud and never appears to stop running, and it's yelling about things that aren't any longer or things that might take place. Neither of these is the present reality, and they only serve to hush the intuition.

You can carry out more active practices to enhance it once you get a feel for what your intuition feels like — for example, keeping a 'hunch' journal. Here, you document any feelings you have about things. Do you get the sense it might drizzle tomorrow? Do you have a hunch about somebody you just met at work? Did you turn on the television to a game show and sense one particular entrant will win? Compose these inklings down and refer back to them later to see if you were right. Ultimately, you'll be able to tell the difference in between when it's your intuition genuinely talking to you, and when it's your rational brain tossing out possible projections.

It's also excellent to spend time with just your intuition. This is a similar procedure to meditation in that you're sitting still and closing your eyes. However, instead of trying to let all thoughts flow away to attain a state of best calm, instinctive meditation is when you open the floodgates to your intuition and pay attention to the visions and impressions that come out. Sit with it for a few minutes a day, and make a note of your impressions. Did you see particular colors? Or a scene, like space or a landscape? Did you see a face, and was it somebody you know or someone you've never seen before? What feeling did you obtain from any of these? Record them, and then document if you see these visions exposed in reality. Remember, though, that just seeing something in reality that your intuition exposed to you does not indicate it's an essential vision that's going to affect the course of your life. What it suggests is that you're working out that intuitive muscles. Your intuition is reaching out further and further and picking up on information that you otherwise would've missed out on. It's helping you to connect the external and the internal so they can operate in tandem. If you make your intuition strong, then when something important is on the horizon, there will be no mistaking it. You'll know it immediately.

The exact same, too, can be said of your tarot readings. Between meditation and remaining in the now, you'll train your brain to decrease, take a breath, and evaluate what's actually taking place in reality and not what you think may occur. This head space is crucial to reading with intuition. To look at the cards and instead of thinking, "This is what this ought to suggest," you check out the cards and simply let the intuition opened by the present moment and meditation guide your ideas.

Chapter 11: Where Should You Use the Tarot?

Tarot For Self-Reflection

One terrific way to make day-to-day use of your tarot deck is to pull a card for each day. Consider this the day's "style" - things you must understand that this day might reveal, shed light upon, be interested in, or bring towards you, in addition to things that might be moving away and no longer influencing your life.

A tarot journal is essential here, as you will want to recall at previous days' readings to see if you can recognize a pattern in how things have actually been going.

It's not what the cards are telling you; it's what you see in the cards. Some people have a problem with the fact that a single tarot card might suggest "anything," depending upon how you analyze it. And that's exactly the point of this workout. Tarot cards are based upon archetypes - universal imagery that generally means the very same thing to the viewer, no matter background, culture, or citizenship. What catches your creativity when you look at a card is a message to yourself, from yourself. The subconscious mind understands a lot more about what's going on than the majority of us provide it credit for - but it does not speak in words; it speaks using images. That's why our dreams are typically so vibrant and quirky. Tarot cards provide the subconscious mind a language it can associate with so that it might impart knowledge and valuable lessons for us to utilize in our daily lives.

In some cases, our mindful mind lies to us or is just blinded by feelings or other people's viewpoints. Picture if your automobile's dashboard unexpectedly went dark. How would you know how quickly you're driving? Would you be able to inform me if your engine required attention? The conscious mind can't look after everything by itself, and it needs some aid. When something in our lives requires to be observed, our subconscious mind is there to stir our intuition. Don't think of tarot as "magic," necessarily (although it's entirely appropriate if you do). Imagine that it is a kind of tool that you can utilize for self-guided treatment.

Tarot For Daily Focus

There are a few various ways to go about this. One way is to merely shuffle your entire deck, and pull each early morning either a card or each night prior to you go to sleep (the card you draw is a sign of what the next day will bring). A second technique is to separate your deck into two decks: the significant arcana and the minor arcana. You can select to pull your day-to-day card from the significant arcana deck and pull a second card for an explanation or information from the small arcana deck if you need more info.

Your daily card can be looked upon for any of these themes or ideas:

• what you must focus on that day
• what you need to be aware of
• something that requires your attention
• the day's technique for success
• the very best method to browse this day happily and peacefully

Before you draw, if one of these subjects resonates with you, state it aloud before you shuffle, cut the deck one time, and pick your card, and as always, jot down your impressions when you see which card you've drawn. Take your time with this part of the procedure - do not rush it.

The benefit of daily focus cards is that the cards you draw can direct your attention towards something you may not have recognized. If you have been having a challenging week, for example, in which you believed you lacked the guts or initiative to deal with a particular issue, drawing, say, The Chariot or the King of Swords may offer you the push to believe otherwise and believe in your abilities some more.

Pulling a daily card is frequently like sending out a message to yourself: it can be a message of love, a message of hope, or a message of encouragement. It can also be a message of caution, or to curb a bad habit. Whatever it is, the tarot card and its message will become another tool in your mental and emotional toolkit.

Tarot For Meditation

In this manner of making use of the tarot does not include arbitrarily choosing a card. Instead, pick a card that represents what you wish to boost or draw better in your life. You may spread the cards out, face-up, and select one that resonates with you for this exercise.

Meditation is not a complicated job, but its benefits have actually been clinically shown in research study after research study. Meditation has the power to form the brain, a phenomenon called neuroplasticity. This suggests the brain is capable of changing its structure, depending upon our thoughts, our practices, and our way of life. Contemplating a routine basis has actually been proven to cause a higher production of serotonin and other positive, mood-enhancing hormones in the brain, along with decreasing the areas of the brain that release stress hormones.

To meditate, all you truly require is a location to sit, some time to sit there, and a dedication to concentrate on breathing and excellent posture. Ten minutes of your lunch break is perfectly acceptable for a newbie to meditate. You might select a comfortable chair to sit in as long as your spinal column can be straight and even while sitting. Your feet must be flat on the ground, or, if you select to sit on the flooring, cross your legs if you have the ability to. Always remember to keep your spine straight and your breathing deep and even -

and from the stomach. Your shoulders must never move when breathing effectively.

If you like to focus on a certain thing, pick the card that best represents that to you. You can shuffle the deck while you focus on your thought, then cut the deck when and pick the top card for your focal tool. Set the card where you can easily see it in detail, then start to meditate-- ideal posture, deep, regulated breathing.

When first finding out to meditate, it's perfectly natural that your thoughts will come crowding in, often somewhat chaotically. Permit them to go through; pay them no attention. Mindfulness meditation is the practice of acknowledging things as you meditate, but not contemplating them. Instead, concentrate on the card itself. The Sun card, for example, reveals the sun with a lovely, peaceful face. A cheerful child. A white horse. Sunflowers grow in the distance. You may enable yourself to notice feelings while contemplating this card. "I feel at peace." "I feel confident." If you feel your eyes start to go out of focus, allow that to occur - this is natural and excellent practice in meditation. You can continue looking at the card, or past the card, without scrutinizing it.

That's all there is to it. Always tape-record your impressions in your tarot journal later on, so that you can review previous meditations to observe your personal journey with the tarot cards.

Tarot For Creativity

You might be starting to observe that the tarot deck is a fast-track hotline straight to your subconscious. This resource can be invaluable to your imaginative work. When browsing a rough spot in an innovative project, you can pull a card to ask yourself:

- What do I wish to convey at this point in the story?
- Which feelings am I purchasing this piece?
- What should I produce next?
- What aspects of my ability am I overlooking?
- What should I work on enhancing?

When doing this, it can be valuable to look beyond "conventional meanings" and, instead, take hints from your first responses to the cards you draw. Add them to your journal with a description of what you're dealing with at the time, or what you hope to be dealing with in the future.

Tarot cards can help authors learn more about their own characters better. Understanding the reasons particular characters make the options they do can help writers craft richer, more credible stories. Bear in mind that tarot cards are based upon archetypes, and every character has an archetype that they closely resonate with. Additionally, as tarot cards already narrate-- in the significant arcana and throughout each small arcana suite-- several cards can be pulled to offer the author an idea of which instructions to take their own story.

Tarot For Manifestation

Tarot cards are not only for the receiving of info. They can likewise be utilized to send our desires for symptom out into deep space. By utilizing a tarot card to work towards your goal or dream, you are likewise setting your own mind to grab that objective.

A powerful exercise that can be done to manifest dreams and objectives is to develop your own tarot card.

Start by picking a card that finest represents your objective or dream. Then, on a piece of posterboard, material, or paper board, put together images cut from publications that best communicate your interpretation of that tarot card. Make sure to consist of images that accompany your objective. Set this tailored tarot card in a place where you'll have the ability to see it every day.

You can utilize this method to reach such objectives as:

- buying a home
- landing a dream task
- getting a promo
- doing well in school
- obtaining a new level of health or fitness
- traveling to a location you've constantly longed to go

A Tarot Spread For Self-Realization

Here's a spread you can do when you want to look inward and check in with yourself. After you shuffle and cut the deck, pick seven cards:

1. Which motivations am I concealing from myself?
2. Which qualities are my most favorable ones?
3. Which qualities are my most unfavorable ones?
4. In which ways am I deceitful to myself?
5. What do I need to be more accepting of?
6. What do I need to let go of?
7. Which is my next life lesson?

The responses may require some guts on your part, but practicing this spread now and again can assist you to continue track for emotional health and better life choices.

Tarot For Unique Occasions

When preparing a dinner celebration, wedding event, or any other special event, constructing the theme of that occasion around a tarot card can be an enjoyable, creative method to set about things. Many of the tarot cards match themes of beverage, food, and event, such as the Empress, the Moon, the 3 of cups, and the 4 of wands.

A Tarot Experience

An enjoyable method to utilize the tarot when you have a day to yourself is to draw one card in the early morning to give you a clue as to where to go out to. Perhaps you draw a card with a forest in the background-- travel to your regional nature preserve or arboretum. Take your deck with you, and pull a second card to inform you where you'll next be going. Bring your journal along to make notes of your impressions.

Sometimes, doing this can reveal a lot more about what's going on in one's life than a mere reading can communicate. This video game can be especially helpful if you've found yourself doing not have energy, stuck in a rut, or unable to make a crucial decision.

Tarot For Magic

Whether you meddle a little moon magic or a seasoned practitioner of Wicca, tarot cards can include a potent focus on your altar or magic workspace. To include a heady dose of good luck and luck, add "The Magician," "The Sun," or "The World" to your spells, taking cues from the card itself to help you add components, colors, and components.

Utilizing among the face card of the Minor Arcana can assist you to feel as if you have a mentor present to make your spells genuinely successful. You can ask these masters for guidance, drawing additional cards after your work is total to get a tailored message from them.

Conclusion

Thank you for reaching the end of the Tarot for Beginners: All You Need to Know in Tarot, Cards, Card Reading, and Interpretations.

The next action is to decide which tarot deck you want to get started with. A word about tarot decks: lots of professional tarot historians choose the timeless decks because of the importance and imagery. There are numerous lovely, fun, and exciting divination decks there to check out, however, many of them are crafted with a particular way of taking a look at things, or with a specific method of self-exploration in mind. They can be highly beneficial, and I recommend attempting a few of them out, nevertheless, to get started, I agree with tarot historians and scholars and suggest that your first deck be the Rider-Waite. Once you feel comfy with that deck, by all means, check out the wealth of understanding and art that is out there. You might even be influenced to produce your own deck - which is a fantastic practice to assist you with your own self-discovery.

Lots of barriers in our lives can be conquered if we had a little help. Tarot can be that helpmate, in its amazing power to direct one's focus within and find out about why we decide that we do, what requires to be cultivated in our lives to cultivate fantastic success, and what we need to let go of in order to discover happiness and achievement in our lives.